Notes On The Apocalypse

Notes On The Apocalypse

With An Appendix Containing Dissertations On Some Of The Apocalyptic Symbols

by David Steele, Sr.,
Pastor of the Reformed Presbyterian Congregation, Philadelphia.

Remove not the ancient landmark...

Printed 2006 by Landmark Project Press

Full Title: Notes On The Apocalypse With An Appendix Containing Dissertations On Some Of The Apocalyptic Symbols, Together With Animadversions On The Interpretations Of Several Among The Most Learned And Approved Expositors Of Britian And America.

This edition is a reprint of the 1870 edition printed by Young & Ferguson in Philadelphia, U.S.A. All original spellings, formatting, and footnotes have been retained.

This work is public domain and may be reproduced or used for any purpose without restriction or acknowledgement. A complete e-text version is available on the Landmark Project website.

Landmark Project Press
Edmonton, Canada
www.landmarkproject.net
press@landmarkproject.net

ISBN 0-9780987-0-6

CONTENTS

Publisher's Preface..3
Dedication...5
Preface..7
Introduction..11
Chapter I..13
Chapter II..25
Chapter III...35
Chapter IV...45
Chapter V..55
Chapter VI..67
Chapter VII...77
Chapter VIII...83
Chapter IX..93
Chapter X..101
Chapter XI..107
Chapter XII...127
Chapter XIII..147
Chapter XIV...163
Chapter XV..185
Chapter XVI...189
Chapter XVII..199
Chapter XVIII...205
Chapter XIX..211
Chapter XX...219
Chapter XXI...231
Chapter XXII..239
Appendix...251

PUBLISHER'S PREFACE

It is my privilege to provide this reprinting of the great work by David Steele, Notes on the Apocalypse. While mostly ignored in our present day (and largely ignored by the Protestant community even in his own day), the truth contained herein demands its resurrection. There is great value in studying and understanding the material covered in these pages and Steele does an admirable job by presenting it clearly and honestly.

Though dwarfed by such expansive, yet comparable, volumes as Horae Apocalypticae (Elliott) and Commentary on Revelation (Durham), Notes on the Apocalypse serves as a competent yet accessible defense of historicist and post-millenial eschatology. Notes on the Apocalypse is rightly considered a commentary as Steele breaks down the book of Revelation into chapters and verses and explains each in turn. Steele also recognizes that he is not the first to treat the topic and takes time to discuss when he is in agreement with past authors as well as when "he has been obliged in important points to dissent" (particularly in the Appendix).

Keen readers will notice his marking of the start of the 1260 years as being either the year 606 (Pope declared head of the universal church) or 756 (Pope also became a "temporal prince"). From our vantage point we can see his earlier choice as being inaccurate, for the period would have concluded in 1866 when we have no indication from history that noteworthy events took place. His other consideration, 756, would conclude in 2016. The accuracy of that date, however, is left solely to our Lord's unveiling in the coming years.

David Steele is perhaps best known for his instrumental work in the Reformed Presbytery of the 19th century. They were a small but vocal group who, in 1840, called out the Reformed Presbyterian Church in North America for backsliding from their church's historical lineage (both in the United States and Great Britian) and after much discussion found the problems to necessitate separation from them to form a new and faithful church. Michael Wagner, Ph.D. concludes in discussing this act of separation, "those who remain faithful to God must contend for the Christ-honouring biblical attainments of the past (Phil. 3:16, 1 Tim. 4:6, Eccl. 3:15), and that is what David Steele did in his generation. Certainly contemporary Christians can learn from his example." (Forgotten Hero: The Autobiography of David Steele, Wagner)

Along with having a significant influence in virtually all of the Reformed Presbytery's official disseminations, Steele produced a number of theological magazines including "The Contending Witness", "The Reformation Advocate" and "The Original Covenanter", all of which he edited and was also a contributing author. He also penned a number of other books including "The Two Witnesses" and an autobiography entitled "Reminiscences: Historical and Biographical".

Originally published in 1870, this book has made a modest resurgence in recent years. It is presently available online from a number of sources (four at last count including Landmark Project) and is also available in audio format through Still Waters Revival Books.

My hope is that in reading this book, you find the truth of Scripture expounded with sincerity and veracity. Also, that as you read this concluding book of the holy canon, it is illuminated "to show unto his servants things which must shortly come to pass." May God bless the faithful exposition of His Word and the efficacy of it in the hearts of all readers thereof.

In Christ,
Jordan Dohms
Edmonton, 2006.

DEDICATION

TO THE REV. JOHN CUNNINGHAM, LL.D.,
Missionary from the Reformed Presbyterian Church to the Jews in London, England.

REV. AND VERY DEAR FRIEND AND BROTHER:—

Although we are "separated upon the wall, one far from the other," we are not altogether precluded from mutual salutation. Placed by our Master on two hemispheres, between which the electric current bears frequent tidings, our respective positions are advantageous for noting the events of providence. These constitute the signs of the times, and are the counterpart of prophecy. Prophecy and providence reflect light upon each other, and both are helpful to the interpretation of each; but He alone who is the "Wonderful Counsellor," can cause us to understand either.

In submitting the following work to the public, I venture to do so under your auspices, if not under the sanction of your name. And I embrace the present occasion, Rev. Sir, to bear willing testimony to your acknowledged scholarship,—your profound erudition, especially in Natural Science and Philology. I do also cheerfully and joyfully recognise you as a public witness; and at the present time of general defection, as an official and *consistent* witness in the British Isles for the integrity of our Covenanted Reformation,—that reformation which in its fuller development is destined to secure the rights of God and man in reorganized society. Such, I believe to be one of the cheering lessons which may be learned by Christ's witnesses from searching the Apocalypse.

That you, Dear Sir, may be long preserved, sustained and comforted by the providence and grace of the Most High, amid all your self-sacrifice, privation and reproach which you endure for the truth's sake, is the prayer of

Your brother in covenant bonds,
DAVID STEELE.
PHILADELPHIA, *February 1st, 1870.*

PREFACE

The Apocalypse is one of the most sublime and wonderful dramatic exhibitions presented for human contemplation. Internal evidence concurs with authentic history, in demonstrating to the devout and intelligent reader, its divine origin. God, angels and men, are the principal actors. Men's natural curiosity may find entertainment in this book; and from no higher principle, many have doubtless been prompted to attempt a discovery of its mysterious contents. What is true, however, of supernatural revelation in general, is equally true of this book:—"The natural man receiveth not the things of the Spirit of God, neither can he know them, because they are spiritually discerned."

To the right understanding of the Apocalypse, so far as the prophetical parts of it are contemplated, the following prerequisites would seem to be indispensable:—

- A competent knowledge of what may be termed the fundamental doctrines of the gospel: such as the unity of the Divine Nature; the distinction of persons in the Godhead; the atonement and intercession of Christ; the total depravity and renovation of human nature; the resurrection and final retribution, etc.
- Acquaintance with symbolical language, as the only language common to all men since the confusion of tongues.
- Familiarity with the typical dispensation, from which most of the symbols are taken.
- Freedom from all political bias.

No expositor of the Apocalypse appears to have possessed all these qualifications, however few and simple. The most learned and judicious interpreters of this book have been divines of Britain and of the United States.

After so many laborers employed in this harvest, the reader may ask,—What remains to be gleaned? To this inquiry, it may be sufficient to remind the devout Christian, that as the Apocalypse is the end of the Bible, so "the harvest is the end of the world;" and during the intermediate time "the Lord of the harvest is sending forth laborers." Prophecy has engaged the attention and occupied the thoughts of the writer, more or less, for the last thirty years. He has consulted the views of most of the distinguished and approved interpreters of the book of Revelation; among whom the following are named, viz.: *Mede, Sir Isaac* and *Bishop Newton, Durham, Fleming, Gill, Whitaker, Kett, Galloway, Faber, Scott, Mason, McLeod*; and many others: from all whose labors, he has derived much instruction; and from all of whom he has been obliged in important points to dissent.

The immediate occasion of this undertaking, was the urgent request of the people of his charge, that the substance of a course of lectures delivered in ordinary Sabbath ministrations, might be put into a more permanent form, for their future edification.

In the early centuries of the Christian era, so wild, enthusiastic and corrupt were the sentiments of some Millenarians, that this book ceased in great measure to be read or studied; and even its divine authority came to be questioned by many learned and pious men. As the "Dark Ages" of Popery resulted from neglect of the sacred Scriptures in general, so even among the first reformers the Apocalypse was viewed with suspicion as to its claim to inspiration. It is probable that many of the unlearned will hear with wonder, and doubt the assertion, that even the great reformer Luther rejected the Apocalypse, as being no part of the sacred canon! The same judgment he formed of the epistle by James! With characteristic boldness, he wrote as follows:—"The epistle of James hath nothing evangelical in it. I do not consider it the writing of an apostle at all.... It ascribes justification to works, in direct contradiction to Paul and all the other sacred writers.... With respect to the Revelation of John, I state what I feel. For more than one reason, I cannot deem this book either apostolic or prophetical, ... and it is sufficient reason for me not to esteem it highly, that Christ is neither taught nor known in it."[1] Such was the estimation in which that distinguished reformer held *two* inspired books of the New Testament at the dawn of the Reformation. How great the increase of scriptural light since his day!

---

1. Life of Martin Luther. Pp. 173, 174. London. 1855. Luther afterwards became convinced of his error.

The grand design of this book, as declared by its divine Author, is, "to show unto his servants things which must shortly come to pass," ... "to testify these things in the churches:"—to make known beforehand, to those styled his "witnesses," the certainty of a great apostacy,—the rise, reign and overthrow of the Antichrist, that "when it came to pass, they might believe," and exemplify before the world "the patience and the faith of the saints." During that protracted period, the witnesses could neither know their duty nor sustain their allotted trials without these necessary instructions.

From the position of the witnessing church—"in the wilderness" during the whole time of Antichrist's reign, which is also the position of the apostle John when viewing in vision the "woman upon the beast;" (ch. xvii. 3,) *that* appears to be the *only advantageous position* from which to view the actors in this wonderful scene. And since few have voluntarily "gone forth to Christ without the camp, bearing his reproach," or submitted to wear the mourning garments of "sackcloth," it is not at all surprising that the Apocalypse—emphatically a *Revelation*—should continue to be, to many, a "sealed book." But on the other hand, "blessed is he that readeth, and they that hear the words of this prophecy, and keep those things which are written therein."

As this work is intended for the instruction and edification of the unlearned, rather than for the entertainment of the learned, words of foreign extract are used as seldom as possible. Practical remarks and reflections are rarely introduced; the principal aim being simply to ascertain and present to the reader the mind of the Holy Spirit. How far this object has been accomplished, is of course left to the judgment of the honest inquirer. The reader, however, in forming his judgment of the value of these Notes, may be reminded of that inspired rule in searching the Scriptures,—"Comparing spiritual things with spiritual." To assist him in the application of this divine rule, many chapters and verses are quoted from other parts of the Bible, but especially within the Apocalypse itself; that by concentrating the various rays upon particular texts or symbols, their intrinsic light may be rendered more luminous. Thus the interpretation given, if correct, may be confirmed and illustrated.

INTRODUCTION

The heavens and the earth did not make themselves. The material universe furnishes to the intelligent creature a visible demonstration of the "eternal power and godhead of its Author." Besides, a *sense of Deity* is essential to humanity; and a supernatural revelation is not necessary to convince rational beings that there is a God. Man is a dependent being in common with all other creatures, and all creatures depend upon a first cause. That cause is God. Dependent as a creature, man may know something of the natural perfections of his Maker; and possessing a conscience, which implies accountability to a superior, he may know,—he *must* know, something of the moral attributes of God.

In view of these positions, we may account for the fact, too often overlooked by the reader of the Bible, that the Holy Spirit directed the first of all historians to begin his narrative *so abruptly*. Assuming that the reader is already assured of *God's being,* Moses proceeds at once to account for the origination of the material universe. In simple narrative he writes,—"In the beginning God created the heaven and the earth." Thus God's being, and the eternity of his being are assumed as known by the first inspired penman; a fact or principle not to be disputed. True, the being of God has been questioned, but only by "fools"—"brutish people;" who, by their atheistical suggestions have proclaimed to their fellows their "brutish folly." (Ps. xiv. 6, xciv. 8, 9.)

As the Bible takes for granted that mankind have had a previous revelation in their own physical and moral constitution,—in the visible heavens and earth; the same is true of the last book of the Bible, the Apocalypse. It assumes that the reader has some competent knowledge of the preceding books of the sacred Scriptures. The reader is supposed to be acquainted with the patriarchal and Mosaic dispensations of the Covenant of Grace. Moreover, the moral law, as inculcated in the Old Testament; the Levitical priesthood and ministry, as being "shadows of good things to come;" the "doctrine according to godliness," taught in the gospels and epistles of the New Testament,—are all taken for granted and supposed to be received with a divine faith by all who would profit by this last book of the sacred canon.

It is further assumed in the Apocalypse, that the humble inquirer into the mind of the Holy Spirit has a knowledge of ancient history, of the character and destiny of Egypt, Babylon, etc. And finally, it is requisite that the successful inquirer into the mind of God be acquainted with the language of symbols; and, above all, that he be resolved, with the inspired writer John, to take a position with the mystic woman *in the wilderness*.

With these few preliminaries, we proceed:

CHAPTER I.

1. *The Revelation of Jesus Christ, which God gave unto him, to show unto his servants things which must shortly come to pass; and he sent and signified it by his angel unto his servant John:*
2. *Who bare record of the word of God, and of the testimony of Jesus Christ, and of all things that he saw.*
3. *Blessed is he that readeth, and they that hear the words of this prophecy, and keep those things which are written therein; for the time is at hand.*

Verses 1-3.—Here, our divine Mediator appears in the continued exercise of his prophetical office "in his estate of exaltation." While present with his disciples on earth, he told them he had many things to say to them, but they could not hear them then. (John xvi. 12) Upon his ascension he fulfilled his own and his Father's promise in sending the Holy Spirit to guide them into all truth—bring all things to their remembrance, and show them *things to come.* (v. 13.) The fulfilment of this promise we have in the whole of the New Testament,—doctrines, facts and predictions.

Jesus said,—"Of mine own-self I can do nothing." (v. 30.) The same is true of his teachings as of his works:—"The words that I speak unto you, I speak not of myself," (xiv. 10.) In all that "Jesus began both to do and to teach," (Acts i. 1,) he was instructed by his Father. These things are all plainly implied in the first verse. Indeed, the official actings of the three Persons in the Godhead had been frequently taught by Christ during the time of his personal ministry; and they are more fully and frequently recorded by the beloved disciple than by any other evangelist, in that gospel which still bears this apostle's name. Thus, it appears that although this book is called a "Revelation of Jesus Christ," he is not the ultimate author. It is a revelation "which God gave unto him." By God here, we are to understand the person of the Father. The reader is thus conducted to the divine origin of all supernatural revelation,—the eternal purpose of God. (Heb. i. 1, 2.) The object of the whole Bible, in the evolvement of the divine economy of man's redemption, appears to be the unfolding of the ineffable mystery of the Trinity, and displaying the perfections of the Godhead, to his own glory as the highest and last end.

The channel through which the divine will comes to the church, is exhibited in the beginning of this book. Originating with God the Father, passing to the Mediator, communicated to a holy angel; by his ministry it is made known to John, who reveals it to the church! How beautiful the order here! How wonderful and condescending on the part of God!

Although we commonly and justly designate the whole Bible by the name "Revelation;" yet we are to consider that this book is so called by way of eminence. Doubtless it is so styled by its divine Author because it reveals events which were then future, and which could not be discovered by human sagacity. But this holds equally true of other parts of the Scriptures, especially those parts which are prophetical. It may be that this book is called "Apocalypse" because of the opposition which it was to encounter from Antichrist, as also because of its singular and intended use to a peculiar portion of professing Christians. As on the one hand the Romish church, and too many who protest against her encroachments, prohibit or discourage the disciples of Christ from reading this book; so, on the other hand, it has been of singular use to others in strengthening their faith and ministering to their comfort.

John "bare record of the word of God and of the testimony of Jesus Christ and of all things that he saw." A question arises here,—What is the difference, if any, between the "word of God" and the "testimony of Jesus Christ?" Or is there any distinction intended by the Holy Spirit? Most readers as well as expositors view these expressions as identical. We shall meet with them, or their equivalent, frequently hereafter; and it may be proper at the outset to inquire a little into this familiar phraseology. (See chapters i. 9; vi. 9; xii. 11, 17; xx. 4, etc.)

Recognising the inspired rule of interpretation,—"comparing spiritual things with spiritual," we refer to Psalm lxxviii. 5, where "testimony and law" are obviously distinguished. The same distinction will be found in Isa. viii. 16, 20. The prophet refers the reader to *two tests* of doctrine and practice: first the "law." But as the spouse of Christ is unable, in her perplexity, to apply the law to the present case in a manner satisfactory to herself, she is directed by her Lord, (Song i. 8,) to "go forth by the footsteps of the flock." That is, search and ascertain how the disciples applied the law in similar circumstances, and imitate their approved example. This is a rule recognised and often inculcated in the New Testament. (Heb. vi. 12.)

The inspired penman in Psalm lxxviii. 5, refers to the covenant transaction at Mount Sinai, where the "law" was exhibited as an appendix to the covenant of grace—"added to the promise." (Gal. iii. 19.) The reader will find this whole matter set before him, perhaps to his surprise and delight in Exod. xx. 1-17. The Lord (Jehovah) is the God (Elohim) of his people. How shall they know that he is *their* God? By the law?—No, for that is a rule to all men. They know by the *testimony* as distinct from the law. Testimony consists of *facts*. God's people knew that he was their God, because he "brought them out of the land of Egypt, out of the house of bondage." This was "the doing of the Lord,"—"the testimony of Jesus Christ." And so it is an important and precious truth to us at the present day.—"The preface to the Ten Commandments teacheth us, that God is the Lord (Jehovah) and *our* God."—This great historical fact is the controlling motive to acceptable obedience to the moral law. To this, among other truths of the gospel, every faithful minister will "bear witness" with the apostle John.

John also bore witness to "all things that he saw," as presented to him in a succession of visions to the end of this book, in view of some of which, he "wondered with great admiration." (xvii. 6.)

In the third verse there is a "blessing" pronounced on all such as "hear, read and keep those things which are written in the words of this prophecy." A mere reading and hearing of the Apocalypse will not secure the blessing. It is suspended on the *keeping*. "Blessed is he that *keepeth* the sayings of the prophecy of this book." (Ch. xxii. 7.) The divine and compassionate Author of this prophecy, who "knoweth the end from the beginning," foresaw the violent and ignorant opposition even to the *reading* of it, which would be encountered by those for whose special direction and comfort it was given. While the "man of sin" would attempt to deprive the church of the light of the Bible in general, the great "Antichrist" would join him in special hostility to this book. The judgment of the former is, that the Bible in the hands of the people will generate *heresies*; of the latter,—the Apocalypse is so "hard to be understood" as to be unintelligible. A revelation, and yet unintelligible! This is very nearly a contradiction. Such sentiments betray rebellion against the authority, and a reflection upon the wisdom and beneficence of God. All Christians acknowledge, as Peter says of the writings of Paul, that in this book are "some things dark and hard to be understood:" but there have been always and now are, some disciples who do not subscribe to the teaching of most expositors of this book,—that their actual fulfilment, alone, will interpret these predictions.—Doubtless it was in view of such discouragements that our Lord prefixed and repeated the special blessing. And this promised blessing of the Master himself is sufficient to countervail all the discouragements and hostility of the adversaries, thrown in the way of the reader and expositor. Moses "endured as having respect unto the recompense of the reward." Let us copy his example. "He is faithful that promised." Let the pious reader, therefore, disregard the counsel to "omit the reading, of this book in family worship," as we have sometimes heard; whether it be tendered by Papist, Prelate or Presbyterian, because it is directly contrary to the express command of Christ, (John v. 39,) and because by following such counsel, he would forfeit the special blessing here promised.

4. *John, to the seven churches which are in Asia: Grace be unto you, and peace, from him which is, and which was, and which is to come; and from the seven Spirits which are before his throne;*
5. *And from Jesus Christ, who is the faithful Witness, and the First-begotten of the dead, and the Prince of the kings of the earth. Unto him that loved us, and washed us from our sins in his own blood,*
6. *And hath made us kings and priests unto God and his Father; to whom be glory and dominion for ever and ever. Amen.*

Vs. 4-6.—Here we have the customary salutation, addressed to the churches of Asia Minor. Many other churches had been organized in other parts of the earth at this date; (A.D. 96:) but the special reason why John saluted these seven, and addressed an epistle to each, would seem to be his vicinity to them in the place of his present sojourning, and probably his personal acquaintance with them in the exercise of his ministry among them, (v. 11.) His prayer for these churches is substantially the same as that prefixed to most of Paul's epistles. Grace and peace are inseparable in the divine arrangement. "There is no peace, saith my God, to the wicked." (Isa. lvii. 21.)

The solitary pilgrim in his place of banishment, contemplating the Abrahamic covenant, and realizing that grace and that peace in which he desires his fellow disciples to share, sets before us the threefold source whence these divine influences flow. First, "from him which is, and which was, and which is to come;" a description of God the Father, whose personal subsistence has priority in the Godhead, and who occupies the like priority in voluntary relationship and economic standing. From the Father personally, as the representative of Trinity, we have seen (in verse 1,) this book emanated; and now from the same we are taught that "grace and peace" come to fallen man. Second, John's prayer here, differs from Paul's usual form in the beginning of his epistles; for Paul omits the Holy Spirit, commonly saying,—"Grace be to you, and peace from God the Father, and from our Lord Jesus Christ," (as in Gal. i. 3.) In this last book of Scripture we have the co-equal Three introduced as co-operating in the work of man's redemption. Thus our attention is directed to the "seven Spirits which are before the throne;" by which we are to understand the Holy Ghost, in his essential equality with God the Father, but in the place of official subordination. The Holy Spirit is *one* personally, but *seven* in his manifold gifts and graces, with special reference to the "seven churches." And whereas the divine Spirit, in the order of his personal subsistence and operation is *third*, here he occupies the *second* place in the order of revelation. Third, The special reason for reserving the notice of our Saviour to the last place, is doubtless that the "beloved disciple" may take occasion to leave on record an expression of his admiration of the Mediator's person, one of whose names is "Wonderful," (Isa. ix. 6;) and that he might exemplify the ruling principle of his own heart,—"We love him, because he first loved us." (1 John iv. 19.) The apostle dwells upon the personal glory of Immanuel, contemplating him in his threefold office of prophet, priest and king.—He is "the faithful witness" in his prophetical office. "The only begotten Son, which is in the bosom of the Father, he hath declared him." (John i. 18;) "who, before Pontius Pilate, witnessed a good confession." (John xviii. 37.) He is "the first-begotten of the dead." He "died unto sin once," as an expiatory sacrifice to atone for the guilt of an elect world. Being a "priest for ever after the order of Melchizedek," "he ever liveth to make intercession,"—"death hath no more dominion over him," as it had over Lazarus and many others who "came out of the graves after his resurrection." (Matt, xxvii. 52, 53.) *Among all*, he has the preeminence. (Col. i. 18.) He is "the Prince of the kings of the earth." There is not in the sacred volume a title of our Redeemer more full or expressive than this, on his headship or royal office. A *prince* is of royal parentage. Such is the understanding of mankind in all civilized nations. Joseph in Egypt typified, in part, the kingly office of Christ; and Solomon on the throne of Israel partially typified him in his dominion: but as Balaam foretold that he should be "higher than Agag," (Num. xxiv. 7,) so we may say he is higher than Joseph,—"A greater than Solomon is here." "Pharaoh said unto Joseph, Thou shalt be over my house, and according unto thy word shall all my people be ruled: only in the throne will I be greater than thou." When the Father says to the Son, "Thy throne, O God, is for ever and ever," (Ps. xlv. 6,) this is consistent with "excepting him that did put all things under him." (1 Cor. xv. 27.) Although we are not warranted to say with some, "The Father is the fountain of the Godhead, we may warrantably and boldly say, the Father is the *fountain of authority*. (John vi. 38.) The dominion of the Mediator is universal, reaching "from the roofless heaven to the bottomless hell." It is comfortable to the disciples to know this in anticipation of the rise and reign of Antichrist. He is, by the appointment of the Father "head over all things," (Eph. i. 22,)—"able to save to the uttermost all that come unto God by him," to "consume with the spirit of his mouth, and destroy with the brightness of his coming, that Wicked, the Man of Sin." (2 Thess. ii. 8.)

In view of the personal dignity and mediatorial dominion of Christ, the apostle gives expression to his admiration and wonder at the amazing love and condescension displayed by him on behalf of himself and all others, on whom that love was fixed from everlasting, and whose guilt and pollution were taken away by the atoning and cleansing blood of the Lamb. To these saving benefits is to be added the honour to which the redeemed are advanced as "kings and priests,—a royal priesthood." The living Head is "a priest upon his throne," (Zech. vi. 13,) and all the members are assimilated to him. (1 Pet. ii. 5, 9.)

7. *Behold, he cometh with clouds; and every eye shall see him, and they also which pierced him; and all kindreds of the earth shall wail because of him. Even so, Amen.*

Verse 7.—How animated the language, sublime the conception, and awe-inspiring the sentiment here! Time is annihilated! The end is seen from the beginning, and all eyes are directed to the sovereign Judge of the world, as he comes in majesty to fix the final destiny of all the children of Adam! These have constituted only two classes since the world began. "Every eye shall see him," but the eye will affect the heart very differently. The hearts of some, with holy Job, will be filled with joy unspeakable, (Job xix. 26, 27;) but others, with mercenary Balaam, will be inspired with terror and dismay. (Num. xxiv. 17.) Of "them that pierced him," who shall be able to abide his indignation? Judas, Caiaphas, Herod and his men of war; Pontius Pilate, and all who have consented to the counsel and deed of them, "must appear before his judgment seat." "All kindreds of the earth," covering all the combinations of "Antichrist" during the definite period of twelve hundred and sixty years, "shall wail because of him," (Rev. xiv. 10, 11.) Assured of the equity of Messiah's judgment, the apostle, in the exercise of "like precious faith with all them that believe," subjoins his hearty assent,—"Even so, Amen:" "So let all thine enemies perish, O Lord." Doubtless the design of the Holy Spirit in this verse is to furnish ground of encouragement to those who were to be engaged in the protracted conflict with the powers of darkness foreshadowed in the prophecy of this book.

8. *I am Alpha and Omega, the beginning and the ending, saith the Lord, which is, and which was, and which is to come, the Almighty.*

Ver. 8.—The same divine person, to whom the apostle directs the doxology in the 6th verse, is introduced in the 8th: that is, the Lord Christ. He claims eternity and omnipotence. He describes himself here in the *very words* which in the 4th verse are descriptive of the eternal subsistence of the person of the Father. "Alpha and Omega," the first and last letters of the Greek alphabet, are explained in the words,—"the beginning and the ending." This language is not to be understood as expressing or defining the duration of the Godhead only; but it points also to the divine purpose and providence. To the same purpose speaks our Redeemer under the name of Wisdom:—"The Lord (the Father) possessed me in the beginning (head, purpose) of his way, before his works of old." (Prov. viii. 22.) In joint counsel with the Father, ere the wheels of time began to move, and being "almighty" to execute the purposes of God, he is perfectly qualified to act as the final Judge of the world. And in the great and last day "every tongue must confess that he is Lord, to the glory of God the Father." (Phil. ii. 11.) "For to this end Christ both died, and rose, and revived, that he might be Lord both of the dead and living." (Rom. xiv. 9.)—"God is judge himself." (Ps. 1. 6.)

> 9. *I John, who also am your brother, and companion in tribulation, and in the kingdom and patience of Jesus Christ, was in the isle that is called Patmos, for the word of God, and for the testimony of Jesus Christ.*

Ver. 9.—Again, the inspired writer addresses the Christians in Asia, acquainting them very briefly and simply with his present local situation; not so much to move their sympathy with him, as to express his unabated affection for them:—"I am your brother, and companion in tribulation." Although the "like afflictions were accomplished in his brethren," the Devil was permitted to "cast" only "some of them into prison." But it is remarkable that John utters not a word, much less manifests any resentment, against the persecutor. He was "in the isle that is called Patmos:"—but he does not say who sent him there. Historians tell us that he was banished by Domitian, the Roman emperor; others say, by Nero; but the former is more probable. This island is proverbially barren. It is situated among a number of islands in the Aegean sea, a point of the Mediterranean running northward between Europe and Asia, and not very remote from most of the churches here addressed.

The ground of controversy between John and his persecutors was "the word of God, and the testimony of Jesus Christ." Of these he "bare record." (v, 2.) "This," say most expositors, "was the cause of John's banishment." This unguarded language confounds the difference between a *cause* and an *occasion*. John had given no cause of banishment to his enemies. The true cause of their hostility was their hatred of the "word of God and the testimony of Jesus Christ." For these John contended earnestly, as Jude enjoined; (ver. 3:) just as Paul and others were "bold in their God to speak the gospel of God with much contention." (1

Thes. ii. 2.) We have here the standing ground of strife between the believer and the infidel; between Christ and Belial, between the church and the world. There is a divine hand interposed all along in this warfare, and the conflict will terminate only in the extermination of one of the parties. (Gen. iii. 15; Rev. xx. 10.)

> 10. *I was in the Spirit on the Lord's day, and heard behind me a great voice, as of a trumpet,*

Ver. 10.—The beloved disciple had often "tasted the good word of God," while the bosom-companion of Christ in the time of his ministry on earth: His "heart burned within him." (Luke xxiv. 32.) Especially had this been his happy experience on the holy Sabbath. Now that his condition is solitary, being by violence "driven out from the inheritance of the Lord," (1 Sam. xxvi. 19,) his gracious Master favours him with a special visit. Did he not say to his disciples while he was yet with them,—"I will not leave you comfortless? I will come to you." (John xiv. 18.) The Comforter was promised to supply the want of the Saviour's bodily presence, (v. 16,) and now John is "in the Spirit," and it is "the Lord's day,"—the Christian Sabbath. We may well suppose this disciple never was happier, no, not when he was "leaning on Jesus' bosom." He would not now envy the emperor or any of his persecutors in all their outward peace and prosperity. He was in an ecstasy,—"whether in the body or out of the body he could not tell:" but his soul was susceptible of the impressions of Christ's love, and of the intimations of his sovereign will. "Shall I hide from Abraham the thing which I do?" (Gen. xviii. 17.) "Surely the Lord God will do nothing, but he revealeth his secret unto his servants the prophets." (Amos iii. 7.) John does not boast as Balaam,—"falling into a trance, but having his eyes open:" yet he heard and saw as distinctly and clearly as if his perceptions had come through the medium of his bodily ears and eyes. "He heard behind him a great voice as of a trumpet," not to alarm, but to engage attention.

> 11. *Saying, I am Alpha and Omega; the first and the last: and, What thou seest, write in a book, and send it unto the seven churches which are in Asia; unto Ephesus, and unto Smyrna, and unto Pergamos, and unto Thyatira, and unto Sardis, and unto Philadelphia, and unto Laodicea.*

V. 11.—Christ speaks, asserting his eternity, and consequently his equality with the Father. This book being written in the Greek language, our Saviour names and appropriates to himself the first and last letters of the alphabet in that language, and gives the interpretation,—"the first and the last," as in v. 8. John is directed to write and send to the seven churches all that is contained in this last book of the Bible. The churches are named here, and in the second and third chapters they are addressed severally in a letter to each. It may be noted that besides the general commission to preach the gospel to every creature, apostles had a special call to *write*; and sometimes a prohibition,—"write not," (ch. x. 4.) Many of the most learned and godly divines whom we would consider best qualified, have never left any writings for the instruction of posterity; whilst others less qualified, either in respect of literature or piety, or not at all qualified, have filled the world with books without a special call from Christ. (John xx. 30, 31; xxi. 25.)

> 12. *And I turned to see the voice that spake with me. And, being turned, I saw seven golden candlesticks;*
> 13. *And in the midst of the seven candlesticks one like unto the Son of man, clothed with a garment down to the foot, and girt about the paps with a golden girdle.*
> 14. *His head and his hairs were white like wool, as white as snow; and his eyes were as a flame of fire;*
> 15. *And his feet like unto fine brass, as if they burned in a furnace; and his voice as the sound of many waters.*
> 16. *And he had in his right hand seven stars; and out of his mouth went a sharp two-edged sword; and his countenance was as the sun shineth in his strength.*

Vs. 12-16.—His attention being arrested, the apostle "turned to see the voice,"—that is, the person from whom the voice came. A glorious vision was presented to his view,—"seven golden candlesticks" or lamp-bearers, in allusion to the golden candlestick with the seven lamps as placed in the tabernacle. (Exod. xxv. 31-40.) "In the midst of the candlesticks appeared one like unto the Son of man," the Mediator, clothed in sacerdotal garments, supplying oil for the light, after the example of Aaron and his sons. (Exod. xxvii. 20, 21.) The "garment" may signify his mediatorial righteousness,—the "golden girdle" the preciousness of his love,—"his head and his hairs white like wool," his purity and eternity,—"his eyes as a flame of fire," his omniscience, by which he searches the reins and hearts, and sees the end from the beginning; "his feet like unto fine brass," the stability of his appointments and the excellency of his providential dispensations,—"his voice," the irresistible energy of his word to quicken, terrify or destroy at his pleasure. (John v. 25, Heb. xii. 26.) "The sharp two-edged sword" will represent his awful justice against the impenitent who resist his righteous authority. "With the breath of his lips shall he slay the wicked." (Is. xi. 4; Luke xix. 27.) "His countenance as the sun shining in his strength," disclosed to the beloved disciple such splendor as to overwhelm him. The like display of divine majesty was insupportable to Saul of Tarsus when on his way to Damascus. (Acts xxvi. 13.) To the workers of iniquity, "our God is a consuming fire." (Heb. xii. 29.) It is a certain truth,—"The vengeance of the gospel is weighter than the vengeance of the law." (Heb. x. 28, 31.) "Let us therefore fear."

17. *And when I saw him, I fell at his feet as dead. And he laid his right hand upon me, saying unto me, Fear not; I am the first and the last:*
18. *I am he that liveth, and was dead; and, behold, I am alive for evermore, Amen; and have the keys of hell and of death.*
19. *Write the things which thou hast seen, and the things which are, and the things which shall be hereafter;*
20. *The mystery of the seven stars, which thou sawest in my right hand, and the seven golden candlesticks. The seven stars are the angels of the seven churches; and the seven candlesticks which thou sawest are the seven churches.*

Vs. 17-20.—We have the effect of the vision upon the beloved disciple. He who had leaned on Christ's bosom at supper, and who had seen his Master transfigured on the holy mount, was now utterly overwhelmed with the effulgence of his glory. John "fell at his feet as dead." So it was with Daniel, "a man greatly beloved." (Daniel x. 4-8.) But the compassionate Saviour dispelled his fears, as in all similar cases; making known to his astonished servant his supreme deity and real humanity, as "the first and the last," who died for the sins, and was raised again for the justification of his people. (Rom. iv. 25.) He is "alive for evermore,"—become "the first fruits of them that slept." (1 Cor. xv. 20.) He "dieth no more. Death hath no more dominion over him." (Rom. vi. 9.) And so complete is his victory over the king of terrors, the last enemy of the believer, that he hath "the keys of hell and of death." He has the "key of the bottomless pit," (xx. 1;) having triumphed over principalities and powers, making a show of them openly. (Col. ii. 15.) Whether Christ used the word, "amen," to ratify the truth of his immortality; or whether this is an expression by John of his joyful acquiescence in that truth, is not material: we know on satisfactory evidence, that our Lord is a prophet and king, as well as a priest, "after the power of an endless life." (Heb. vii. 16; Rom. xiv. 9.)

John is next commanded to write,—*First*, "the things which he had seen;" that is, the description of the foregoing vision:—*Second*, "the things which are;" that is, the actual condition of the church, as delineated in the diverse characters of the seven churches addressed, as in the next two chapters:—*Third*, "the things which shall be hereafter:" that is, the prophetical part of the book, from the beginning of the fourth chapter to the close, as containing the prospective history of the church and of the nations, as she was to be affected by them, or they by her, till the consummation of all things. This is the division of the book made by the divine Author himself, and it is a natural and intelligible one. All attempts of learned and pious men by other divisions to render this mysterious part of the Bible more clear to the unlearned reader, tend only to display the ingenuity of the writers,—not to say their temerity, while they "darken counsel by words without knowledge." Such artificial divisions are as unfounded, in the apprehension of sober expositors, as the attempts of impious Arians and others, to turn the historical narrative of the creation and fall of man into an allegory!

The meaning of the "seven stars and seven candlesticks" is then explained to John. The word, "are," is used in a figurative sense, and not to be taken literally. It means here, *symbolize, represent* or *signify*. It is to be interpreted in the same sense as in the following places of sacred Scripture:—"It *is* the Lord's passover." (Exod. xii. 11.) "That rock *was* Christ." (1 Cor. x. 4.) "This *is* my body." (Matt. xxvi. 26.) None but a Papist will have any difficulty here, or perhaps,—a Lutheran!

CHAPTER II.

Some commentators, among whom may be mentioned the learned Dr. Gill, a leading Antipedobaptist minister of England, have imagined, that the seven epistles addressed to the Asiatic churches, contain a mystical prophecy of the church general, covering the whole period of her history from the apostolic age till the end of the world. According to this fancy,—for it is nothing more than a fancy; the church in Smyrna, will represent the church's condition in the second stage of her history, when Arianism prevailed! And the Laodicean must represent her last, and so her worst condition! How will this harmonize with the 20th chapter, where she appears in triumph over all her antichristian foes? This is given as a specimen of the unbridled fancy and licentious imagination with which even good men may be tempted to approach the reading and interpreting of this important and instructive part of God's word. But Peter informs us that some persons in his time, "wrested" those parts of Paul's writings which were "dark and hard to be understood:" and this was not the worst of their conduct, for they treated "the other scriptures also" in the same reckless and irreverent manner, which were neither dark nor hard to be understood. (2 Pet. iii. 16.) These epistles are no more mystical or prophetical than those of the apostle Paul. They are simply and properly descriptive, although like all other epistles, they are applicable to the church general in all ages, and equally suited to the case of individuals, as is clear in the close of each:—"If *any man* have an ear, let *him* hear."

1. Unto the angel of the church of Ephesus write; These things saith he that holdeth the seven stars in his right hand, who walketh in the midst of the seven golden candlesticks;
2. I know thy works, and thy labour, and thy patience, and how thou canst not bear them which are evil: and thou hast tried them which say they are apostles, and are not, and hast found them liars:
3. And hast borne, and hast patience, and for my name's sake hast laboured, and hast not fainted.
4. Nevertheless, I have somewhat against thee, because thou hast left thy first love.

5. *Remember therefore from whence thou art fallen, and repent, and do the first works; or else I will come unto thee quickly, and will remove thy candlestick out of his place, except thou repent.*
6. *But this thou hast, that thou hatest the deeds of the Nicolaitans, which I also hate.*
7. *He that hath an ear, let him hear what the Spirit saith unto the churches; To him that overcometh will I give to eat of the tree of life, which is in the midst of the paradise of God.*

Vs. 1-7.—This first epistle, addressed to the church in Ephesus, comes from the Lord Jesus, who holds the stars in his right hand; who gives commission to the ministry, gives them authority as his ambassadors to negotiate with mankind, communicates to them the light which they diffuse in the world, sustains them in their respective spheres, and controls them as they move in their orbits. He walks in the midst of the candlesticks, as the sun in the system of nature, trimming and snuffing the lamps that they may burn more clearly.

This is the second epistle sent from Christ to the church of Ephesus. Paul, who is thought to have planted this church, (Acts xviii. 19,) had written to those Christians some thirty years before, while he was a prisoner in Rome. (Eph. i. 4; vi. 20.) Paul and John were nothing more than Christ's amanuenses,—"the pen of a ready writer." (Ps. xlv. 1; 1 Cor. iii. 7.)—"The angel of the church" is at once a symbolic and collective name, including also the idea of representation:—not a pope or any other prelatic personage. No doubt in our Saviour's estimation the saints take precedence here of the "bishops (overseers.) and deacons," as they do in Phil. i. 1; Eph. iv. 8-12. All ecclesiastical officers are Christ's gift to the church; but the object or recipient of the gift is more valued than the gift. And just here is the point where prelates "do greatly err, not knowing the Scriptures." They have arrogated to themselves the honourary title of "clergy;" and for the sake of distinction, and to give plausibility to their ambitious pretensions, call the membership of the church the "laity,"—contrary to the express decision of the unerring Spirit. Peter cautions the "elders" that they be not as "lords over God's *heritage*,"—*lot, clergy;* where it is obvious that the body of the people, as distinguished from their rulers, are denominated the *clergy*. Moreover, it is evident to any unbiased reader, that the membership, and not a bishop only, are addressed by our Lord in these epistles; as when he says,—"some of you." (v. 10.) Hence it may be inferred that there is no proof in these epistles on which to erect the antichristian hierarchy of diocesan prelacy; and consequently that ecclesiastical government is by divine right, lodged in the hands of a plurality of presbyters.

Christ notices what is commendable, before he administers reproof. "I know thy works."—There seems to be an incompatibility between the "patience" commended, and not being able to "bear them which were evil." But patience under persecution or any other providential dispensation, is perfectly consistent with an enlightened zeal against error and immorality. Indeed, the two graces,—patience and zeal, are inseparable in themselves, and as connected with all the other graces of the Holy Spirit.—There were such in the primitive church, who claimed to be apostles, and who, upon trial, were discovered to be impostors. Paul, in the exercise of the miraculous gift of "discerning of spirits," could, without presbyterial examination of witnesses, personally detect "false apostles, deceitful workers" in Corinth. (2 Cor. xi. 13.) But John was not at Ephesus, and therefore the ordinary rulers are approved by Christ for the faithful exercise of discipline. Persons who falsify the doctrines and corrupt the order and ordinances of divine appointment, are the worst of liars, and having been by competent authority "found" to be such; they may be so called without breach of charity. When discipline is neglected or relaxed, error and tyranny soon enter, with "confusion and every evil work." But when false teachers have gained followers and influence in the church, the friends of truth and order will be in danger of yielding to the pressure. They are liable to become "weary and faint in their minds," (Heb. xii. 3;) but zeal for their Master's honor will animate them to contend for the faith so as to secure his approbation. It is remarkable that so much labor, patience, zeal etc., should be found in this church while chargeable with having "fallen from first love." Habits contracted in the fervor of early affection to Christ, may continue to influence an individual or a church, when the fervency of affection is sensibly abated. This state of feeling the exercised Christian will confess and lament. Nothing but repentance and reformation in such a case will procure the approbation and restore the favor of Christ. Continued impenitence is threatened with removing "the candlestick," the gospel, ministry and ordinances.

The Nicolaitans were a sect of corrupt professors of Christianity of whose doctrines and deeds little or nothing is certainly known. It is most generally supposed that they were a sort of Antinomians, who turned the grace of God into lasciviousness; and there is a tradition, not well sustained, that their heresy was derived from Nicolas, a proselyte of Antioch, one of the seven deacons of whom we read, Acts vi. 5. The similarity of name seems to have suggested this fancy; for there is no historical evidence that one who was "of honest report, full of the Holy Ghost and wisdom," was permitted thus to fall away. Their deeds, however, were hateful to Christ, and therefore hateful to his real disciples: for one of the infallible marks of a state of grace is to hate what,—yes and whom,—our Lord hates. (Ps. cxxxix. 21, 22.) All who read or hear these things are interested in them, whether they will hear, or whether they will forbear. What Christ saith in each of these epistles, the Spirit saith; and what is said to each church is said to all the seven; that is, to the whole visible church. "To him that overcometh" false apostles, the deeds of the Nicolaitans, any doctrines or practices in opposition to the truth of Christ, or militating against the honor of Christ; to such he "will give to eat of the tree of life," from which Adam was excluded upon the breach of the first covenant. (Genesis iii. 22-24.) What the first Adam lost by the fall, the last Adam will restore with interest, (1 Cor. ii. 9.) The felicity of the saints in glory can be represented only by sensible things; and even then but very imperfectly. (1 Cor. xiii. 12; 1 John iii. 2.)

8. *And unto the angel of the church in Smyrna write; These things saith the first and the last, which was dead, and is alive;*

9. *I know thy works, and tribulation, and poverty, (but thou art rich,) and I know the blasphemy of them which say they are Jews, and are not, but are the synagogue of Satan.*

10. *Fear none of those things which thou shalt suffer: behold, the devil shall cast some of you into prison, that ye may be tried; and ye shall have tribulation ten days: be thou faithful unto death, and I will give thee a crown of life.*

11. *He that hath an ear let him hear what the Spirit saith unto the churches; He that overcometh shall not be hurt of the second death.*

Vs. 8-11.—Smyrna is the second in order of the seven churches addressed through the ministry as the official representatives. Our Saviour here assumes those titles mentioned in ch. i. 17, 18, which bespeak his divine personal dignity and voluntary humiliation, his eternal Godhead and true manhood,—"God manifest in the flesh," having by death triumphed over death, to deliver them who through fear of death were all their life-time subject to bondage. (Heb. ii. 15.) This church was subjected to "tribulation,"—persecution in name, substance and person. The members were either of the poorer sort of the citizens of Smyrna, or rendered poor by fines,—"the spoiling of their goods."—"But thou art rich," rich in faith, in good works, in the gifts and graces of the Spirit, the earnest of the heavenly inheritance.—In this place a colony of Jews had gained such social influence as to move the populace, and even the local magistrates, to offer violence to the servants of God. It does not appear that these Jews were professing Christians of any creed, but just such as Paul often encountered in Judea and elsewhere. (Acts xvi. 19-22.) The devil instigated the Jews, and they the Gentiles; and both, the magistrates, to silence the testimony of Christ's witnesses, by which all were tormented. The design of the devil, who was a murderer from the beginning, was to *destroy* that church; but Christ's design was to *try* her members. Only *some* were to be imprisoned, and the time of trial would be limited to "ten days,"—a definite for an indefinite, but short time. Those who resist the truth contradict its advocates, and blaspheme the holy name of God, though professing to be either Jews or Christians, are a "synagogue of Satan." "A crown of life" is promised to such as proved "faithful unto death." They shall not be "hurt of the second death;" that is, eternal death. (Ch. xx. 14, 15.)

12. *And to the angel of the church in Pergamos write; These things saith he which hath the sharp sword with two edges;*
13. *I know thy works, and where thou dwellest, even where Satan's seat is: and thou holdest fast my name, and hast not denied my faith, even in those days wherein Antipas was my faithful martyr, who was slain among you, where Satan dwelleth.*

14. *But I have a few things against thee, because thou hast there them that hold the doctrine of Balaam, who taught Balak to cast a stumbling-block before the children of Israel, to eat things sacrificed unto idols, and to commit fornication.*
15. *So hast thou also them that hold the doctrine of the Nicolaitans, which thing I hate.*
16. *Repent; or else I will come unto thee quickly, and will fight against them with the sword of my mouth.*
17. *He that hath an ear, let him hear what the Spirit saith unto the churches; To him that overcometh will I give to eat of the hidden manna, and will give him a white stone, and in the stone a new name written, which no man knoweth saving he that receiveth it.*

Vs. 12-17.—To the church in Pergamos reproofs and threatenings are addressed by him who has the "sharp sword." Satan had his throne in this place, whence he assailed the true doctrine and disciples of Christ by heresy and persecution. In such a great fight of afflictions there was one distinguished, like Stephen, for boldness and fortitude, who "resisted unto blood, striving against sin." And wherever there is a "faithful martyr" for Christ, who "holds fast his name, and will not deny his faith" at the risk of his life, his divine Lord will condescend to register his name among that noble company who "by faith have obtained a good report." (Heb. xv. 2.) The "doctrine of Balaam" and that of the Nicolaitans led to gross immoralities in apostolic times as of old in the days of Moses. (Num. xxxi. 16.) And thus it appears, that old heresies, which have been condemned, are afterwards revived under new names, and patronized by new leaders. In such a case, we have the authority of Christ for calling them by the same names of those whose principles they adopt, and whose example they emulate. It was no breach of charity, therefore, by our forefathers to designate those who "delated" them to the cruel persecutors in Scotland by the name of "Ziphites," or to call the archtraitor Sharp,—"a Judas." The Lord Jesus "hates the doctrine" as well as "deeds of Nicolaitans," which are subversive of truth and godliness. Those who oppose the doctrines of Balaam and the Nicolaitans in any age when these are popular, must expect persecution. But when "troubles abound for Christ's sake, consolations much more abound by Christ." This is to "eat of the hidden manna." Also, the "white stone" or pebble,—the token of justification,—will be given to the conqueror in the Christian conflict. The allusion here is to the mode of procedure in courts of judgment among the ancient Greeks. White stones were cast for acquittal; black for condemnation. The manna is *hidden*, and so is the *white* stone, both signifying the sustaining and consoling evidence of the Comforter,—the Holy "Spirit witnessing with the spirit" of the persecuted believer, that he is a "child of God." It is the same thing as the "hundred-fold in this life," promised by Christ. (Matt. xix. 29.)

It is worthy of notice, in the condition of this church, that while among a minority may be found an "Antipas,—faithful martyr" for the cause of Christ, against those who hold the doctrine of Balaam and the Nicolaitans: the majority are called upon to "repent,"—evidently for conniving at the destructive errors and immoralities of those seducers. And unless the discipline of the church was employed to "purge out these rebels;" the Master would take the work into his own hand, and "fight against them with the sword of his mouth:" and then such as screened or spared these sinners might expect to partake of their just punishment. Rulers in the church "must give account for those over whom they watch."

18. *And unto the angel of the church in Thyatira write; These things saith the Son of God, who hath his eyes like unto a flame of fire, and his feet are like fine brass;*
19. *I know thy works, and charity, and service, and faith, and thy patience, and thy works; and the last to be more than the first.*
20. *Notwithstanding, I have a few things against thee, because thou sufferest that woman Jezebel, which calleth herself a prophetess, to teach and to seduce my servants to commit fornication, and to eat things sacrificed unto idols.*
21. *And I gave her space to repent of her fornication; and she repented not.*
22. *Behold, I will cast her into a bed, and them that commit adultery with her into great tribulation, except they repent of their deeds.*
23. *And I will kill her children with death; and all the churches shall know that I am he which searcheth the reins and hearts: and I will give unto every one of you according to your works.*
24. *But unto you I say, and unto the rest in Thyatira, (as many as have not this doctrine, and which have not known the depths of Satan, as they speak;) I will put upon you none other burden:*

25. But that which ye have already, hold fast till I come.
26. And he that overcometh, and keepeth my works unto the end, to him will I give power over the nations:
27. And he shall rule them with a rod of iron; as the vessels of a potter shall they be broken to shivers; even as I received of my Father.
28. And I will give him the morning-star.
29. He that hath an ear, let him hear what the Spirit saith unto the churches.

Vs. 18-29.—The most lengthy epistle is sent to the church in Thyatira. He who is the "Son of God," a divine person, possessing the essential attributes of omniscience and immutability, has more to say to this church than to any of the rest. Commending, as usual, whatever was commendable,—their "works, charity, service," etc.; "and the last to be more than the first:" he has, nevertheless, "a few things against them,"—especially "suffering that woman Jezebel to teach." Is this "woman Jezebel" to be taken in a literal or figurative sense? Analogy seems to require a metaphorical sense. If, in the preceding epistle, "Balaam" is not to be understood literally and personally, but figuratively and representatively, so Jezebel represents an individual, or rather as that other woman, (ch. xvii. 4.) a faction or sect, who propagated destructive heresy. Jezebel was daughter of Ethbaal, King of the Zidonians, whom Ahab married contrary to the express law of God. (1 Kings xvi. 31; Deut. vii. 3.) She was a violent persecutor of the Lord's people, because she was given to idolatry; and she was an instigator of all the cruelty perpetrated by that wicked king, "whom Jezebel his wife stirred up." As Ahab suffered his wife to control his policy, "giving him the vineyard of Naboth," etc., so it appears, the rulers in this church are blamed for permitting "a woman to teach," contrary to the law of Christ. (1 Tim. ii. 12.) She "called herself a prophetess,"—why not then require her to show her credentials? Permitted to usurp the functions of a public teacher, she "seduced Christ's servants" to join in the abominable rites of the heathen. Spiritual fornication, especially when conducted by female agency, has always issued in that which is literal. This may be verified from the time of Noah and Balaam till the erection of nunneries under the sanction of the "man of sin." The distinction here between "committing fornication" and "eating things sacrificed unto idols," intimates that the "adultery" is to be taken in a literal sense. Time was allowed for repentance, "and she repented not." All this time the rulers were culpable: therefore the Lord himself, as before, will interpose to rectify such gross sin and scandal. This he would do by visiting these impenitent transgressors with some incurable disease which would issue in certain death. So he did in the church of Corinth. (1 Cor. xi. 30.) By this example he would teach "all the churches, that it is he who searcheth the reins and hearts,"—demonstrating his divine omniscience.—"But unto you I say." Where now is to be discovered, in this address of the Saviour, that "presiding minister," or diocesan bishop, whom the anti-christian prelates affirm our Lord addresses in all these epistles? "And unto the rest in Thyatira,"—still no prelate addressed; but those laborious and patient ones previously commended, who "had not known the depths of Satan." Those deceivers pretended to instruct their deluded followers in the "deep things of God;" but Christ calls them "depths of Satan." It is usual with the devil's factors to delude credulous persons with pretending to teach them deep mysteries,—"curious arts." (Acts xix. 18, 19.)

To such as withstood the adversary and his allies, Christ would give no additional injunctions to those which they had received. And to animate them to continued fidelity and fortitude in future conflicts with these enemies of all righteousness, he holds forth an ample reward. He shall share in the honor of his Master, conferred on him by his Father. Whatever may be comprehended in this promise, it can be made good to the victorious Christian only by Him who is divine. None else has "power over the nations," but he to whom "all power is given in heaven and in earth." (Matt, xxviii. 18.) "The morning star" may signify Christ himself, (ch. xxii, 16,) or the "first fruits of the Spirit," (Rom. viii. 23,) or the full assurance of grace. (2 Peter i. 19.)

As before, what "Christ saith, the Spirit saith;" and the instruction, warning and threatening sent to the church in Thyatira, was addressed to all churches and to every human being endowed with an "ear to hear." It is assumed in the beginning of the Apocalypse, that only some will have sufficient education to "read the words of the prophecy of this book;" and such is the condescension of our gracious Master, that those who, by reason of invincible ignorance, cannot *read*, yet may share in the reward promised to such as "hear and keep" the sayings of this book.

And no doubt thousands have received this reward since the begun decline of Popery, who were privileged to hear and to "know the joyful sound" of the gospel proclaimed by the heralds of the Reformation. In the times of Luther, Calvin, Knox, and others, who were their compeers and successors, many were called from darkness to light, in continental and insular Europe, who could not read.

All are commanded to "search the Scriptures." Now to be able to obey this reasonable command, either all must be instructed in the knowledge of Hebrew and Greek,—the two languages in which the Bible was originally written, or the Bible must be translated into the languages of all nations. But the former supposition is impracticable, and therefore the latter is dutiful. And after all that has been done, and is yet to be accomplished, in translating the sacred writings into the languages of the nations of the earth, the "angels of the churches" will be employed by the chief Shepherd in feeding his flock.

CHAPTER III.

1. *And unto the angel of the church in Sardis write; These things saith he that hath the seven Spirits of God, and the seven stars; I know thy works, that thou hast a name that thou livest, and art dead.*
2. *Be watchful, and strengthen the things which remain, that are ready to die: for I have not found thy works perfect before God.*
3. *Remember therefore how thou hast received and heard, and hold fast, and repent. If therefore thou shalt not watch, I will come on thee as a thief, and thou shalt not know what hour I will come upon thee.*
4. *Thou hast a few names even in Sardis which have not defiled their garments; and they shall walk with me in white: for they are worthy.*
5. *He that overcometh, the same shall be clothed in white raiment; and I will not blot out his name out of the book of life, but I will confess his name before my Father, and before his angels.*
6. *He that hath an ear, let him hear what the Spirit saith unto the churches.*

Vs. 1-6.—As hitherto in these epistles we do not discover a "presiding minister" above an elder, so neither do we in this one find any hint of a "bishop and pastors." All Christ's bishops are elders, and "all are brethren." (Acts xx. 17, 28.) Prelacy,—that is, preferring one pastor before another in office, is expressly prohibited by the church's only Lawgiver. (Matt. xx. 25, 26.) The attempts to annul this law of Christ has caused more sin and suffering to his disciples than any one external agency of the devil. The whole history of the church furnishes the evidence of this.

The church in Sardis is addressed by him who "hath the seven spirits of God and the seven stars," who has authority by office to give the quickening influences of the Spirit to the dead, and his reviving influences to the dormant; for revival presupposes life. Their "works were not perfect before God," however they might appear to men. The majority were in a languishing condition, had "given themselves over to a detestable neutrality" in the Lord's cause. And as the whole body is justly characterized by the major part; this church is described as "dead." "Be watchful,—remember,—repent." These duties point out the prevailing sins, namely, slothfulness, forgetfulness and security. Where these predominate, "things that remain are ready to die." And there is no other remedy but that of applying to the "Seven Spirits of God," which Christ is ready to shed abundantly on all who make believing application.

Christ threatens to "come as a thief" upon those who do not "watch." In similitudes, we are not to indulge a licentious fancy in our attempts to interpret them. The objects of the thief's visit and that of Christ are not the point of resemblance; for "the thief cometh not but for to steal, and to kill, and to destroy." The point, and the only point of resemblance, is the suddenness of the visit. Ignorance or neglect of this rule of interpretation has been a fruitful source of error, especially in expounding Revelation.

In this epistle, the order hitherto observed by the Saviour is reversed. What was praiseworthy in other churches was first noticed. Here the commendation follows the reproof. "Thou hast a few names," etc. A virtuous minority are "undefiled in the way." They have nobly withstood the prevailing contamination, and therefore Christ will admit them to fellowship and honor. The victor shall be "clothed in white raiment,"—grace shall be perfected in glory; and their names, which were inscribed in the book of life,—the register of the church of the first-born, shall be confessed by Christ "before his Father and before his angels," as having "followed the Lamb," when others went back like Orpah. (Ruth i. 15.) Let those who, having "put their hand to the plough," are tempted to "look back," consider "what the Spirit saith" to the church in Sardis.

7. *And to the angel of the church in Philadelphia write: These things saith he that is holy, he that is true, he that hath the key of David, he that openeth, and no man shutteth; and shutteth, and no man openeth;*
8. *I know thy works: behold, I have set before thee an open door, and no man can shut it: for thou hast a little strength, and hast kept my word, and has not denied my name.*

9. Behold, I will make them of the synagogue of Satan, which say they are Jews, and are not, but do lie; behold, I will make them to come and worship before thy feet, and to know that I have loved thee.
10. Because thou hast kept the word of my patience, I also will keep thee from the hour of temptation, which shall come upon all the world, to try them that dwell upon the earth.
11. Behold, I come quickly: hold that fast which thou hast, that no man take thy crown.
12. Him that overcometh will I make a pillar in the temple of my God, and he shall go no more out: and I will write upon him the name of my God, and the name of the city of my God, which is new Jerusalem, which cometh down out of heaven from my God; and I will write upon him my new name.
13. He that hath an ear, let him hear what the Spirit saith unto the churches.

Vs. 7-13.—This church, like the one in Smyrna, is "without rebuke," in the midst of similar trials.—Christ's message is prefaced, as usual, by some description of himself, implying his supreme deity and authority. "He that is holy, he that is true," is more than a creature. As "there is none *good* but one, that is God;" so, "there is none *holy* as the Lord," (Jehovah,) (1 Sam. ii. 2.) Here is another, among many plain proofs, of our Saviour's proper divinity. His divine authority is held forth in his "having the key of David," etc. A key is the symbol of authority, (Matt. xvi. 19,) and the reference is to that prophecy, (Isa. xxii. 20-24,) in which the mediatorial dominion of Christ is set forth, by calling Eliakim to the place of authority in the room of Shebna. "The key of the house of David will I lay upon his shoulder." It is in virtue of this extensive grant of power from the Father, that the Lord Christ has a right, *as Mediator*, to send his ambassadors into all nations, to call sinners (rebels) back to their rightful allegiance; and also to execute deserved punishment upon all who do harm to his servants. (Ps. cv. 15.) In the exercise of his rightful authority, he has set before this church an "open door" of liberty, of opportunity, of activity; that she may put forth her "little strength" in keeping Christ's word and confessing his name amidst opposition, reproach and violence; for it is obvious, that when impostors fail to reach their objects by deceit, they will resort to forcible measures. Because this church was unable to purge herself by corrective discipline,—having but "a little strength," therefore Christ declares his purpose to strip these lying Jews of their cloak of hypocrisy, and exhibit them in their true character a "synagogue (church) of Satan." (James ii. 2.) Seeing that in apostolic times there were apostles, ministers, churches of the devil, is it to be supposed that we violate the law of charity, if in our own degenerate age, when heresies abound, when ecclesiastical order is trampled upon, we venture to apply the language of the Holy Spirit to unholy and profane amalgamations? No, it is part of the special business of Christ's witnesses to unmask specious hypocrites and warn of danger from false teachers, (2 Cor. xi. 13-15; Gal. i. 6, 7,) that "their folly may be made manifest to all men." (2 Tim. iii. 8, 9; 2 Peter ii. 1, 3.)—The cruel enemy, who in the day of prosperity boasts of his success, in the day of adversity becomes the most arrant coward and cringing suppliant,—whether it be Saul or Shimei. (1 Sam. xv. 30; 2 Sam. xix. 18.) Haughty persecutors have been changed to humble suitors for an interest in the prayers of their victims,—"to worship before their feet." "The word of Christ's patience" may signify any truth or doctrine of the Bible which is of supernatural revelation. The same idea is suggested by the phrase, "the present truth,"—any divine truth which may come to be opposed or denied, especially as it may bear upon the personal glory of our Redeemer. Love to Christ is often tested by an enlightened and firm adherence to the "truth as it is in Jesus," when "false apostles will sell it for a mess of pottage." (Prov. xxiii. 23; 2 Cor. xiii. 8.) The first promise here is of a temporal kind, of protection in time of general danger. The "temptation" thus predicted may refer to some of those "ten persecutions" waged by the Roman emperors against the Christians, as that of Trajan in particular; but doubtless, like many other predictions, it was to have more than one fulfilment. The expression, "all the world" does indeed sometimes mean the Roman empire, (Luke ii. 1;) but perhaps it would be rash to affirm, that it is to be always thus limited. Like "the kingdom of heaven,—the kingdom of God,"—phrases which have unquestionably a two-fold signification, so it will be safer to consider this expression as of a similar kind. All other churches would be exposed to trial, from which this one would be exempted. The trial might consist of persecution, or the spreading of heretical principles and wicked practices, followed by apostacies. At such a time of trial, a firm adherence to the "doctrines which are after godliness," would be imperative duty, and the only way to secure the victor's crown. The gracious reward of fidelity here promised is a permanent and honorable place in the heavenly temple,—the temple of Christ's Father, whose name the citizen of the New Jerusalem should bear for ever, and should be known and recognised as "fellow-citizen with the saints." These names may be safely interpreted as importing, "son, daughter of the Lord Almighty, citizen of Zion, Christian." As "the disciples were first called Christians at Antioch," so their gracious Master will "confess their names before his Father and the holy angels." (Acts xi. 26; Rev. iii. 5.)

14. And unto the angel of the church of the Laodiceans write: These things saith the Amen, the faithful and true Witness, the beginning of the creation of God;
15. I know thy works, that thou art neither cold nor hot: I would thou wert cold or hot.
16. So then, because thou art lukewarm, and neither cold nor hot, I will spue thee out of my mouth.
17. Because thou sayest, I am rich, and increased with goods, and have need of nothing; and knowest not that thou art wretched, and miserable, and poor, and blind, and naked.
18. I counsel thee to buy of me gold tried in the fire, that thou mayest be rich; and white raiment, that thou mayest be clothed, and that the shame of thy nakedness do not appear; and anoint thine eyes with eye-salve, that thou mayest see.
19. As many as I love, I rebuke and chasten: be zealous therefore, and repent.
20. Behold, I stand at the door and knock: If any man hear my voice, and open the door, I will come in to him, and will sup with him, and he with me.
21. To him that overcometh will I grant to sit with me in my throne, even as I also overcame, and am set down with my Father in his throne.
22. He that hath an ear, let him hear what the Spirit saith unto the churches.

Vs. 14-22.—It appears that in Paul's time a Christian church had been planted in Laodicea. (Col. ii. 1; iv. 16.) This church had the benefit of his ministry as well as that of Ephesus: and as both these churches were comparatively near to all the other five, we may suppose that a man of his zealous, active and persevering character and habits, would "impart unto them some spiritual gift." (Rom. i. 11.)

It is evident that this church had degenerated more than all the others. In her there is nothing to commend. Her officers and members are described in their real character by him who is the "Amen, the faithful and true Witness, the beginning of the creation of God." Each of these titles speaks the divine dignity of Christ. They are all to be understood in an absolute, not in a comparative sense. As "there is none *good* (absolutely so,) but one; that is, God," Matt. xix. 17; so Christ only is the "Amen" in such sense that he "cannot lie" as a "witness.'" He "speaks that which he has seen with his Father." (John viii. 38.) Jesus is, moreover, the "Beginning;" the author, owner and sovereign ruler of "the creation of God." This is clearly taught in Col. i. 15-18, where the same person, who (in v. 18) is called "the beginning," as here; is (in v. 17,) said to "be before all things;" by whom (v. 16,) "were all things created, that are in heaven, and that are in earth."—Creation is a work proper to God only. But our Redeemer has "created all things." Now, according to Heb. iii. 4, "he that built all things is God;" therefore he of whom these things are spoken is "the Most High God." And so said the inspired prophet long ago, "For thy Maker is thine husband." (Isa. liv. 5.) In the language of Jeremiah, (x. 11,)—thus do we say to Arians, Socinians, and other self-styled Unitarians,—"The gods that have not made the heavens and the earth, even they shall perish from the earth, and from under these heavens:" and their blinded votaries, "except they repent, shall all likewise perish."—However far the body of this church had declined, it does not appear that they had yet, as a community, gone the length of "denying the Lord that bought them."

Spiritual pride, self-sufficiency, seems to have been the prevailing sin among these degenerate professors. Like the Pharisee, they would boast of their riches, the spiritual gifts which they possessed, by which they flattered themselves that "they were not as other men." Possibly they might excel in knowledge, that "knowledge which puffeth up;" in utterance,—"great swelling words of vanity," by which they gained both "filthy lucre" and the admiration of an ignorant and carnal multitude. Such is too often the actual condition of ministers and people, when they are all the while under the power of sin, and wholly "blind" to their spiritual destitution. Self-deception is fatal; and it would be just in the Lord Jesus to give such persons up to their own hearts' lusts. So he threatens,—"I will spue thee out of my mouth," as a man's stomach loathes that which is nauseating. The like figure is used by Isaiah, (lxv. 5,) personating his Lord when describing similar characters:—"These are a smoke in my nose,"—intolerably offensive.—To us the case of this church would appear hopeless. It is not so, however: on the contrary, he assures them that these sharp rebukes proceed from love. "As many as I love, I rebuke, and chasten." (Heb. xii. 6-8.) And from the "counsel" which he gives, as farther evidence of his love, we learn wherein this church was lacking,—in grace, justifying righteousness, and the saving self searching illumination of the Holy Spirit. As this church had not the promise of exemption from the coming "temptation," (v. 10,) the "gold tried in the fire" of persecution will be indispensable to preserve any from apostacy, whereby their cloak of hypocrisy would be removed, and they be exposed to "shame."—Christ "stands and knocks."—If the church refuses him admittance, yet if but one will "hear his voice and open the door," he will certainly communicate such consolations,—the "joy of his salvation," that it may be said they sup together. (Song v. 1.)

This, as before, is the "hundred-fold," promised in this life, as a foretaste and pledge of heavenly felicity.—There is added, a participation in his honor and authority; for those who suffer with him shall also reign with him. (2 Tim. ii. 12.) Whilst "this honour is to all his saints," it is to be conferred upon them by Christ. This assertion may seem to contradict what Christ said to the mother of Zebedee's sons, (Matt. xx. 23,)—"to sit on my right hand, and on my left, is not mine to give."—No, it is not his to give,—"but, except to them for whom it is prepared of his Father." Then it is his to give,—his right. Of the honor and felicity promised to such as "fight the good fight of faith," none can have an adequate conception without actual experience. (1 John iii. 2.)

GENERAL OBSERVATIONS.

Although the fundamental doctrine of the *Trinity in Unity* be not expressly taught or asserted in these epistles, it is nevertheless often and plainly presupposed. Each epistle begins and closes with express mention of two divine persons as equally the author. What Christ says, the Spirit says to these churches. But there is a *third* divine person often mentioned who is called "God," and "Father." (Ch. ii. 7, 18, 27, etc.;) and in the first verse of chapter third, one speaks who has the seven Spirits of God," where the *Trinity* is included. Thus, while in these epistles this important doctrine of the adorable Trinity,—a doctrine which lies at the very foundation of a sinner's hope, is obscurely revealed, as being clearly discovered in the preceding parts of the Holy Scriptures; the subsequent part of this book of Revelation is intended, among other objects, to demonstrate *the distinct subsistence and economical actings* of the co-equal and eternal Three, in the protection and salvation of the church, and in the control and moral government of the universe.

Again, on the groundless and chimerical assumption of those expositors who view these epistles as prophetical of seven successive periods of the destiny of the church general, the last estate would be worse than the first,—Laodicea being the worst of all. But this is obviously contrary to the description contained in ch. xx. 1-10, where the saints are represented as in possession and exercise of all their purchased and social rights. Neither does authentic history prove that the church of Christ was more prosperous under the "ten persecutions" by the heathen Roman emperors than in the apostolic age, as the superior condition of the church in Smyrna to that of Ephesus would require. The very contrary is true; and hence the groundlessness of such interpretation, however respectable the names of its authors. The object of our Saviour in all the instructions, counsels, warnings, rebukes and threatenings addressed to these several churches is doubtless the real benefit of his people in after generations;—just as his dealings with the church in Old Testament times, "were written for our admonition and learning." (Rom. xv. 4; 1 Cor. x. 11.) Moreover, some persons have inferred from our Lord's treatment of these churches, a *divine warrant* for the existence, and an imperative Christian duty for the charitable recognition, of all the conflicting and antagonistic organizations of our time, popularly styled Christian churches. But as the designation, "Christian churches," is in the apprehension of some too general, the term "evangelical" is used by them as restrictive of the term "Christian." Still the question will present itself,—What constitutes a church "evangelical?" And this question is still without any definite answer. Perhaps no two persons would include in one category the same denominations of professing Christians. For example,—Is a community to be considered a Christian church in which the "doctrine of Balaam" is taught? Does the law of charity require the recognition of an organization as a Christian church, in which a "Jezebel would be suffered to teach, and to seduce the servants of Christ?" Is that a Christian church which denies the supreme deity of Christ, and rejects the seals of the covenant of grace,—the only charter of the Christian church's existence, on earth? Or is that combination to be viewed as a Christian church which has no regular ministry, but expressly rejects the "pastors and teachers" of Christ's appointment and the morality of the sabbath? These, and many other questions of similar or analogous import, will suggest negative answers to all who fear God, respect his authority, and are free from the bewildering effects of popular error.

It ought to be considered that all these *seven* churches were *one church*, as originally constituted, having the same,—that, is, a divine, scriptural organization. And although in the divine forbearance, they were still owned by Christ, notwithstanding the errors, heresies and immoralities which had crept into them; yet it is manifest that he threatens some of them with divorce, total extinction in case of impenitence. He has indeed fulfilled his awful threats in making them a desolation. Is it reasonable to suppose that he would reorganize these, or recognise others which incorporate the same or the like corruptions in doctrine and practice for tolerating which he has "removed their candlestick," or "spued them out of his mouth?" (*Absit blasphemia*.) To say so, or write so, does not manifest the "charity which rejoiceth not in iniquity, but rejoiceth in the truth." Alas! the present condition of the church general contains frequent evidences, that our Saviour's affectionate counsels, solemn warnings, and awful threatenings, are neither duly pondered nor dutifully regarded.

CHAPTER IV.

With this chapter the prophetical part of the Apocalypse begins. This is the place where the third division of the book commences, of which intimation had been given to John.—"Write ... the things which shall be hereafter." (Ch. i. 19.) The third is therefore much the largest part of the whole book, comprising all from the 4th to the 22d ch. It is also to be noticed that the fourth and fifth chapters are properly of the nature of an introduction to what follows, presenting to view, as it were, a grand theatre on which are to be exhibited the dramatic characters and events which constitute the outline of history in the church and the world from the apostle's time till the consummation of all things.

Expositors commonly frame and lay down some rules by which they suppose symbolic language in general, and the symbols of this book in particular, may be interpreted. On examination, however, it will be discovered that the learned are not agreed either in the nature or number of such rules, and sometimes an expositor who has exerted his ingenuity most in devising canons of interpretation, forgets to apply them.

All languages, whether spoken or written, are more or less metaphorical, interspersed with what are called figures of speech. It is customary to represent nations and tribes, whose language abounds in symbols, as but little advanced in civilization; and to view oriental nations as more disposed to indulge in tropes and figures than those of the west; but perhaps this relative estimate of the modes of speech in the eastern and western hemispheres will admit of some modification, when we consider the gesticulations and similes by which the aborigines of America attempt to give expression to their ideas. The word *hieroglyphics*, signifying sacred sculpture, derived from the ancient mode of writing by the priests of Egypt, has received conventional currency among the learned, as descriptive of any writing which is obscure, "hard to be understood." And all who read this book will find some of it "dark" indeed. The divine Author intended that it should be so, (ch. xiii. 18;) yet he calls it emphatically, a "Revelation."

We have already noticed, that the symbols in this book are taken from the ceremonial law in part, and part are taken from the works of creation. The heavens and the earth present to our senses a variety of material objects; some more, some less calculated to arrest our attention. Among these, the sun, moon and stars,—earth and sea, mountains and rivers, occupy prominent places. To facilitate our knowledge of these, and prompt reference to any part of them, we generalize or throw them into groups. Thus we speak familiarly of the "solar system," the "animal, vegetable or mineral kingdom." Now, just transfer these systematized objects from the material and physical, to the moral and spiritual world. Then consider what relation any one object bears to the system, and what influence it has upon the other objects of which it is a part, and its import may be generally, satisfactorily and certainly ascertained. Thus the same canons or rules which we apply in the interpretation of other writings, will be equally available in "searching the Scriptures,"—never, never forgetting that it is the Spirit of Christ that "guides into all truth," or his own all-comprehensive rule of interpretation, "comparing spiritual things with spiritual." (1 Cor. ii. 13.)

In order to the right observance of the divinely prescribed rule, "comparing spiritual things with spiritual," we must often refer to the prophecies of the Old Testament,—to the second and seventh chapters of Daniel in particular, because that prophet, while the church was captive under the power of literal Babylon, was favoured with a discovery of the purpose of God, that a succession of imperial powers should afterwards arise to "try the patience and the faith of the saints." As in the case of Pharaoh, so in the whole history of the rise, reign and overthrow of succeeding persecuting powers, Jehovah's design was precisely the same,—"to make his power known, and that his name might be declared throughout all the earth." (Ex. ix. 16; Rom. ix. 17.) In connexion with this, he would "glorify the riches of his grace on the vessels of mercy, which he had afore prepared unto glory," by sustaining them in the furnace of trial.

1. *After this I looked, and, behold, a door was opened in heaven: and the first voice which I heard was as it were of a trumpet talking with me; which said. Come up hither, and I will show thee things which must be hereafter.*

2. And immediately I was in the Spirit; and, behold, a throne was set in heaven, and one sat on the throne.
3. And he that sat was to look upon like a jasper and a sardine stone: and there was a rainbow round about the throne, in sight like unto an emerald.

Vs. 1-3.—"After these things," contained in the three preceding chapters, the glorious vision of the mediatorial person, and the writing and sending of the seven epistles; there seems to have intervened a pause. While John was in expectation of farther discoveries of "things which were to be thereafter," "behold, a door was opened in heaven," the place of Jehovah's special residence. But as this "heaven" is sometimes the theatre of *war*, (ch. xii. 7,) of course it is not to be taken literally. As a symbol it generally signifies organized society, over which the Most High presides. The "door opened" afforded the means to John of seeing the objects within. The "voice as of a trumpet," which arrested his attention, was that of Christ,—the "voice of the Lord, full of majesty." (Ps. xxix. 4; ch. i. 10, 11.) John was in his own apprehension, like Paul, "caught up into the third heaven," that he might behold in glorious succession "things which must be hereafter." Why *must* they be? Simply because such was the "purpose of Him who worketh all things after the counsel of his own will; who is wonderful in counsel and excellent in working; whose counsel stands, and who doeth all his pleasure." (Eph. i. 11.) Can a rational creature work without a plan? And shall mortal man be more rational than his Maker? The objects which were presented to John are not to be understood as *material* objects. It was requisite that he should be "in the Spirit," before he could see them. The exercise of his bodily senses, the organs of sensation, must be suspended, that he might have a perception of the objects presented in vision. As the "spirits of just men made perfect" in glory, in a disembodied state, are still conscious and active; so are we warranted to conceive of souls yet in the body as being in a state analagous,—falling into a trance. (Acts x. 10.) The first object seen by John was a "throne set in heaven," the emblem of sovereignty. "One sat on the throne," who cannot be described, only in an obscure manner by comparison, being "the invisible God, whom no eye hath seen, nor can see." Yet we know with certainty it is the person of the Father, because he is in the next chapter plainly distinguished from "the Lamb." Seated on the throne,—and "in the throne he is greater than the Mediator." A relation between these divine persons was shadowed forth in Egypt between Pharaoh and Joseph. (Gen. xli. 40.) Occupying the throne of the universe, the Father sustains the majesty of the Godhead, and represents the persons of the adorable Trinity; for the idea is equally unscriptural and absurd, that either person appears or acts (*ad extra*) in absolute or essential character. (Is. xlii. 1; John x. 18; xiv. 31.) He that "sat, was ... like a jasper and a sardine stone,"—not like any human form, but in allusion, perhaps, to the Shekinah or visible glory above the mercy-seat in the most holy place, he appeared in the essential purity or holiness of his nature and awful justice,—one "who will by no means clear the guilty." The rainbow is the familiar emblem or "token of the covenant." Its being "round about the throne" teaches us, that God "in wrath remembers mercy." As "green" is the color most pleasing to the natural eye, so is the rainbow of covenant mercy most grateful to the penitent sinner, contemplated by the eye of faith. God is "ever mindful of his covenant." (Ps. cxi. 5.)

Ever since the revelation of mercy to fallen man, God deals with mankind, not in essential or absolute character, but by covenant in economical standing. All along since that epoch in the history of this world, "the Father judgeth no man, but hath committed all judgment unto the Son." As yet, however, the Son is not brought upon the stage in the apostle's present view. The Son has his appropriate place in the vision, where he will appear as Mediator. In the conflict to be carried on for twelve hundred and sixty years by the combined powers of earth and hell "against the Lord and his Anointed," we have the agencies exhibited in these two chapters *only on heaven's side*. The opposing hosts will afterwards appear.

> 4. *And round about the throne were four and twenty seats; and upon the seats I saw four and twenty elders sitting, clothed in white raiment; and they had on their heads crowns of gold.*
> 5. *And out of the throne proceeded lightnings, and thunderings, and voices: and there were seven lamps of fire burning before the throne, which are the seven spirits of God.*

Vs. 4, 5.—To John's view, the "throne" seen from one side would appear to be surrounded by a segment of a circle, within which were "four and twenty seats," (thrones,) occupied by an equal number of "elders." In society divinely organized "elders" have always been the legal representatives of God's covenant society in civil and ecclesiastical relations. (Exod. iii. 16; Acts xx. 17.) These "four and twenty elders" represent the collective body of God's people under the Old and New Testaments,—the "twelve tribes of Israel" and the "twelve apostles." (ch. vii. 4; xxi. 12-14.) Their "white raiment" and "crowns of gold" indicate their legal state and moral purity,—their justification and sanctification, as also their promotion to honour, to "reign as kings." (ch, i. 6; v. 10.) ["*reign on the earth,*" ch, xx. 4.] Allusion is had to the terrific scene at Sinai by the "lightnings," etc., when "Moses did exceedingly fear and quake," importing that God, "our God, is a consuming fire" to all his impenitent, especially antichristian, enemies, even under the milder economy of the New Testament. (Heb. x. 28-31; ch. xx. 10.) The "seven lamps of fire" are explained to mean "the seven spirits of God," in allusion to the golden candlestick in the temple, (Exod. xxxvii. 23; Zech. iv. 2,) and signifying the gifts and graces of those who are "baptized with the Holy Ghost and with fire."

6. *And before the throne there was a sea of glass like unto crystal; and in the midst of the throne, and round about the throne, were four beasts full of eyes before and behind.*
7. *And the first beast was like a lion, and the second beast like a calf, and the third beast had a face as a man, and the fourth beast was like a flying eagle.*
8. *And the four beasts had each of them six wings about him; and they were full of eyes within: and they rest not day and night, saying, Holy, holy, holy, Lord God Almighty, which was, and is, and is to come.*
9. *And when those beasts give glory, and honor, and thanks, to him that sat on the throne, who liveth for ever and ever,*
10. *The four and twenty elders fall down before him that sat on the throne, and worship him that liveth for ever and ever, and cast their crowns before the throne, saying,*
11. *Thou art worthy, O Lord, to receive glory, and honour, and power; for thou hast created all things, and for thy pleasure they are and were created.*

Vs. 6-11.—The "sea of glass before the throne" is a symbol taken from the "brazen sea" in the temple, in which priests and victims were to be washed. (Exod. xxx. 18; 1 Kings vii. 23.) This sea represents the same thing as the "fountain opened," (Zech. xiii. 1,) which denotes the atoning and cleansing blood of Christ. (Ch. vii. 14.) All who offer "spiritual sacrifices, acceptable to God," must first be washed; for the "Lord had respect to Abel" *first*, and then to his "offering," (Gen. iv. 4.)—Next, John saw "four beasts." The translation here is faulty, as noticed by many expositors. Different words in the original Greek,—not only different, but in some respects opposite in signification, ought not to be rendered by the same English word; for this tends to mislead the unlearned leader. He is thus bewildered instead of being enlightened. There are several beasts besides these, introduced as instructive symbols in this book. Two are mentioned in ch. xiii. 1, 11, altogether different from these,—so different as to be antagonistic. Instead of "beasts," they should have been called "animals" or "living beings;" for even the phrase "living *creatures*" hardly covers or conveys the whole import of the Greek word. The position of these "four animals" is worthy of special notice:—"in the midst of the throne, and round about the throne." How can this be? Well, if the "seats" and the "elders" occupying them are "round about the throne," in a segment of a circle, as viewed by John, then it will be readily perceived that the "animals" seen from the same quarter would appear to him as occupying a space forming a smaller segment of a circle between the elders and the throne. Thus we have the relative positions, (*a*) the throne, (*b*) the "four animals" next to the throne, and lastly, (*c*) the "four and twenty elders." The places occupied by these several parties are pregnant with scriptural instruction, as may appear when we come to the latter part of ch. 6.

In the mean time, what do these "four animals" represent? Not the adorable Trinity, as some learned men have imagined; nor holy angels, as more learned men have supposed and laboured to prove. These "animals" are worshippers; (v. 8,) therefore they are not the Object of worship. They are culpably blind who mistake the creature for the Creator. (Rom. i. 25.) Other expositors have attempted, with greater plausibility, but no better success, to prove these animals to be symbolical of angels. For this purpose, reference has been made to Isaiah's vision of the *seraphims*, (ch. vi. 2,) and also to the "four living creatures" which appeared in vision to Ezekiel, (i. 5-10.) The identity of John's "animals" and Ezekiel's "living creatures" is argued especially from their number, "four," and their "faces" being the same. To the thoughtful and unbiased reader it is sufficient to reply,—that John's "animals" acknowledge themselves to have been *redeemed* by the blood of the Lamb, (ch. v. 8, 9,) an expression which is inapplicable to angels. As the "four and twenty elders" and the "four animals" comprise the whole company of the *redeemed*, as distinguished from the higher and lower orders of God's worshippers, (ch. v. 8-14,) and as the "elders" represent the whole church, it would seem to be reasonable to suppose, that these "animals" are the symbols of the gospel ministry. And to this agree their functions as exercised in the farther developments of this book, as we shall see.

One plausible objection to this interpretation is grounded on the fact that their "faces" are the same as those of Ezekiel's angels,—"of an ox, or young calf, of a lion, of a man, and of an eagle." But each of the "cherubims" had "four faces" whereas these "animals" have but *one* face each. Nor ought it to be thought incongruous that faithful ministers are represented as possessing some of the properties of holy angels, when we find them called by the same name: (ch. i. 20;) and also, when we find the Master directing them to imitate and emulate holy angels in their services. (Matt. vi. 10; Ps. ciii. 20, 21.) These "animals," emblematical of the gospel ministry, are in number "four," answerable to the universality of their mission into the four quarters of the earth,—"all the world." (Matt, xxviii. 19; Mark, xvi. 15.) So the "four winds," (ch. vii. 1,) mean all winds. As the "lion, which is the strongest among beasts, and turneth not away for any," is distinguished for courage and magnanimity; so, as a symbol, it represents a ministry of courageous and heroic spirit. Luther in continental, and Knox in insular Europe, may be named as displaying this prominent feature of ministerial character. The "calf" or young ox, symbolizes "patient continuance in well-doing" amidst trials, such as "cruel mockings," etc. The "face as a man" indicates sagacity, "Christian prudence," together with active sympathy. The "flying eagle" is emblematical of penetration and discrimination,—"ability to teach others," from a spiritual insight into the divine character and purposes,—an experimental acquaintance with "the God of glory." All these properties are not to be supposed ordinarily in any one minister, but as distributed among the ministry at large,—"according to the measure of the gift of Christ,"—the Holy Spirit "dividing to every man severally as he will." (Eph. iv. 7; 1 Cor. xii. 11.) It may be remarked, that in some cases all these properties may be discerned in great measure in the same individual. In the gifts and grace of the apostle Paul, may be discovered the *boldness* of the *lion*, the *patience* of the *ox*, the *compassion* of the *man*, and the *soaring flight* of the *eagle*. Our covenant God endows his servants for the service to which he calls them, always making good the promise,—"As thy days, so shall thy strength be." The "six wings," of course, are expressive of the activity of the ministry,—"in season, out of season," emulating the heavenly seraphims in serving the same Lord. They were "full of eyes before, behind, within." They are to "take heed to themselves, and to the ministry which they have received in the Lord, that they fulfil it." (Col. iv. 17; 1 Tim. iv. 16.) They are to regard the operation of God's hand in providence, so as to "have understanding of the times, and know what Israel ought to do." (1 Chron. xii. 32.) They are to "try the spirits whether they are of God;" and "after the first and second admonition, to reject heretics." (Tit. iii. 10.) They are to "oversee the flock," (Acts xx. 28;) and to "watch for souls, as they that must give account" to the Master. (Heb. xiii. 17.) And we may say with Paul,—"Who is sufficient for these things?" Modern prelates, who arrogate to themselves the exclusive use of the Scriptural official name "BISHOP," generally manifest that they are *only* bishops, (*two-eyed*) and not the *many-eyed* servants of Christ, symbolized by the "four animals" of our text, or the "overseeing *elders*" charged at Miletus by the apostle Paul. (Acts xx. 17.) "While these men slept, the enemy sowed tares."—In direct acts of worship, these "animals,"—the ministers, take the lead, answerable to another official name,—"guides, in things pertaining to God." (Heb. xiii. 7; [Greek] v. 1.) They are, as well expressed by another phrase, the "sworn expounders of God's word," and authoritative rulers in his house. Destitute of legislative power, which in ecclesiastical affairs pertains to Christ alone; they are the authorized administrators of all the laws by which his household is to be governed. (Heb. xiii. 7, 17.)—The language of adoration here is the same uttered by the seraphim. (Isa. vi. 3) The "holiness" of God is that adorable character which is most attractive to holy angels and redeemed sinners, being the principal feature of the divine image reflected by themselves. (Matt. xxv. 31; Jude 14; 1 John iii. 2.) The glorious Being seen by John, as sitting on a throne, is the same who was seen by Isaiah, (vi. 1;) and precisely in the same attitude; but called by different names. By Isaiah he is denominated "the Lord of Hosts,"—by John, "the Lord God Almighty." The context proves,—especially ch. v. 1; that John in vision contemplated God in the *person* of the *Father*; whereas we are assured, in John xii. 41, that Isaiah saw him in the *person* of the *Son*. Thus we may understand our Lord's words addressed to Philip, (John xiv. 9.) "He that hath seen me hath seen the father." (See Heb. i. 8; Col. i. 15.)

Led by the "four animals,"—the ministry of reconciliation; the "four and twenty elders," representing all the redeemed of mankind, "fall down before him that sat on the throne" in prostrate adoration of that glorious Being whose "eternal power and Godhead" are demonstrated in the volume of creation. We are thus taught that motives to acceptable worship of God are *primarily* to be found in the *perfections* of his *nature* as our beneficent Creator,—perfections possessed by him in essential character, independently of all his works of creation and redemption. His "worthiness" of worship is inherent in himself, but outwardly manifested to intelligent creatures by the work of creation, of which he is the first Cause and the last End,—the efficient and final Cause. This doctrine, understood by the intellect and unbraced in the heart, would greatly tend to "hide pride from man." (Job xxxiii. 17.) Aside from the doctrine of the "cross," which is still counted "foolishness" by our modern self-styled "philosophers, psychologists and freethinkers;" there is enough here revealed of this eternal One to humble the "proud looks and haughty hearts" of these "enemies of the King." Without repentance, "he that made them will not have mercy on them; and he that formed them will show them no favour;" for notwithstanding their pride of superior intellect, he whose judgment is according to truth, has pronounced them a "people of no understanding." (Isa. xxvii. 11.) It is no disparagement to those in places of highest earthly dignity, as David; nor to the wisest of all men, as Solomon: to "cast their crowns before the throne" of this only universal Monarch; saying, "Thou art worthy, O Lord, to receive glory and honor and power; for thou hast created all things, and for thy pleasure they are and were created;" "and let the whole earth be filled with his glory." (Ps. lxxii. 19.)

CHAPTER IV.

CHAPTER V.

> 1. And I saw in the right hand of him that sat on the throne a book written within and on the backside, sealed with seven seals.

V. 1.—The dividing of the books of Scripture into chapters and verses is not by inspiration. Fallible men have used their discretion in this respect, as they still do, by parceling chapters into sections, paragraphs, &c. And so, although we have passed to another chapter, the vision is the same. The inspired penman had looked upon the great King surrounded by part of his retinue. In earnest expectation of farther discoveries, he beheld "in the right hand of him that sat on the throne a book written within and on the back side," (or *outside,* as in some copies.) The book was "sealed with seven seals." This volume was in the form of a *roll,* as the word *volume* signifies. The form of a book is determined by the kind of material on which one writes. This has consisted of great variety in the successive ages of the world. The first of which we have any notice in history is *stone.* When Job, in his affliction, was sustained by faith in the promised Redeemer; and when he would emphasize and transmit an expression of that faith to future generations; he thought of the nearest expedient familiar to his mind:—"Oh that my words were now written.... that they were graven with an iron pen.... in the rock forever," (Job xix. 23, 24.) On the same material the law was written at Horeb, (Exod. xxiv. 12.) No doubt this was the usual method of recording events in Egypt in the time of Joseph, as the word "hieroglyphics" or *sacred sculpture,* appears to imply. Next, it appears that the inside bark of trees was used for this purpose, as of birch, which has a natural tendency to *curl* or *roll* together when dry. Hence the word *library,* and volume, or *rolled bark.* The royal archives, or "house of the rolls," is thus explained, (Ezra. vi. 1.) "Vellum," or dressed skins of beasts, appears to have been next used; then linen and cotton; and as now put through a chemical process, these are the material in most common use at the present day. Thus contemplating the symbol in the text, we may trace in our thoughts the gradual advancement of this department of science and the mechanic arts. The second stage of progress had been reached in John's time, from stone to the bark of timber. The "book" appears to have been of cylindrical form, but whether in one piece or in seven separate pieces, revolving on a common axis, it is not easy nor perhaps important to determine. It is of much greater importance to know that the "book" is emblematical of the decrees of God. This will appear by comparing Psalm xl. 7, where we find the same symbol employed to represent the record of covenant agreement or stipulation between the Father and the Son, and to which our Saviour appeals as evidence in his case. (Heb. x. 7.) While the symbol may be safely considered as involving all the purposes of God; it signifies here more especially the following part of the Apocalypse, containing, as it were, a transcript from the great original.—"Seals" are for security and secrecy. Both may be included in the case. And indeed their being "seven" in number—a number of perfection, would seem to confirm this two-fold meaning. The sealed book, symbolical of the decrees of God, comprehending all events of all time, teaches us the doctrine expressed in plain words thus:—"Known unto God are all his works from the beginning of the world," (Acts xv. 18.) The complex symbol also teaches more forcibly than in words,—"My counsel shall stand, and I will do all my pleasure," (Is, xlvi. 10.) Some have suggested a little change in the punctuation. Instead of placing the comma, after the word "side," place it after the word "within," the meaning would then be, that the "book was written only on *one* side, namely on the side *within*." We do not accept the suggestion. The reason is sufficient for its rejection, that the material in the time of the apostle, was too costly to leave one-half of it *blank*; and here our divine Lord "speaks to us of heavenly things" through the medium of earthly things with which we are familiar.

2. And I saw a strong angel proclaiming with a loud voice, Who is worthy to open the book, and to loose the seals thereof?
3. And no man in heaven, nor in earth, neither under the earth, was able to open the book, neither to look thereon.

Vs. 2, 3.—Proclamation is made by a "strong angel," the Almighty Monarch's herald to the universe, challenging all creatures to the task of opening the seals. His "loud voice" reverberates throughout illimitable space, that all concerned might hear. The challenge is not, "who is *able?*" but, "who is *worthy?*"—Who is "worthy," by personal dignity, or distinguished and meritorious services, "to open the book and to loose the seals thereof?" No response comes from any quarter to break the solemn silence. The whole creation is mute. "Who hath known the mind of the Lord? or who hath been his counsellor?" "O the depth of the riches both of the wisdom and knowledge of God! How unsearchable are his judgments and his ways past finding out!" (Rom. xi. 33, 34.)—"And no man in heaven," &c. The word "man" is in this place, as in many others, an imperfect and inadequate supplement. In some places it is calculated to mislead the "unlearned and unstable," as John x. 28, 29, (in some copies,) Heb. ii. 9. The former text, as supplemented by the word "man," contradicts the apostle, Rom. viii. 39. The meaning here is obviously that no *creature*,—angel or man, was worthy or "able" to "open the book." To holy angels, devils, and the dead "under the earth," the purposes of God are as inscrutable as they are to us, until they are revealed. (Eph. iii. 10; 1 Pet. i. 12.)

4. *And I wept much, because no man was found worthy to open and to read the book, neither to look thereon.*

V. 4.—John understood by the symbol which he saw, that its contents were of deep significance. A sanctified curiosity and anxiety, more powerful than that of the Ethiopian eunuch, (Acts viii. 34,) occupied his soul. But the book is sealed and there is no visible interpreter! (Is. xxix. 11.) The "beloved disciple" is much affected. He has more than once or twice "beheld the glory of God," and cannot but earnestly desire to know more of his mind. "Hope deferred maketh his heart sick." He "wept much." His covenant God "has seen his tears." He "will heal him," (2 Kings xx. 5.)

5. *And one of the elders saith unto me, Weep not: behold, the Lion of the tribe of Juda, the Root of David, hath prevailed to open the book, and to loose the seven seals thereof.*

V. 5.—From a quite unexpected quarter comes a hint! How could John anticipate relief from such a source? "One of the elders" is made the messenger of joyful tidings. As Aquila and Priscilla took to them the eloquent Apollos, and "expounded unto him the way of God more perfectly," (Acts xviii. 26,) so one of the elders—one of the humble disciples was the instrument of comfortable instruction to the aged apostle! The prophet Daniel was similarly affected by a partial exhibition of the same important events; but his anxiety to know the meaning of the vision, though allayed, was not fully gratified, as that of John. (Dan. xii. 8, 9,) "Go thy way, Daniel, for the words are closed up and sealed." The desire of the best of God's people to know his purposes may be sometimes excessive, as exemplified by the disciples of Christ, (Acts i. 7.) "It is not for them to know the times and the seasons which the Father hath put in his own power." So much, however, is revealed as may be necessary to their present support and comfort; and the rest they "shall know hereafter," (John xiii. 7.) But as the events involved in the secret purpose of God, were concealed from Daniel; because not to be evolved till near "the time of the end:" so in John's time, when as in Abraham's case, "the time of the promise drew nigh"—the time was approaching when the interests of God's people would be greatly affected by these events; it became needful that the book should be unsealed and its contents made known. "The time was at hand." Accordingly, John is exhorted by the elder to dry up his tears, for to the unspeakable joy of himself and of the whole creation, the announcement is made,—"Behold, the Lion of the tribe of Judah, the Root of David, hath prevailed to open the book, and to loose the seven seals thereof." Here our attention is called away back to the famous prophecy of dying Jacob, (Gen. xlix. 9, 10,) and also to the subsequent and concurrent declaration of the evangelical prophet, (Isa. xi. 1, 10.) Christ is the "Lion of the tribe of Judah" in reference to his human nature; "for it is evident," from the inspired tables of his genealogy, "that our Lord sprang out of Judah," (Heb. vii. 14;) and it is no less evident that he is the Root of David, in respect to his divine nature, (John i. 1, 3; Isa. ix. 6; 1 Cor. xv. 47.) The "one Mediator between God and men," partaking of the nature of each party, is "worthy"—alone worthy, by reason of personal dignity, to "open the book." It is also to be noticed that *worthiness* is not his only qualification. In view of the challenge published,—"who is worthy?" the answer is, this champion "hath *prevailed!*"—Isaiah saw him in vision, victorious over enemies—"travelling in the greatness of his strength," (Isa. lxiii. 1.) To his *personal* worthiness is to be added the unrivalled merit of his achievements in conflict with hostile powers, (Gen. iii. 15; Isa. liii. 12; Col. ii. 15.)

6. *And I beheld, and, lo, in the midst of the throne and of the four beasts, and in the midst of the elders, stood a Lamb as it had been slain, having seven horns and seven eyes, which are the seven Spirits of God sent forth into all the earth.*

V. 6.—In this verse we have the Lord Jesus Christ introduced to the view of John and the intelligent universe in his sacerdotal or priestly office, "a lamb, as it had been slain." In the order of nature and of merit, his priestly office precedes his prophetical and kingly offices. This is evident from the position which he occupies in relation to the throne and royal retinue. He stands in the attitude of a priest "in the midst of the throne and of the four animals," etc. As seen here, our Saviour does not *sit on the throne.* He appeared in a standing posture. His position was obviously *before* the throne. As the priestly function required, he stood nearest to the object of worship, between the ministers and the throne,—in the inmost circle. There he exhibited the scars received in war; the wounds made by the sword of divine justice; (Zech. xiii. 7;) the holes in his hands and side by the nails and soldier's spear. (John xix. 34; xx. 23.) This "Lamb slain,"—typified by all the spotless lambs offered in sacrifice by divine appointment from the time of Abel, had been marvellously restored to life, as no other victim had ever been. (John x. 18; ch. i. 18.) The "seven horns and seven eyes," symbolize the power and wisdom of the Mediator. "It pleased the Father that in him should all fulness dwell." (Col. i. 19.) He "giveth not the Spirit by measure unto him." (John iii. 34; Heb. i. 9.) Christ was privy to all the purposes of his Father, (John v. 20,) and the extent of his knowledge is limited in him *as Mediator,* only by the authority and will of the Father. "Of that day and that hour ... knoweth no man ... neither the Son." (Mark xiii. 32.) The same interesting and important truth is taught by the Father's holding the book in his hand, as also in plain words, (ch. i. 1,)—"the Revelation of Jesus Christ which God gave unto him." "No man knoweth the Father but the Son." (Matt. xi. 27.) In office-capacity the Lord Christ is qualified to unfold and execute the decree of God. (Ps. ii. 7,) as more fully appears in the following part of the book.

7. *And he came and took the book out of the right hand of him that sat upon the throne.*

V. 7.—The Lord Jesus approaches his Father's throne to receive the roll. And with the prophet we may ask,—"Who is this that engaged his heart to approach?" (Jer. xxx. 21.)—With all who are honored to surround the throne, we may joyfully answer in the words of the Psalmist,—It is the "Lord, strong and mighty in battle." (Ps. xxiv. 8.) "He took the book."—This action symbolically signified the authoritative commission given by the Father and received by the Mediator to proceed in the execution of the divine decree, and in discharge of his threefold office as prophet, priest and king,—especially and more formally his prophetical and kingly offices.

> 8. And when he had taken the book, the four beasts and four and twenty elders fell down before the Lamb, having every one of them harps, and golden vials full of odours, which are the prayers of saints.

V. 8.—No sooner does the "Lamb take the book," than all spectators are apprized of the act, and instantly give expression to their confidence and joy. Among all the worshippers before the throne, the "four animals" take precedence, and lead by their own example as before, (ch. iv. 9.) They gave "glory" etc., to God creator, as in the person of the Father; and now in the presence of the Father's manifested glory, they prostrate themselves before the "Lamb," in obedience to the Father's command, "That all men should honor the Son, even as they honor the Father." (John v. 23.)—The "four and twenty elders,"—the representatives of all the children of God, cordially join the ministry in these acts of solemn worship. Some of the furniture employed in the temple worship, is here introduced, to harmonize with the rest of the symbolic scenery. "Harps and golden vials" signify praise and prayer. Our modern advocates for instrumental music in God's worship, to be consistent, must associate with the "harps," the "incense-cups" and the "golden altar:" for all belonged alike to the service of the temple. Even in the time when such "vessels of the ministry" were in use with divine approbation, the Psalmist had greater clearness,—more evangelical conceptions of the temporary use of those "beggarly elements whereunto many desire again to be in bondage" than they seem to have. (Gal. iv. 9.) He knew, even then, that "incense and the evening sacrifice" represented spiritual worship. (Ps. cxli. 2.) Others there are, who question whether Christ as Mediator be the *formal* object of worship? While they acknowledge his supreme deity as God equal with the Father, they are in doubt on his assuming human nature, whether, "as such, he is the object of worship!" Such doubts are groundless, as unanswerably shown in this place, and in many others, such as John xx. 28: xxi. 17; Ps. xlv. 11; xcvii. 7; Heb. i. 6. All these worshippers appear to know that the nature of the *altar* at which they worship determines the kind of oblations to be offered: namely,—"spiritual sacrifices, acceptable to God by Jesus Christ." (1 Pet. ii. 5.)

9. *And they sung a new song, saying, Thou art worthy to take the book, and to open the seals thereof: for thou wast slain and hast redeemed us to God by thy blood out of every kindred, and tongue, and people, and nation;*
10. *And hast made us unto our God kings and priests, and we shall reign on the earth.*

Vs. 9, 10.—"They sung a new song." They all agreed in the matter, as well as in the divine object of worship. "Now will I sing to my well beloved a song of my beloved touching his vineyard." (Isa. v. 1.) Agreed as to the object and matter of the song none is silent in Immanuel's praise,—no *select choir*, not one who *worships by proxy*. Such belong to a different fellowship. This is the "song of the Lamb," which joined to the "song of Moses," constitutes the whole of the "high praises of the Lord," leaving no place for the vapid, empty, bombastic, amorous and heretical effusions, of uninspired men, whether of sound or "corrupt minds."—The burden of the song is the same as the "Song of Songs" and the forty-fifth Psalm,—"Christ crucified,"—Christ glorified, "the praises of him who hath called them from darkness into his marvellous light." The key-note among them all is the work of redemption. "Thou hast redeemed us to God by thy blood,"—*us*, and not others in the same condition. Others may talk of a ransom that does not redeem: but these dwell with emphasis upon the price and power that brought them "out of every kindred, and tongue, and people, and nation." This happy and joyful company never conceived the idea that, in order at once to vindicate Jehovah's moral government and give the most impressive demonstration of his opposition to sin, he subjected his beloved Son to untold sufferings, which should be equally available by all his enemies, but *specially intended for none in particular*! They never imagined that their adorable Creator was under a natural necessity of "seeking the greatest good of the greatest number," that he might thereby escape the just imputation of *partiality*. Such impious conceptions imply distributive injustice on the part of God, when he "spared not the angels that sinned, but cast them down to hell." (2 Pet. ii. 4.) Neither man's chief end nor God's is the happiness of creatures,—no, neither in creation nor redemption, as is clear to unsophisticated reason, and plainly determined by the Spirit of God. (See ch. iv. 11; Isa. xliii. 7, 21; Eph. i. 12.) The manifestation of his own perfections,—his own glory, is the highest and ultimate end of Jehovah in all his purposes and works. "The Lord hath made all things for himself." (Prov. xvi. 4; Rom. xi. 36.) Now, if the Lamb has redeemed the whole human family, as some affirm; then it will follow that all must be saved, or Christ died in vain, in reference to them that are lost: and besides, the "Judge of all the earth" would be chargeable with exercising distributive injustice, in exacting double payment, first from the Surety, and then from the sinner! "That be far from God." "He is just and having salvation,"—"a just God and a Saviour." (Zech. ix. 9; Isa. xlv. 21.) As there can be no liberty without law, so there can be no mercy without justice, though there may be "justice without mercy." (James i. 25; ii. 13.) This worshipping company, the representatives of the universal church, ascribe their redemption to the blood of Christ. It is their declared faith that pardon is grounded on atonement, that "without shedding of blood is no remission." (Heb. ix. 22; Lev. xvii. 11; ch. i. 5.) They believe, moreover, that as the obedience of Christ unto death, his doing and dying, is an adequate satisfaction to law and justice; so by compact between the Father and the Son, his penal sufferings avail the believing sinner for pardon. Thus it is, that "if we confess our sins, he (God the Father,) is faithful and *just* to forgive us our sins." (1 John i. 9.) This doctrine the apostle, as the mouth of the whole church, had already avowed: (ch. i. 5, 6;) and now again we have it repeated and incorporated in the song of praise. Thus, while "Christ crucified is to the Jews a stumbling block, and to the Greeks foolishness;" to them who are saved this humbling doctrine is "the power of God and the wisdom of God." (1 Cor. i. 24, 25.) God's glory and the saints' honor and felicity equally spring from the slaying of the Lamb. These good things the blood of Abel's sacrifice spake in type soon after the fall: and here we have the same things proclaimed as the faith of all believers. (Heb. xi. 1.)

By this blood they are consecrated a "royal priesthood" to offer up spiritual sacrifices; and there is a period in the world's eventful history, when they shall "reign on the earth." Of the nature of this *reign* there are two views entertained. That of the Millenarians, under the supposed corporeal presence of Christ, which is *too gross,* after the manner of carnal Jews: the other *too refined* and remote, after the manner of carnal Christians, who "will not have this man to reign over them,"— *except in the church.* Such Christians come very near the views and sentiment of those who exclaimed,—"Not this man, but Barabbas." (John xviii. 40.) Of the nature of Christ's royal dominion we will have occasion to treat in other parts of the Apocalypse; but we take occasion to remark, that his kingly office is formally and meritoriously founded on the efficacy of his sacrifice: "Thou art worthy, for thou wast slain."—That the saints shall "reign in glory" in company with their Saviour is a precious scripture truth; but it is not the truth taught in the words,—"we shall reign *on the earth.*" This is not the place to enter on a full discussion of the doctrine here avowed; yet the following may be adduced as part of the warrant of this doctrine. (Dan. vii. 27; Rev. xx. 4.)

11. *And I beheld, and I heard the voice of many angels round about the throne, and the beasts, and the elders: and the number of them was ten thousand times ten thousand, and thousands of thousands;*
12. *Saying with a loud voice, Worthy is the Lamb that was slain to receive power, and riches, and wisdom, and strength, and honour, and glory, and blessing.*

Vs. 11, 12.—Here we have the concurrence of holy angels, as seen by John in vision, with all the redeemed in acts of solemn worship offered directly to the Lamb.—"Many angels," how many? Some divines have actually attempted, by arithmetical rules, to compute the number! Such employment may amuse, but it cannot edify. The definite here mentioned for indefinite numbers, may be easily computed; (as in Dan. vii. 10; Ps. lxviii. 17;) but still we would labor in vain "to find out the account;" for we are expressly told that they are "innumerable." (Heb. xii. 22.) Like the ransomed children of Adam, they are "a great multitude which no man can number." (ch. vii. 9.) Why then attempt that which the Holy Spirit has pronounced impossible? "Vain man would be wise." It is of much more consequence for us to contemplate their position, relations and employments. Their *position* is "round about the throne," beholding the "Lamb as it had been slain." The law of their creation could not reveal to them this object of adoration. That they may know their duty to the Mediatorial Person as their moral Head, it is requisite that they be directed by a new revelation. Accordingly, we find a "new commandment" issued from God the Father expressly to them. (Ps. xcvii. 7; Heb. i. 6.) "Worship him, all ye gods;" that is, "Let all the angels of God worship him." By the development of the eternal counsels of God in his dealings with the church, these "principalities and powers in heavenly places," discover with adoring wonder more and more of the "manifold wisdom of God." They *stoop down*, as it were, "to look into this" mysterious economy, (Eph. iii. 10, 11; 1 Pet. i. 12.) They are humbly but intensely desirous to discover still more of "the hidden wisdom which God ordained before the world unto the glory" of their fellow worshippers. (1 Cor. ii. 7.) Such is their position.—They are related to the Lamb as his subjects by the Father's grant and command. "He (Jesus) is gone into heaven ... angels ... being made subject unto him." (1 Pet. iii. 22.) They are also related to the "elder" and "animals," the members and ministers of the church. Said one of them to John,—"I am thy fellow-servant." (ch. xix. 10.) Angels are not ashamed to call them "fellow-servants," whom the Lord Jesus "is not ashamed to call his brethren." (Heb. ii. 11.) As the "four animals" are nearer the throne than the "elders," so are the "elders" nearer the throne than the angels. These are ranged, in John's view, in the outside segment of the circle. All the redeemed, ministry and membership, are "nearer of kin" to the Lamb than angels are. "He took not on him the nature of angels, but he took on him the seed of Abraham." (Heb. ii. 16.) All believers are "members of his body, of his flesh and of his bones." (Eph. v. 30.) He has highly advanced human nature, by taking it into real and indissoluble union with his divine person. This is the special ground of nearness and intimacy between Christ and his brethren. And O, how ought we to emulate holy angels in adoring this precious Redeemer! "He loved the church and gave himself for it," (Eph. v. 25,) and he loved and gave himself for every member of the church. (Gal. ii. 20.)

The employments of this innumerable company of angels, besides "ministering for them who shall be heirs of salvation," (Heb. i. 14;) consist much in admiring contemplations of the glory of the "Lamb slain, and in ascriptions of praise to him who is "worthy to receive power," etc. In this they cordially harmonize with the redeemed, whose delightful exercise is "to show forth the praises of him who hath called them out of darkness into his marvellous light:" (1 Pet. ii. 9:) and all the honor, thus ascribed to the Mediator by both classes of worshippers, is intended to terminate ultimately on the person of God the Father. (Phil. ii. 9-11.) The Father "hath committed all judgment unto the Son, that all men," yes, and all angels, "should honor the Son, even as they honor the Father." (John v. 22, 23.)

13. And every creature which is in heaven, and on the earth, and under the earth, and such are in the sea, and all that are in them, heard I saying, Blessing, and honour, and glory, and power, be unto him that sitteth upon the throne, and unto the Lamb, for ever and ever,
14. And the four beasts said, Amen. And the four and twenty elders fell down and worshipped him that liveth for ever and ever.

Vs. 13, 14.—In addition to angels and men, we have here enumerated "every creature" in the whole vast universe, co-operating in the worship of the two divine Persons as associated in concerting and executing the plan of redemption. Thus the "host of heaven" and all inferior creatures according to their several capacities unite in ascribing "blessing, and honor, and glory, and power, unto him that sitteth upon the throne, and unto the Lamb for ever and ever." And we may say with Nehemiah,—They are both "exalted above all blessing and praise." (Neh. ix. 5.) Fallen angels and reprobate men are excluded, from the nature of the case, and by the unalterable laws of the moral government of the Most High, from any participation in this service. (Ps. cx. 1; 1 Cor. xv. 24, 25; Luke xix. 27.)—Can any one who denies the supreme deity of the Lord Jesus, or who refuses to worship him, ever join the society of these worshippers? Or, supposing the possibility of their admission, could they be otherwise than miserable? O the "blasphemy of them who say they are Jews!"—This is one of the sublime doxologies framed by the Holy Spirit, for the use of all creatures on special occasions, but not to be abused by "vain repetitions" as by Papists and Prelates. The like specimens of the "high praises of the Lord" we have in Ps. lxix. 34.—As the three ranks of worshippers here presented in vision to John, beautifully harmonize in holy exercises, each in its appropriate sphere; so the "animals and elders,"—the rulers and ruled of the church, take precedence of all others in acts of solemn worship, and also close the solemn service, saying,—"Amen."

The "sealed book" being delivered by the Father into the possession of the Mediator, the whole creation awaits with confidence and joy the development of the counsels of God, as they may affect the destinies of his redeemed people. The "Lamb has prevailed to open the book," and his established character is sufficient guarantee for success in accomplishing the responsible work assigned him by his Father. This feeling of confidence is expressed by the worshippers, not only by the matter of their praise, but also by the closing word, "amen;" which word is expressive of their "desires and assurance to be heard."

CHAPTER VI.

1. *And I saw when the Lamb opened one of the seals; and I heard, as it were the noise of thunder, one of the four beasts saying, Come and see.*
2. *And I saw, and behold a white horse: and he that sat on him had a bow; and a crown was given unto him: and he went forth conquering, and to conquer.*

Vs. 1, 2.—The apostle "saw when the Lamb" proceeded to disclose the contents of the book by breaking the seals in regular succession. It is not requisite to suppose that each of the seals covers an exactly equal part of the roll. These parts may be quite different in quantity or length. It is obvious, however, that upon the breaking of any one seal, that part of the roll which the seal was intended to cover, would be disclosed to a spectator's view,—the whole of such part and no more. We shall find as we advance that the several parts of this book are in fact very different in extent. When the seventh and last seal is opened, the whole contents of the book must of course be disclosed: and it will appear that the last of the seals contained a much greater part of the roll than any of the others. To a superficial reader this may be apparent from the circumstance that within the compass of this short chapter, six of the seals exhibit their contents.

By the most learned and sober divines the first six seals are considered as disclosing the events which transpired from the time of the apostle John till the overthrow of pagan idolatry in the Roman empire and the accession of Constantine.

Let us consider the contents of these seals in order: Upon the opening "of one of the seals," the first of course, "one of the four animals" with a voice like "thunder, said, Come and see." This was the animal like a "lion," emblematical of those bold and dauntless servants of Christ who took their life in their hand and "went every where preaching the word," (Acts viii. 4.) Many expositors, of secular notions and affinities, imagine that some one of the Roman emperors is to be understood as represented by him who rides on the white horse,—Vespasian, Titus, or

Trajan. To name such figments is enough to confute them in the mind of such as have spiritual discernment. "White" is not the divinely chosen symbol of bloody warriors or persecutors. It is most frequently the emblem of purity, legal or moral. (Matt. xvii. 2; Rev. iii. 4, 5.) "White horse" may represent the gospel, the Covenant of Grace or the church. In this "chariot," (Song iii. 9,) or upon this horse, as it were, Christ, "the captain of salvation" in apostolic times, "went forth conquering, and to conquer." Much opposition from Jews and Gentiles was raised against his gospel, especially upon his exaltation to his mediatorial throne: but the opening of this seal discloses the Father's purpose to bear out his Son in extending his rightful conquests. (Isa. xlii. 4.) "The Lord gave the word; great was the company of those that published it." (Ps. lxviii. 11.) The "bow and the crown" as symbols, combine the military and regal character of Christ, indicating his victories and succeeding exaltation. He shall wound the heads over the large earth; therefore shall he lift up the head. (Ps. cx. 6.) He is the "Prince of peace," and the primary object of his mission by the Father is, to establish "truth and meekness and righteousness" in the earth. Yet he is a "Lamb," but a Lamb that makes war; and "in righteousness he doth judge and make war." (ch. xix. 11.) In this last cited text we have an irrefragable proof of the correctness of our interpretation of the symbols under the first seal. The rider's name is, "The Word of God," (v. 13.)

3. *And when he had opened the second seal, I heard the second beast say, Come and see.*
4. *And there went out another horse that was red; and power was given to him that sat thereon to take peace from the earth, and that they should kill one another: and there was given unto him a great sword.*

Vs. 3, 4.—The opening of the "second seal" furnishes occasion for the "second animal" to cry, "Come and see." It is the customary business of faithful ministers to invite the disciples of Christ to a contemplation of his providential procedure. "Come, behold the works of the Lord." (Ps. xlvi. 8.) This is the call of the ministry represented by the symbol of a "calf or young ox." "Patient continuance in well doing" is the special duty of Christ's servants in times of suffering. And such seems to be the import of the emblem, the "red horse." By the horse, singly considered, we are to understand a *dispensation* of *providence*. So we are to view it as a symbol in Zech. i. 8; vi. 1-8. The prophet said, "O, my Lord, what are these?... And the man answered,—These are they whom the Lord hath sent to walk to and fro through the earth." We speak familiarly of a "dispensation of the gospel,"—the "white horse." Our attention is now called to a "red horse,"—*fiery*, as the word imports. The character of the dispensation is thus indicated as bloody. Wars should prevail so as to "take peace from the earth." "They should kill one another." The instrument of slaughter is seen,—"a great sword." *Mutual* slaughter does not seem to harmonize with the idea of persecution, by which the saints only "are killed all the day long." History records that insurrections, battles, massacres and devastations of an extraordinary kind took place in the first half of the second century, by which more than half a million of the Jews perished by the hand of the pagans; and a still greater number on the opposite side were slain by the Jews. Thus the two parties who rivalled each other in opposing the gospel and the progress of Christ's kingdom, were made by him the instruments of their mutual destruction. For he it is who directs the movements and course of providence, the "red horse." "Behold what desolations he hath made in the earth!" "In this text," says an eminent expositor, "earth signifies the Roman empire." ... "Daniel, ... whose sealed prophecy is explained by the opening of the Apocalyptical seals, denominates the Roman empire, 'the fourth kingdom upon earth.'" We humbly suggest, that this does not render the Roman empire *synonymous* with *earth*, any more than the Chaldean, Persian, or Grecian. And indeed the monarchs of those empires put forth as extensive claims to universal empire as ever the Cesars did. The word *earth* is to be interpreted always by the context. Like the term *world*, it may sometimes signify the Roman empire, as Luke ii. 1. But in other cases even within the compass of the Apocalypse, it is not to be so understood without manifest confusion, as in ch. xvi. 1, 2. The contents of *all* the vials are there said to be poured out upon the earth; but *earth* is afterwards the special *object* of the *first only*. It follows that this term cannot be uniformly and safely in this book interpreted as identical with and limited by the Roman empire. The importance of accuracy here may become more apparent in our future progress.

CHAPTER VI.

5. And when he had opened the third seal, I heard the third beast say, Come and see. And I beheld, and, lo, a black horse; and he that sat on him had a pair of balances in his hand.
6. And I heard a voice in the midst of the four beasts say, A measure of wheat for a penny, and three measures of barley for a penny; and see thou hurt not the oil and the wine.

Vs. 5, 6.—The third of the four "animals" calls attention to the disclosures made by breaking the "third seal." Hie "had a face as a man," (ch. iv. 7,) indicating, as already said, active sympathy, affectionate counsel and seasonable exhortation in calamitous times. Christian ministers need "the tongue of the learned to speak a word in season to him that is weary," when the judgments of God are abroad in the earth; for some of these press, most sensibly, on the poor. Such is the character of the dispensation symbolized by the "black horse." Scarcity of bread is the judgment represented here by the combined symbols. "Our skin was black like an oven, because of the terrible famine." (Lam. v. 10; Zech. vi. 2.)—The rider "had a pair of balances in his hand." The word translated "balances," literally rendered, signifies a *yoke,—pair,—couple.*—In popular use, it came to signify an instrument for weighing commodities, from the counterpoising (double) scales. This symbol indicated famine,—that people should "eat bread by weight and with care;" (Ezek. iv. 16;) and this is confirmed by the "voice in the midst of the four animals:"—"A measure of wheat for a penny," etc. The quantity of food, and the price, as here announced, would seem to the English reader to express plenty and cheapness. But when it is understood that the "measure of wheat" was the ordinary allowance for a laboring man, and "a penny" the usual wages for *one day*; a little more than a *quart*, for about *fifteen cents*: it may be asked, How could the laboring man procure food and clothing for himself, his wife and children? It is said that three times the quantity of "barley" could be had for the same money; but being a coarser and less nutritious grain, it would reach but little farther in sustaining a family. Famine usually falls heaviest on the middle and lower classes of society. Even in such times the "rich fare sumptuously every day." Accordingly, "the oil and the wine,"—some of the staple productions of Canaan,—are exempted from the providential blight sent upon the necessaries of life. (Gen. xliii. 11.)

According to history, from the year 138, till near the end of the second century, a general scarcity of provisions was felt, notwithstanding all the care and foresight of emperors and their ministers to anticipate the scourge. The Pharaohs on the throne had no Joseph to lay up in store in the "years of plenty." But when our New Testament Joseph would thus fight against the persecutors of his saints by the judgment of famine; he gave previous intimation here to his disciples of the approaching calamity, as his manner is to his own. (Luke xxi. 20-22.)

7. And when he had opened the fourth seal, I heard the voice of the fourth beast say, Come and see.
8. And I looked, and behold a pale horse; and his name that sat on him was death, and hell followed with him: and power was given unto them over the fourth part of the earth, to kill with sword, and with hunger, and with death, and with the beasts of the earth.

Vs. 7, 8.—"It is better to go to the house of mourning than to go to the house of feasting," according to the judgment of the wisest of mere men; (Eccl. vii. 2,) and so we are invited here by a spiritually-minded ministry,—"like a flying eagle." A scene of lamentation, mourning and woe, is disclosed at the opening of the "fourth seal."—All the symbols betoken augmented severity in the judgments. There is "pestilence" added to the sword and famine. "The pale horse," or *livid green*, is the emblem of pestilence. The Mediator conducts the destroying angel to fulfil the will of God. "Before Him went the pestilence;" and by a combination of awful symbols, the king of terrors,—"death," is represented as slaying his victims, and "hell followed with him," satiated with his prey. "Sword, hunger, death and beasts of the earth," were commissioned to lay waste the fourth part of the then known world.

If we are to interpret the "beasts of the earth" literally, then we may easily perceive how the depopulation produced by the other calamities would make way for their increase and destructive ravages. But if we understand these "beasts" as symbolizing the persecuting powers; then adding these to all the other destructive agencies,—especially to the "pale horse," the chief symbol in the group; we may readily perceive the force of the combined emblems, a concentrating, as it were, of all destroying agencies. Historians inform us, that "a pestilence arising from Ethiopia, went through all the provinces of Rome, and wasted them for fifteen years." This, added to the sword of war and persecution, which lasted sixty years, according to some interpreters, or from 211 to 270, would seem to exhaust the events symbolized by the series of the seals, except the seventh, so far at least as the sufferings of the church are concerned. For under the fifth and sixth seals, as will appear, nothing of a calamitous nature befalls the righteous.

9. *And when he had opened the fifth seal, I saw under the altar the souls of them that were slain for the word of God, and for the testimony which they held:*
10. *And they cried with a loud voice, saying, How long, O Lord, holy and true, dost them not judge and avenge our blood on them that dwell on the earth?*
11. *And white robes were given unto every one of them; and it was said unto them, that they should rest yet for a little season, until their fellow-servants also, and their brethren, that should be killed as they were, should be fulfilled.*

Vs. 9-11.—At the opening of the fifth seal, none of the "four animals" calls attention to its contents. This fact may indicate that no new development of providence is intended, but rather the effects of the preceding three, produced upon the church and saints of God; as the sixth discloses the penalty inflicted on his and their enemies.

John saw the "souls of them that were slain."—Souls are visible only in vision, (ch. xx. 4.) These souls were not slain, but they were the souls of them, the persons, that were slain. (Matt. x. 28.) The enemy could kill the body only, an essential part of the human person, although the chief aim was to kill the soul. The ground of their suffering was the same, as that of John, (ch. i. 9.) And from the first of this honoured class,—Abel, mentioned in the Bible, to the last,—Antipas; the cause is the same, and the distinguished name is the same. They are "martyrs for the word of God, and for the testimony which they held." And however tenaciously a person may hold other principles, even though he should die for them, he is not a martyr. The aphorism is true,—It is not suffering for religion, but "the *cause* that makes the martyr,"—suffering unto death from love to "the truth as it is in Jesus."

These souls were "under the altar," in allusion still to the outward means of grace under the Old Testament economy. It is not very material, perhaps, whether we understand the altar for sacrifice or that for incense, the comfortable doctrines, often taught in the Scriptures, are here illustrated. *First*, That the redemption of the sinner is by the atoning sacrifice of Christ. *Second*, That after death,—especially by martyrdom, the soul is safe "under the altar,"—in fellowship with the Saviour. *Third*, That the soul, "made perfect in holiness," retains a deep conviction, that "vengeance belongs to God," (ch. xviii. 20; xix. 1-3.) *Fourth*, That "the spirits of just men made perfect," both desire and need instruction relative to the future evolution of the divine purposes. Adoring the infinite perfections of God, acknowledging his holiness and acquiescing in his faithfulness; they cannot but desire a farther display of his vindictive and distributive justice, as indispensable to the manifestation of the divine glory, the vindication of the claims of the divine government, the asserting of their injured rights, and the completing of their eternal felicity. Accordingly, we find their earnest plea admitted. "It was said unto them, that they should rest."—Their repose can never be disturbed. The "white robes" in which they are arrayed, are not spun out of their own bowels, like the spider's web, either by their services or sufferings; but they are the well known emblems of the imputed righteousness of their Redeemer,—fine linen clean and white, the only righteousness of saints, (ch. xix. 8). Persecution did not terminate under the preceding seals. Others, their "fellow-servants and brethren, should be killed as they were." The honorable roll of martyrs was not yet completed. The "little season" is a very indefinite period in our mode of computation. But "with the Lord, one day is as a thousand years,"—(2 Pet. iii. 8.) This "season" seems to comprehend the whole period of persecution. Now, as we shall see, the Roman empire, whether pagan or Christian, is still a ravenous beast,—"devouring Jacob."

The policy of Rome pagan was to dictate the state religion. The idol gods of the conquered provinces were generally adopted and enrolled among those of the Pantheon. There was a niche for any and every god but "Jacob's God." As he would permit no rival, (Exod. xx. 2, 23; Is. xlii. 8;) so the populace "would have none of Him," (Acts xvi. 19-21.) Such we will find to be the policy of Rome Christian. There is no "communion between light and darkness."

12. And I beheld when he had opened the sixth seal, and, lo, there was a great earthquake: and the sun became black as sackcloth of hair, and the moon became as blood;
13. And the stars of heaven fell unto the earth, even as a fig-tree casteth her untimely figs, when she is shaken of a mighty wind:
14. And the heaven departed as a scroll when it is rolled together; and every mountain and island were moved out of their places;
15. And the kings of the earth, and the great men, and the rich men, and the chief captains, and the mighty men, and every bond-man, and every free-man, hid themselves in the dens, and in the rocks of the mountains:
16. And said to the mountains and rocks, Fall on us, and hide us from the face of him that sitteth on the throne, and from the wrath of the Lamb:
17. For the great day of his wrath is come, and who shall be able to stand?

Vs. 12-17.—The sixth seal is opened, like the rest, by the hand of the Mediator, and here "his right hand teacheth terrible things." "By terrible things in righteousness wilt thou answer us, O God of our salvation." (Ps. lxv. 5.) The awful scene disclosed would seem to be a beginning of answer to the importunate cry of the "souls under the altar," as in the foregoing vision.

Many expositors since the time of Cyprian in the third century, have understood this seal as disclosing the scene of the last judgment. No doubt the symbols here employed are suited to that event; but the series of seals, trumpets and vials, not to speak of events still more remote, wholly precludes such an interpretation. All the symbols under the sixth seal betoken revolution. Such is their established and well known import in other parts of Scripture.

The "earthquake" is more than a shaking of the earth. It is a *concussion* of the heavens also. As Haggai is interpreted by Paul, we learn the civil and ecclesiastical change of the Jewish polity by the "shaking of the heavens and the earth." (Hag. ii. 6; Heb. xii. 26, 27.) The day of final judgment is so often referred to as certain, that no special prediction was needed to assure us of that event. Indeed, the description of the day of judgment is commonly employed by the prophets to represent revolutions among the nations. So it is in reference to the overthrow of Babylon, (Is. xiii. 13.)—of Egypt, (Ezek. xxxii. 7, 8,) of Jerusalem, (Matt. xxiv. 7, 29.) The "sun, moon and stars" are emblems of civil officers, supreme and subordinate, as well as of military commanders. Their consternation and despair, now that they are cast down from their exalted position, as heavenly luminaries darkened and hurled from their orbits, betray their apprehension of deserved and inevitable wrath. Indeed we may view the last three verses of this chapter, as exegetical or explanatory of the preceding three. The whole frame of imperial power underwent a change which is commonly called a revolution. And the grandeur of the complex symbols, borrowed from the closing scene of time, was never more appropriately employed by the Spirit of prophecy, than in the present instance, to portray the total overthrow of pagan power, idolatry and tyranny. The most conspicuous instrument in the Mediator's hand by which this great revolution was effected, is well known in history as "Constantine the Great." The great lights of the heathen world, the powers civil and ecclesiastical, were not eclipsed, but extinguished, heathen priests and augurs were extirpated and idolatrous temples were closed. Christianity was professed by the emperor himself, and his authority exerted for its recognition and diffusion throughout his dominions. Thus did the God of Israel "avenge his own elect, who cried to him night and day from under the altar;" and thus did he afford unto them a "season of rest."

Constantine, however, was more of a politician than divine. To the student of history he will appear in many respects a striking prototype of William Prince of Orange, who on a less extended scale answers as an antitype in the latter part of the seventeenth century. Neither of them exemplified in their lives the "power of godliness". Like Charles the Second, they did not consider primitive apostolic Christianity "a religion for a gentleman." Constantine combined in his character the properties of the lion and the fox. He was crafty and ambitious. Usurping the prerogatives of Zion's King, he assumed a blasphemous supremacy over the church, and proceeded to model her external polity after the example of the empire. Among the Christian ministry, he found mercenary spirits who pandered to his ambition,—"having his person in admiration because of advantage." Advancing these to positions of opulence and splendor, he could certainly rely upon them to support him in his schemes of aggrandizement. Thus the mystery of iniquity, whose working Paul discovered in his time, was nurtured to its full development in Heaven's appointed time. (2 Thess. ii. 7, etc.) If on such occasions mighty kings and valiant generals are stricken with dismay, what shall be the terror of all the impenitent enemies of the Lord and his Anointed when the heavens and the earth shall pass away and leave them without these imaginary hiding places from "the wrath of the Lamb!"

CHAPTER VII.

The scenes portrayed by varied symbols in this chapter, are by some considered as a continuation of the sixth seal. We think they may with more propriety be viewed as relating to the events under the four which precede; while they are obviously preparatory to the opening of the last seal in the next chapter.

> 1. *And after these things I saw four angels standing on the four corners of the earth, holding the four winds of the earth, that the wind should not blow on the earth, nor on the sea, nor on any tree.*

V. 1.—The "four angels" represent the instruments of providence. The "four corners of the earth" intend all nations of the world, as then known in geography. (Ch. xx. 8, 9.) The "holding of the winds" is emblematical of the tranquillity consequent upon the accession of Constantine to the imperial throne,—the temporary cessation of desolating wars and persecutions,—the "rest" for which the martyrs prayed. "Thou calledst in trouble, and I delivered thee." (Ps. lxxxi. 7.)

> 2. *And I saw another angel ascending from the east, having the seal of the living God: and he cried with a loud voice to the four angels, to whom it was given to hurt the earth and the sea.*
> 3. *Saying, Hurt not the earth, neither the sea, nor the trees, till we have sealed the servants of our God in their foreheads.*

Vs. 2, 3.—"Another angel ... having the seal of the living God," can be none other but the Lord Christ. His people are "sealed unto the day of redemption with that Holy Spirit of promise," or promised Holy Spirit. (2 Cor. i. 22; Eph. i. 13). He came from the east. There the Son of righteousness arose upon a dark world, and his beams enlightened the kingdoms of Europe, in which multitudes were effectually called during this tranquil period, (ch. xiv. 1). This angel, as having sovereign authority over "earth and sea," and from whom the "four angels" had their commission, now commands them not to "hurt the earth and the sea," till He and the ministers,—the instruments of his grace,—had "sealed the servants of God." This "sealing," while symbolizing baptism, signifies especially the saving work of the eternal Spirit, by which its subjects are to be, and actually are, preserved from apostacy in future and trying times. We shall meet with them again, (ch. xiv. 1.)

The favour shown by Constantine to Christian ministers and converts, induced multitudes to make a profession of Christianity, and of course filled the church with hypocrites. The flattery of those in power has often proved as detrimental to the church's spiritual prosperity as their frowns. (Dan. xi. 32.) Still, the special design of this sealing seems to be the preservation of a chosen remnant,—the witnesses, during the period of the trumpets, when Antichrist should be fully organized.

> 4. *And I heard the number of them which were sealed: and there were sealed a hundred and forty and four thousand, of all the tribes of the children of Israel.*
> 5. *Of the tribe of Juda were sealed twelve thousand. Of the tribe of Reuben were sealed twelve thousand. Of the tribe of Gad were sealed twelve thousand.*
> 6. *Of the tribe of Aser were sealed twelve thousand. Of the tribe of Nephthalim were sealed twelve thousand. Of the tribe of Manasses were sealed twelve thousand.*
> 7. *Of the tribe of Simeon were sealed twelve thousand. Of the tribe of Levi were sealed twelve thousand. Of the tribe of Issachar were sealed twelve thousand.*
> 8. *Of the tribe of Zabulon were sealed twelve thousand. Of the tribe of Joseph were sealed twelve thousand. Of the tribe of Benjamin were sealed twelve thousand.*

Vs. 4-8.—The number sealed was "a hundred forty and four thousand;" of "each tribe twelve thousand." These numbers are not to be taken literally, but comparatively, as contradistinguished from another company, (v. 9.) Neither do we suppose, with many expositors, that Jews by nation are here exclusively intended. At the time referred to, in the fifth century, the "middle wall of partition" had been long removed. (Eph. ii. 14.) Jews and Gentiles were "all one in Christ Jesus." (Gal. iii. 28.) There is no ground to suppose that exactly the same number would be sealed of every tribe. Besides, all the original tribes are not named. Dan is not among them, and Judah is first in order in Reuben's place. The gates of the heavenly Jerusalem are inscribed with the names of the twelve tribes of Israel, (ch. xxii. 12.) In a word, this sealed company is composed of Jews and Gentiles, representing the whole number of true believers, who were enabled by grace to hold fast their profession in trying times, and who experienced more special protection in perilous times. (Ezek. ix. 4-6.)

> 9. After this I beheld, and, lo, a great multitude, which no man could number, of all nations, and kindreds, and people, and tongues, stood before the throne, and before the Lamb, clothed with white robes, and palms in their hands;
> 10. And cried with a loud voice, saying, Salvation to our God which sitteth upon the throne, and unto the Lamb.
> 11. And all the angels stood round about the throne, and about the elders and the four beasts, and fell before the throne on their faces, and worshipped God,
> 12. Saying, Amen: Blessing, and glory, and wisdom, and thanksgiving, and honour, and power, and might, be unto our God for ever and ever. Amen.

Vs. 9-12.—The "great multitude, which no man could number," are evidently distinguished from the number sealed. They are collected from all the nations known at that time. They "stood before the throne and before the Lamb," as accepted worshippers; ascribing "salvation," not to their own merit, but to the free grace of God the Father, and the oblation and intercession of the Lamb. They are now in a triumphant state, as indicated by the "palms in their hands," the usual emblems of victory. "White robes" bespeak their justification. "All the angels" in heaven, signify their hearty assent to the praises of the redeemed by saying, "Amen." Then in an attitude of profoundest reverence, they celebrate the praises of God in strains proper, though not peculiar to themselves. As in ch. v. 11, the angels in this place are disposed and arranged in the outer circle of all the intelligent worshippers. Redeemed sinners stand nearest to the throne, in virtue of their union to Christ, while holy angels, without envy, contemplate, with rapturous emotions, the displays of the "manifold wisdom of God" in his dealings with the church. (Eph. iii. 10.) Thus we may learn to do the will of God on earth, as it is done by the angels in heaven.

13. And one of the elders answered, saying unto me, What are these which are arrayed in white robes? and whence came they?
14. And I said unto him, Sir, thou knowest. And he said to me, These are they which came out of great tribulation, and have washed their robes, and made them white in the blood of the Lamb.
15. Therefore are they before the throne of God, and serve him day and night in his temple; and he that sitteth on the throne shall dwell among them.
16. They shall hunger no more, neither thirst any more; neither shall the sun light on them, nor any heat.
17. For the Lamb, which is in the midst of the throne, shall feed them, and shall lead them unto living fountains of waters; and God shall wipe away all tears from their eyes.

Vs. 13-17.—"One of the elders" asks John,—not for information, but to engage his attention,—"What are these, ... and whence came they?" Ministers may often receive instruction from the members of the church. This elder answers his own questions as the angel did to the prophet, (Zech. iv. 5, 6.) These are the "great multitude,"—probably the same whose "souls" John saw at the opening of the fifth seal, but now appearing in a new aspect: for it is evident that they had been engaged in war. This appears by the "palms" of victory. They had been in "great tribulation" prior to the peaceful reign of Constantine, by Satan's temptations, the spoiling of their goods, imprisonment of their persons, and the sacrifice of their lives,—"not loving their lives unto the death." All these tribulations, however, could not separate them from the love of God. (Rom. viii. 37-39.) They had "washed their robes,"—not in penitential tears, their own martyr-blood, their doing or suffering in the cause of Christ; but their robes were "made white in the blood of the Lamb," who was "made of God unto them ... justification and sanctification." (1 Cor. i. 30.) Could the human mind conceive the idea of rendering linen garments *white* by washing them in *blood*? Never, unless as suggested by the doctrine of Christ crucified, whose "blood cleanseth from all sin." (1 John i. 7.) "Therefore are they before the throne of God,—without fault before his throne," (ch. xiv. 5.) Delivered from the tempestuous storms of war, and the scorching heat of persecution; they are safe in the haven of eternal rest.

Not only are they for ever freed from the sensation of "hunger or thirst;" but they shall drink of the "living fountains of waters, proceeding from the throne of God and of the Lamb," (ch. xxii. 1). "In thy presence is fulness of joy; at thy right hand there are pleasures for evermore." (Ps. xvi. 11.) While this company, brought out of great tribulation, to which they had been subjected in the centuries before the time of Constantine, are represented as in possession of eternal blessedness, the other company of the "sealed" ones, are by this mark furnished with the gifts and graces of the Holy Spirit, to enter the lists with the Dragon in a much more trying and prolonged contest. The latter company, although *preceding* the other, in the order of symbolic revelation; do really in the order of time, succeed them in continuation of the struggle with the powers of darkness. And here we make the general remark, That nearly throughout the Apocalypse the two parties whom we may call the powers of darkness and the children of light, often change their relative positions, and assume different aspects. And in this, there is nothing new, as appears, 2 Cor. xi. 14, 15; vi. 8, 9.

CHAPTER VIII.

Hitherto our observations have been brief, because interpreters are very generally agreed in their views of the first series, the seals, in this interesting book of prophecy. The first six seals, covering the time of heathen Rome's opposition to Christianity, and before the Devil succeeded in enlisting the nominal church of Christ in his interest, do not therefore furnish occasion for much controversy among expositors. Besides, the seventh seal covers much more time than all the others. The first six refer to pagan Rome, and constitute the first period, properly styled the PERIOD OF THE SEALS. The seventh seal, introducing the trumpets, is the second period, called the PERIOD OF THE TRUMPETS. In attempting to unfold their mystical import, greater amplification will be indispensable.

1. And when he had opened the seventh seal, there was silence in heaven about the space of half an hour.

V. 1.—"Heaven" is the ordinary symbol of organized society, whether civil or ecclesiastical or both. "Silence in heaven for half an hour," indicates public tranquillity, together with anxious and mute expectation of coming and alarming events. "Half an hour," a definite for an indefinite duration, as usual, imports that the repose hitherto enjoyed, shall shortly terminate. The respite which the saints enjoyed during the period succeeding the revolution indicated by the opening of the sixth seal, soon came to an end.

2. And I saw the seven angels which stood before God; and to them were given seven trumpets.
3. And another angel came and stood at the altar, having a golden censer; and there was given unto him much incense, that he should offer it with the prayers of all saints upon the golden altar which was before the throne.
4. And the smoke of the incense, which came with the prayers of the saints, ascended up before God out of the angel's hand.

Vs. 2-4.—"Seven angels" appear to John as ministers "standing before

God," ready to execute his commands. To them were given "seven trumpets." Here, as all along hitherto, there is allusion to the former dispensation. Under the Old Testament, trumpets were constructed by divine direction and to be used for diverse purposes. Of the manifold uses of this instrument, that which is here chiefly intended is, to "sound an alarm." (Joel ii. 1; 1 Cor. xiv. 8). Whilst all is suspense, and before the silence is broken by the sounding of the first trumpet, the worship of God is exemplified after the usual manner. An angel, by his official place and work easily distinguished from those having the trumpets, holds in his hand a "golden censer" that with "much incense" he might render acceptable "the prayers of all saints." As the angel who had the "seal of the living God," is distinguished from those that "held the winds," (ch. vii. 1;) so is he here, from those that had the trumpets. Here he appears as the Great High Priest over the house of God; and as "the whole multitude of the people were praying without, at the time of incense;" (Luke i. 10;) so the service of God is thus emblematically represented as conducted according to divine appointment. This Angel therefore is Christ himself. "No man cometh unto the Father but by him." He is the only Advocate with the Father; and through him "we have access by one Spirit unto the Father." (Eph. ii. 18.)

May we not inquire, without presumption, a little into the nature or purport of the "prayers of all saints" at this time of ominous silence? And what could so likely be the burden of their petitions as that of the cry of the souls under the altar, namely, the destruction of the Roman empire? Surely this has been the prayer of God's persecuted servants in all ages:—"Pour out thy fury upon the heathen," etc. (Jer. x. 25; Ps. lxxix. 6). However inconsistent with Christian charity superficial Christians may deem the law of retaliation; we shall find it often urged on our attention as exemplified in this book. It is absolutely essential to the divine government.

> 5. And the angel took the censer, and filled it with fire of the altar, and cast it into the earth: and there were voices, and thunderings and lightnings and an earthquake.

V. 5.—The Lord Jesus, in carrying out the designs of the divine mind, and executing the commission which he received from the Father as Mediator, appears in various characters. Whilst as a priest he intercedes for his people, and by the incense from the golden censer renders their prayers acceptable before God; as a king he answers their prayers by terrible things in righteousness. (Ps. lxv. 5). This work of vengeance is vividly signified by scattering coals of fire on the earth.

From the very same altar, whence the glorious Angel of the Covenant had received fire to consume the incense, he next takes coals, the symbol of his wrath, and scatters them into the earth. These "burning coals of juniper" produce "voices, and thunderings, and lightnings, and an earthquake." "O God, thou art terrible out of thy holy places." (Ps. lxviii. 35; lxxvi. 12). "The Lord our God is a jealous God." Our merciful Saviour once put a strange and startling question to his disciples:—"Suppose ye that I am come to give peace on earth? I tell you, Nay."—For ends worthy of himself, the only wise God has unchangeably decreed that "offences must needs come," (Matt. xviii. 7;) and "there must be also heresies" among professing Christians. (1 Cor. xi. 19.). However, in the administration of providence, judgment without mercy awaits every nation to which the gospel is sent in vain. The voices, thunderings, etc., consequent upon the scattering of the coals, portended the calamities which would be inflicted upon men for their opposition to the gospel and cruel treatment of the saints, in answer to their prayers through the intercession of Christ.

6. *And the seven angels, which had the seven trumpets, prepared themselves to sound.*

V. 6.—The "seven angels now prepare themselves to sound." The first alarm, of course, will put an end to the "silence." It should be noted that while each seal, when broken, disclosed so much of the roll of the book as was concealed by it; the seventh leaves no part unrevealed. The whole contents are laid open. It is otherwise with the trumpets. The reverberations of one may not have ceased when the next begins to sound. Thus, several may be partly cotemporary. Again, it may be questioned whether mankind are to be considered in civil or ecclesiastical organization as the formal object of the judgments indicated by the trumpets. Some expositors view the one, and some the other, as the object, and the contention has been sharp among them. We humbly suggest that neither is the formal object without the other, simply because the *same individuals* constitute the complex *moral person*. The correctness of this view is largely illustrated and abundantly confirmed in the subsequent part of the Apocalypse. Provinces, nations, empires, are no farther worthy of notice in prophecy than as they affect the destiny of the church and illustrate the immutable principles of the moral government of God. He is known by the judgments which he executeth, and nations must be taught that "the heavens do rule." (Dan. iv. 26.) Although the church and the state are, by divine institution, distinct, not united; they are nevertheless co-ordinate, and always exert a reciprocal influence for good or for evil. It has been the policy of Satan to confound this distinction; and alas! with too much success in the apprehension of many. There are not wanting divines who boldly assert, that even among the Jews, under the Old Testament,—"the church was the state, and the state was the church!" We may have occasion to notice hereafter, that this gross error and antichristian dogma, is yet entertained in relation to divinely organized society under the present New Testament economy!

The "voices, thunderings and earthquakes" resulting from the scattering of the coals,—are the harbingers and precursors of coming calamities upon Christendom at the sounding of the trumpets. And these may be emblematical of the contentions, strife and divisions which accompanied the rise and prevalence of the heresy of Arius and the apostacy of the emperor Julian, during the time of comparative public tranquillity from Constantine to Theodosius. The church and the state, as one complex system, we have considered as the object of the judgments to be inflicted under the trumpets. These had, in fact, become incorporated, if not identified, under the reign of Constantine and his imperial successors. But assuming the correctness of the phraseology of secular historians and Christian expositors, when in a *popular sense* they speak of the Roman empire as the object of penal inflictions; we by no means agree with the latter class of writers, when they *limit* the empire to the geographical boundaries as it existed at the time of this prediction. This mistake, if not detected here, will materially affect and control our views of the whole subsequent part of the Apocalypse. Who would not discover the impropriety and absurdity of treating of events now transpiring within the empire of the United States, as if falling out within the limits of the original thirteen as they existed in 1776? But the Roman empire yet exists, and we have sufficient evidence that it will continue till the time of the sounding of the seventh trumpet, (ch. xi. 15.) *Political bias* has prevailed with one class of expositors to exempt the British empire from the stroke of God's wrath, symbolized by both the trumpets and vials. Others, from similar predilections, would exempt the United States and British Provinces from these plagues. Whilst a third class, giving fall scope to the hallucinations of mere imagination, aver their conviction that republican America is the special and doomed object of all these plagues!—Hence, the necessity of caution, sobriety, reverence for divine authority, reliance on the teaching of the Holy Spirit, whom the Saviour has promised to his humble disciples to "guide them into all truth, and to show them things to come." (John xvi. 13.) That the student of prophecy,—especially of the Apocalypse, may realize the fulfilment of this promise, it is indispensably necessary that he be absolutely untrammeled by all antichristian politics. Such cases are very rare, (ch. xiii. 3.)

During the reign of Constantine, that monarch had transferred the capital of the empire from the "city of seven hills" to another locality and founded another metropolis, which as the future seat of imperial rule, and to immortalize himself, he called after his own name, Constantinople. This ambitious enterprise itself virtually divided the empire, preparing the way for its total dismemberment by the trumpets. And now the "seven angels prepared themselves to sound," for all things are ready. The interceding Angel at the "golden altar" has prevailed to obtain a period of tranquillity whilst preparatory steps are in progress towards the next series of events; but that time shall be no longer, or respite from impending judgments, is significantly intimated by the symbolical Angel casting his "golden censer" from his hand, and hurling it into the earth. Then without farther delay,

> 7. The first angel sounded, and there followed hail and fire mingled with blood, and they were cast upon the earth: and the third part of trees was burnt up, and all green grass was burnt up.

V. 7.—"The first angel sounded." The object of this judgment is the *earth*, the population of the empire in general. The judgment itself is, "hail and fire mingled with blood,"—desolating wars, like successive storms of hail mingled with lightning, "hailstones and coals of fire." (Ps. xviii. 12.) The effect is, a consumption of a third part of the "trees and grass," people in high and low degrees. Green trees and grass are the ornaments and products, of a land: and when the earth is an emblem of nations and dominions, trees and grass may represent persons of higher and lower rank.

The careful student of the Apocalypse will discover a striking analogy between the effects of the trumpets and vials as the latter are presented in the sixteenth chapter. This first trumpet therefore produces an effect upon the social order of Christendom, which will continue till the pouring out of the first vial. As the Roman empire in its twofold division is the general object of all the trumpets; so the first four are directed towards the western, and the next two against the eastern member.

The infidel historian Gibbon has unwittingly recorded the fulfilment of these predictions, as Josephus has done those of our Lord respecting the destruction of Jerusalem. Unconscious that he was bearing testimony to the truth of prophecy, Gibbon used with his classic pen the very allegorical language of the inspired apostle. Respecting the incursion of the barbarous Goths, as led by Alaric their chief into the fertile plains of southern Europe, he describes their alarming descent as a *"dark cloud, which having collected along the coasts of the Baltic, burst in thunder upon the banks of the upper Danube."* He who directed Balaam and Caiaphas to utter predictions, doubtless could direct Josephus and Gibbon to attest the truth of prophecy; and this may be one of the many ways in which "he makes the wrath of man to praise him."—The Goths, the Scythians and Huns, first under Alaric and afterwards under Attila, those savage warriors from the northern regions, invaded the provinces of the Roman empire in both sections, carrying all before them like an irresistible tornado,—with fire and sword utterly destroying cities, temples, princes, priests, old and young, male and female,—thus "burning up trees, and green grass."

> 8. *And the second angel sounded, and as it were a great mountain burning with fire was cast into the sea; and the third part of the sea became blood:*
> 9. *And the third part of the creatures which were in the sea, and had life, died; and the third part of the ships were destroyed.*

Vs. 8, 9.—"The second angel sounded." The object of this judgment, is the *sea*. As a great collection of waters, this symbol is explained, (ch. xvii. 15.) "Peoples, and multitudes, and nations, and tongues," indicate the population in an agitated and disorganized or revolutionary condition. The judgment is a "burning mountain," a tremendous object,— consuming and being itself consumed. The mountain is a symbol of earthly power civil or military, and sometimes ecclesiastical.—"Who art thou, O great mountain?" (Zech. iv. 7.) The Almighty says to the king of Babylon,—"Behold, I am against thee, O destroying mountain ... I will roll thee down from the rocks, and will make thee a burnt mountain." (Jer. li. 25; Ps. xlviii. 2.)

The consequence of this judgment is, the third part of the sea became blood, the fish perished, and the shipping was destroyed. Similar language, illustrating these figurative expressions, had been used by the prophets to represent divine judgments denounced against Egyptian power. (Ezek. xxix. 3, etc.) In the eighth verse is contained the explanation of the symbolic language,—"Behold I will bring a sword upon thee, and cut off man and beast from thee."

History verifies this part of the Apocalyptic prediction. Only two years after the death of that northern "scourge of God," Attila, who boasted that "the grass never grew where his horse had trod;" Genseric set sail from the burning shores of Africa; and, like a burning mountain launched into the sea, accompanied by a vast army of barbarous Vandals, suddenly landed his fleet at the mouth of the river Tiber. Disregarding the distinctions of rank, age or sex, these licentious and brutal plunderers subjected their helpless victims to every species of indignity and cruelty. Hence the hostility to arts and science, the tokens of refined civilization,—indiscriminate devastation of life and property perpetrated by the savage warriors, has given rise to the word "Vandalism."

> 10. And the third angel sounded, and there fell a great star from heaven, burning as it were a Lamp, and it fell upon the third part of the rivers, and upon the fountains of waters;
> 11. And the name of the star is called Wormwood: and the third part of the waters became wormwood; and many men died of the waters, because they were made bitter.

Vs. 10, 11.—The object of the third trumpet is the waters as before,—the population of the empire, but not in collective form as a *sea;* rather in a state of separation or disconnected, as "rivers and fountains." Some apply this symbol of a "falling star" to Genseric, but this is incongruous. On the contrary, he was a victorious prince,—a *rising* star. It is more consonant to the truth of history and the chronological series of prophecy, to apply this symbol to the downfall of Momyllus the last of the Roman emperors, who was deposed by Odoacer king of the Heruli, called in derision Augustulus,—the diminutive Augustus. Doubtless the allusion here is to the king of Babylon:—"How art thou fallen from heaven, O Lucifer, (day-star,) son of the morning! How art thou cut down to the ground, which didst weaken the nations!" (Isa. xiv. 12.) A star may indeed signify either a civil or ecclesiastical officer, but the scope and context determine all these judgments to the enemies of the church, and those of her illustrious Head. It is the "vengeance of his temple." We have already found a star the emblem of a gospel minister, and we shall hereafter find it employed in that sense; but it does not seem to refer in the present connexion to any apostate. The name of this star,—"Wormwood," embittering the waters, is a lively emblem of the miseries experienced by the people, in the use of the remaining temporal comforts which the preceding calamities had left.

> 12. And the fourth angel sounded, and the third part of the sun was smitten, and the third part of the moon, and the third part of the stars; so as the third part of them was darkened, and the day shone not for a third part of it, and the night likewise.

V. 12.—The design of all the trumpets is to point out the utter destruction of the Roman empire,—Daniel's "kingdom of iron." (Dan. ii. 40.) For although from the time of Constantine it assumed the Christian name, it nevertheless continued to be a beast. Of this we shall have cumulative evidence as we progress. The first trumpet began to demolish the fabric of antichristian power; and by the fourth the western division was overthrown. For although the northern barbarians under the first, the southern Vandals under the second, and the successors of both, prevailed to bring down the last of the Caesars, yet the ancient frame of government still subsisted. The political heaven, though shaken, was not yet wholly removed, while the Senate, Consuls and other official dignitaries continued to shine as political luminaries in the firmament of power. But as the last of the Caesars fell from power in the year 476, so the last vestige of imperial dominion in the west was removed in 566, when Rome, the queen of the nations, was by the emperor of the east reduced to the humble condition of a tributary dukedom. Most of the saints had their residence at this time in the nations of western Europe and northern Africa, where they were grievously afflicted by the Arian, Pelagian and other heresies; as also exposed to persecution by the civil powers, whom those heresiarchs moved to oppress the orthodox: consequently, the righteous judgments of God fall first upon that member of the empire. The eastern section, however, is destined to become the special object of the judgments indicated by the succeeding trumpets. However interpreters differ in details when explaining the effects produced by the sounding of the first four trumpets, they very generally harmonize in the application of them to the western section of the Roman empire. The luminaries of heaven are darkened, or fall, or are extinguished, while the earth, the sea and the rivers are correspondently affected. Now, these are the well known allegorical representations of divine judicial visitations of guilty communities, as we find in the prophetic writings. See, for example, the case of Babylon, "the beauty of the Chaldees' excellency" (Isa. xiii. 1, 10;) also Egypt,—(Ezek. xxxii. 7, 8.)

> 13. And I beheld, and heard an angel flying through the midst of heaven, saying with a loud voice, Woe, woe, woe, to the inhabitants of the earth, by reason of the other voices of the trumpet of the three angels, which are yet to sound!

V. 13.—Before the fifth angel sounds, a note of warning is given by the ministry, of another angel distinct from the seven with the trumpets. He pronounces a "woe" thrice repeated, upon the inhabitants of the earth, indicating that heavier judgments and of longer duration are about to be inflicted. This announcement was intended to excite attention and awful expectation. This angel's message of "heavy tidings" may be viewed in quite interesting contract with that of a subsequent angel,—"flying through the midst of heaven," (ch. xiv. 6.) How different, yet harmonious, is the ministry of those heavenly messengers!

The first four trumpets, as we have seen, demolished the western division of the Roman empire. About the middle of the sixth century this work was brought to completion. Here, for greater clearness, we may be allowed to anticipate by digressing a little. Assuming now, what shall afterwards appear to be correct, that the Roman empire is Daniel's fourth universal monarchy, and Paul's "let," or hinderance, to the revealing of the "Man of Sin;" since the first four trumpets have dismembered that great power, revealing the "ten toes,—ten horns," or kingdoms; we would expect now to hear of the destruction of that "Son of perdition." But it is not so. That is to be effected by the vials, (ch. xvi.) As the general and grand design of the Apocalypse is to illustrate the divine government, exhibiting the moral world as affecting, or affected by the Christian religion, it seemed good to the Divine Author that the destinies of the eastern section of the Roman empire yet standing, where many of his saints reside, shall come under review. Ecclesiastical history treats familiarly of a *Greek,* as well as a *Latin* church and empire. As the trumpets cover the whole time from the opening of the sixth seal till the final overthrow of the whole fourth monarchy; (Dan. vii. 26; Rev. xi. 15,) it follows that the eastern section must be the object of a part of them. Accordingly, the remaining part of the second period,—the *Period of the Trumpets,* includes the first two of the three, emphatically and significantly styled "woe-trumpets."

CHAPTER IX.

1. And the fifth angel sounded, and I saw a star fall from heaven unto the earth: and to him was given the key of the bottomless pit.
2. And he opened the bottomless pit; and there arose a a smoke out of the pit, as the smoke of a great furnace; and the sun and the air were darkened by reason of the smoke of the pit.
3. And there came out of the smoke locusts upon the earth; and unto them was given power, as the scorpions of the earth have power.
4. And it was commanded them that they should not hurt the grass of the earth, neither any green thing, neither any tree; but only those men which have not the seal of God in their foreheads.
5. And to them it was given that they should not kill them, but that they should be tormented five months: and their torment was as the torment of a scorpion, when he striketh a man.
6. And in those days shall men seek death, and shall not find it; and shall desire to die, and death shall flee from them.
7. And the shapes of the locusts were like unto horses prepared unto battle; and on their heads were as it were crowns like gold, and their faces were us the faces of men.
8. And they had hair as the hair of women, and their teeth were as the teeth of lions.
9. And they had breastplates, as it were breastplates of iron; and the sound of their wings was as the sound of chariots of many horses running to battle.
10. And they had tails like unto scorpions; and there were stings in their tails: and their power was to hurt men five months.
11. And they had a king over them, which is the angel of the bottomless pit, whose name in the Hebrew tongue is Abaddon, but in the Greek tongue hath his name Apollyon.

Vs. 1-11.—The scene of the events announced by the sounding of the first "woe-trumpet," is the eastern Roman empire. A variety of symbols is here employed to represent the judgment to be inflicted. The principal agents and events are,—a "star, locusts, Apollyon their king, their depredations, the time of their continuance."

Neither Boniface III. nor Mahomet answers to the symbol "falling star." Allowing that a star, as a symbol, may represent a person in either civil or ecclesiastical office, no successful aspirants to places of power, as both of these were, can be here understood. Obviously degradation and not elevation is intended. Either dethronement of a prince or apostacy of a theological dignitary must be intended.

No character in history at the time referred to, so well agrees to the symbol of a fallen star as the monk Sergius, who is known to have been the coadjutor of Mahomet. He had been a monk of the Christian sect called Nestorians from Nestorius their leader. This monk Sergius had been excommunicated for heresy and immorality. He was glad to serve the devil as dictator to Mahomet in composing the Koran, which bears internal evidence of having been written by one who was acquainted with the Sacred Scriptures. When this degraded man had finished his task, he was put to death by his master, lest he should betray the imposture.

He opened the bottomless pit, from which issued a smoke darkening the whole face of the heavens. The pit is hell, whence came the smoke,—the diabolical system of delusion. From the same place comes the character afterwards to appear under the aspect of a beast, (ch. xi. 7.) Locusts constituted one of the plagues of Egypt, and they are the emblem of a destroying army. (Exod. x. 14-19; Joel i. 4-6.) And this is their import here. They represent the deluded and destructive followers of Mahomet, who in vast multitudes laid waste the nations of western Asia, southern Europe, and northern Africa. The Saracens, originating in Arabia, the national locality of the literal locusts, in great multitudes like clouds, laid waste the fairest and most populous portions of the earth for a succession of ages.

These symbolic locusts have also the property of scorpions, a poisonous reptile, resembling in some degree a lizard combined with a lobster, armed with a sting in the end of its tail. Wicked and impenitent men are compared to scorpions. (Ezek. ii. 6.) But these locusts are under restraint. They are permitted to hurt only "those men which have not the seal of God in their foreheads." The time of their continuance is "five months," of thirty days each, making 150 years,—"a day for a year." (Ezek. iv. 6.) In the year 606, Mahomet began his imposture by retiring to the cave of Hera. In 612 he appeared publicly as the apostle of his new religion at the head of his deluded followers. Between 612 and 762, he and the warlike chiefs who succeeded him, overran with terrible destruction, Syria, Persia, India, Egypt and Spain. Although the Saracenic empire continued for a longer time, yet from this time it lost the disorderly *Locust* character and became a more settled commonwealth. In the year 762, the city of Bagdad was built by one of the caliphs, who called it "the city of peace." This put a stop to the devastations of the locusts, when the empire began to decline. It was foretold, however, that during the time of successful war by these cruel invaders, they would inflict such miseries upon their wretched victims, that they would earnestly but vainly desire death to put an end to their exquisite torments. It is farther said that these locusts resembled horses, as indeed they do, especially in their heads. The Arabians excelled in horsemanship, and their chief force lay in cavalry. The "crowns upon their heads" may refer to the turbans worn by the Arabians as part of their national costume; or to the kingdoms which they subdued. Flowing hair is also characteristic of these people. Their "teeth" like those of lions indicated their strength and fury to destroy. "Breast-plates of iron,"—defensive armour, indicates self-protection by the most effectual public measures. The sound of their wings may denote the fury of their assaults, and the rapidity of their conquests. But the deadly stings in their tails were their most fatal instruments of torture, symbolizing the poison of their abominable and ruinous religion.

Their king is "Abaddon or Apollyon," the destroyer: for so is his name by interpretation, both in Hebrew and Greek. He is from the "bottomless pit,"—from hell, the vicegerent of the devil. Mahomet in person, and in the person of his official successors, will alone answer to this *duplicate* symbol. This is, without a rational shadow of ground for controversy, the *Great Eastern Antichrist*, sufficiently distinguished from the *Western*. The western combination against real Christianity never attained to power by successful conquest of the nations; but on the contrary by chicanery, insidious policy, flattery of princes and priestcraft. This enemy is described with sufficient accuracy and peculiar precision in the subsequent part of the Apocalypse. Prophecy has a determinate meaning; and we are not at liberty to give loose reins to our imagination: otherwise we shall bewilder, rather than satisfy the devout and earnest inquirer.

12. *One woe is past: and, behold, there come two woes more hereafter.*

V. 12.—Before the time of the sixth trumpet, intimation is given that some pause shall intervene prior to the judgments which are to follow:—"One woe is past."—The object of the first woe is the nominally Christian Roman empire, which still stands in its Eastern section; and is to be totally demolished by the second woe-trumpet: for the Western section, recovering from the effects of the first four trumpets, is the object of the third and last woe. The "man of Sin,"—the "little horn" of Daniel, is actuating the "ten horns" to "scatter Judah," etc., during the time of the Mahometan conquests in the East; by which the whole Roman empire is ripening for the harvest of the vials of wrath.

13. *And the sixth angel sounded, and I heard a voice from the four horns of the golden altar which is before God,*
14. *Saying to the sixth angel which had the trumpet, Loose the four angels which are bound in the great river Euphrates.*
15. *And the four angels were loosed, which were prepared for an hour, and a day, and a month, and a year, for to slay the third part of men.*
16. *And the number of the army of the horsemen were two hundred thousand thousand; and I heard the number of them.*
17. *And thus I saw the horses in the vision, and them that sat on them, having breastplates of fire, and of jacinth, and brimstone: and the heads of the horses were as the heads of lions; and out of their mouths issued fire, and smoke, and brimstone.*
18. *By these three was the third part of men killed, by the fire, and by the smoke, and by the brimstone, which issued out of their mouths.*
19. *For their power is in their mouth, and in their tails: for their tails were like unto serpents, and had heads, and with them they do hurt.*

Vs. 13-19.—At the sounding of the sixth trumpet, a "voice comes from the four horns of the golden altar," the immediate presence of the Almighty. This indicates punishment to be inflicted upon men for corrupting the gospel, similar to the judgment of fire from the "golden censer," (ch. viii. 5.) The effects of the first woe may be supposed to reach from the early part of the seventh century to the latter part of the thirteenth,—the period of Arabian locusts. During the latter part of this time, the Turks were held in check by the Crusaders, who strove to wrest the Holy Land from the infidels. The "four angels" are the four Turkish Sultanies. The river Euphrates is to be taken in this place literally, as designating the geographical locality of these combined powers, which were the instruments employed by the enthroned Mediator, to demolish the remaining part of the Roman empire,—"the third part of men." The time occupied in this barbarous work of slaughter is "an hour, a day, a month and a year," about equal to 391 years; or from the year 1281 to 1672. The Western empire had been overthrown by the first four trumpets, the Eastern nearly ruined under the fifth; and under the sixth it was finally subverted. The numbers which the Turks brought into the field are here said to be "two hundred thousand thousand,"—a definite for an indefinite number as usual, a vast army. And historians tell us that they were, in fact, from four to seven hundred thousand, and a large proportion of them cavalry.

From the year 1672, one of their own historians dates the "Decay of the Othman empire!" Since that date, the Turkish power is well known to have been straitened by the Russian empire.

These eastern warriors and their horses are described by their military costume and their arms. Fire is *red*, jacinth *blue*, and brimstone *yellow*,—the chosen colors of the Ottoman warriors, their military uniform. The heads of their horses "as the heads of lions," denote strength, fierceness and cruelty. "Fire, smoke and brimstone issuing out of their mouths," may be supposed to indicate the employment of gunpowder, first invented about that time, as an element of destruction. The commander at the siege of Constantinople is said to have employed cannon, some of which were of such caliber as to send stones of three hundred pounds weight! Thus their power was in their "mouth:" but like the locusts, "they had in their tails power to do hurt,"—the deadly poison of the Koran. The Turks left behind them wherever they went, as the Saracens had done before, the poisonous and ruinous religion of Mahomet, more durable and injurious to men than all their bloody conquests. By this abominable system of delusion, the remains of the Greek church in the Eastern division of the Roman empire, were almost extirpated; Christianity was nearly extinguished in that part of the world where the gospel had shone brightly, and there Mahometanism continues till the present day. Such has been the desolating effect of the sixth,—the second woe trumpet. Thus the Judge of all the earth punishes impenitent communities. Besides the positive effects of the second wo, we have intimation of some that are negative in the close of this chapter.

> 20. *And the rest of the men, which were not killed by these plagues, yet repented not of the works of their hands, that they should not worship devils, and idols of gold, and silver, and brass, and stone, and of wood; which neither can see, nor hear, nor walk:*
> 21. *Neither repented they of their murders, nor of their sorceries, nor of their fornication, nor of their thefts.*

Vs. 20, 21.—The "rest of the men that were not killed by these plagues," or morally destroyed by becoming Mahometans, by the foregoing calamities, were not brought to repentance of their evil deeds. The population of the Western Latin empire and nominal Christian church, still persisted in their idolatries and immoralities. Both individually and as associated, they openly violated both tables of the moral law. It is evident from these two verses, that the sins enumerated in them were the procuring causes of the divine judgments symbolized by the trumpets,—the two woe-trumpets, all the trumpets,—yes, including the seventh and the last. Professing Christians both in the Greek and Latin churches, after all the plagues inflicted by the angels of the past six trumpets, continue to this day in the practice of worshipping demons, angels and saints, for which they can produce no better arguments than their Pagan predecessors whom the Lord charges with "worshipping devils" here and elsewhere. (1 Cor. x. 20; Ps. cvi. 37.) In their stupid worship of senseless images, consecration of places, etc., who cannot perceive the identity of modern Papists and prelates with those portrayed by the pen of inspiration in the passage before us? The horrible "murders," massacres and bloody persecutions of the saints, are verified in authentic history. Papal bulls, imperial and royal edicts, issued against *heretics*, answer to the second part of this awful picture. Then follow "sorceries," plainly pointing out pretended revelations, false miracles, etc. To these are to be added "fornications," corporeal and spiritual, in a mass of superstitions added to, or supplanting divine ordinances; together with vows of celibacy, monkeries and nunneries,—followed by public license of brothels. And finally,—"thefts." By these are to be understood the illegal exactions and oppressive impositions, by which the nations of Christendom have been plundered of their revenues to enrich the lordly hierarchy of apostate Christendom. This state of things still continuing after the sixth angel sounds his trumpet, and no evidence of repentance; who can doubt that the same community is yet to be visited with the "third woe?" Surely the Lord may justly still say,—"For three transgressions, and for four, (of Antichrist,) I will not turn away the punishment thereof." The eastern church, in which the first corruptions prevailed, was punished by the *first woe* of the Saracens; and this not producing repentance, her ruin was completed by the *second wo* of the Ottomans. So, when God judges, he will overcome; therefore the western church, still persisting in her abominations, without repentance, shall be destroyed by the *third woe*. Let not the pious reader suppose that by these penal inflictions on churches, the church of Christ is to perish. No, no. But, on the contrary, their overthrow is subservient to her preservation. This also will appear with increasing evidence as we proceed with our meditations on this instructive book.

In the mean time it may be well to remark here, at the close of those *woes* which developed the rise and progress of Mahometanism, that the creed of this religious sect is substantially the same as that of those Christians called Socinians. Both presumptuously and arrogantly claim to be the worshippers of *the one God*,—commonly called *Unitarians*. This is one of the "depths of Satan." All who worship, as well as believe in, three co-equal Divine Persons, Father, Son and Holy Ghost, believe in, and worship *one God*, and in this sense are Unitarians.—*the only scriptural Unitarians.* "Whosoever denieth the Son, the same hath not the Father." (John ii. 23.) And the same is true of such who "have not so much as heard whether there be any Holy Ghost." (Acts xix. 2.) "He is Antichrist that denieth the Father and the Son,"—a deceiver and an Antichrist. It is doubtless in view of these soul-ruining heresies, that the beloved disciple tendered the caution,—"Little children, keep yourselves from idols." (1 John v. 21.)

We would expect the tenth chapter to begin with the sounding of the seventh trumpet; but we find it is not so. Indeed, we shall not find any direct intimation of the work of the seventh angel till we come to the fourteenth verse of the eleventh chapter. The sixth trumpet continues to reverberate throughout Christendom for centuries; and during the intermediate time, our attention is called to another scene, which the Lord Jesus deemed necessary as preparatory.

CHAPTER X.

This chapter and the greater part of the next, from the first to the fourteenth verse inclusive, is of the nature of a parenthesis; for the fifteenth verse of the 11th chapter evidently connects the narrative or series of events with the ninth chapter. The ninth chapter closes with an intimation of impenitence on the part of those who had been punished by the plagues of the preceding trumpets. Then it follows, as we have seen, that they are to be still farther visited by the infliction of the closing judgment symbolized by the seventh trumpet. The immediate design, therefore, of interrupting the natural order of the narrative is to place before us the actual condition of society when the seventh trumpet sounds.

1. *And I saw another mighty angel come down from heaven, clothed with a cloud; and a rainbow was upon his head, and his face as it were the sun, and his feet as pillars of fire:*
2. *And he had in his hand a little book open: and he set his right foot upon the sea, and his left foot on the earth,*
3. *And cried with a loud voice, as when a lion roareth: and when he had cried, seven thunders uttered their voices.*

Vs. 1-3.—The majestic description of this Angel agrees to no creature. It is proper to God-man only. It is partly the same display of the Mediator's glory which we had in ch, i. 15. Especially is this the case as to his *face*, his *feet* and his *voice*. The "rainbow" is still the sign of the everlasting covenant. "In wrath he remembers mercy."

This "book" differs from the *sealed* book as a part from the whole, or a codicil from the will to which it is appended. Also, it is distinguished from the former as being *little* and *open*. They do therefore greatly err here, who would make this little book comprehend all the remaining part of the Apocalypse, which would make it larger than the sealed book. The little book is *open*, because it is part of the large one, from which the last seal had been removed by the Mediator. But another reason why the little book is represented as being open, is the fact that the most of the events to which it refers, had transpired prior to the sounding of the seventh trumpet. That trumpet had been without its appropriate object, as presented in any preceding part of the prophecy. To present that object is the special design of the little book. All the events predicted in this book of Revelation are not successive in the order of time, but some are coincident; and the inspired writer of the Apocalypse, on several occasions goes back, as we shall see, in order to explain at greater length, what had been but briefly and obscurely narrated.

The angel set his feet upon the world, as his footstool; by which position is emblematically signified his sovereign dominion over sea and earth. And this is agreeable to his own plain teaching in the days of his public ministry:—"All power is given unto me in heaven and in earth." (Matt. xxviii. 18.) He trod upon the billows of the ocean literally in the state of his humiliation, giving thereby evidence of his power over the mystical waters,—"the tumults of the people." During the popular commotions signified by the trumpets, he said to the raging passions of men and their towering ambition, as to the waves of the sea,—"Hitherto shall ye come, and no further; and here shall your proud waves be stayed." "He maketh the storm a calm, so that the waves thereof are still;" and whether the nations of Christendom are at war or in peaceful tranquillity, he reigns over them as their rightful sovereign;—"his right foot on the sea, and his left on the earth." In possession of universal dominion, he speaks with authority, "as when a lion roareth." Although a lamb slain, the victim for our sins; he is also the Lion of the tribe of Judah, ruling over his own people, restraining and conquering his own and their enemies.

The "seven thunders," etc., give a *premonition* of tremendous judgments, the import of which is to be "sealed up" until it be demonstrated to all the world by the seventh trumpet and vial.

4. *And when the seven thunders had uttered their voices, I was about to write: and I heard a voice from heaven, saying unto me, Seal up those things which the seven thunders uttered, and write them not.*
5. *And the angel, which I saw stand upon the sea, and upon the earth, lifted up his hand to heaven,*

6. And sware by him that liveth for ever and ever, who created heaven, and the things that therein are, and the sea, and the things which are therein, that there should be time no longer.
7. But in the days of the voice of the seventh angel, when he shall begin to sound, the mystery of God should be finished, as he hath declared to his servants the prophets.

Vs. 4-7.—The attitude assumed by the Angel of the covenant is very impressive, instructive and exemplary:—"his hand lifted up to heaven." This is the external attitude of solemnity most becoming the jurant when performing the act of religious worship, the oath. Abraham, in the presence of the king of Sodom, used the same form, appealing to the "Lord, the Most High God, possessor of heaven and earth." (Gen. xiv. 22.) "Kissing the book" has no example in all the Bible; hence it is unquestionably of heathen, and so of idolatrous origin and tendency. No Christian can thus symbolize with heathens, without so far "having fellowship with devils" as really as in eating in their temples. (1 Cor. x. 21.)

The matter of the Angel's oath is,—"that there should be time no longer." Here it is humbly suggested that our excellent translators are faulty as in ch. iv. 6, already noticed. Neither the original Greek text, nor the coherence of the symbolic narrative, will sustain or justify the version. John, like all pious people, when he heard the lion's voice, followed by the "seven thunders," was filled with solemn awe, anticipating the coming dissolution of all things. It was not the only instance of his weakness and misapprehension, (ch. xix. 10;) nor is this infirmity peculiar to the apostle John; for we find other disciples mistaking "the times and the seasons which the Father hath put in his own power." (2 Thess. ii. 1-3.) These Thessalonians had misapprehended the language of Paul in his first epistle to them, when speaking of the end of the world. (1 Thess. iv. 15-17.) To relieve the anxieties of the Thessalonians, relative to the apprehended and sudden coming of the Lord, Paul wrote again to correct their mistake; so it may be supposed that the Angel interposed this solemn assurance to his servant John, for the like purpose, of allaying his forebodings. The words in the original, literally translated, stand thus: "That the time shall not be yet." That is, the "time of the end," as we read in Daniel xii. 9, shall not be, till the seventh trumpet begins to sound. The phrase,—"time of the end," may signify either the final overthrow of antichristian power, or the end of the world, because of the resemblance between the two events. The plain and certain meaning, then, of the Angel's oath is, that the "mystery of God shall be finished" only by the work of the seventh angel. What this mystery is, we will discover in the following chapters. Indeed, it had been long before "declared to the prophets," but still accompanied with comparative obscurity suitable to their time; for the word "declared," is expressive of glad tidings, being the same in origin and significance as that which we translate,—*gospel*, good news. Accordingly, our Saviour directs his disciples, in view of his appearing either to overthrow the Roman power, or to judge the world, in the following words of cheer: "And when these things begin to come to pass, then look up, and lift up your heads; for your redemption draweth nigh." (Luke xxi. 28.) To the prophet Daniel the same event was attested with like solemnity. (Dan. xii. 7.) This is the period to which the suffering saints of God have been long looking forward with believing and joyful hope. As Abraham rejoiced to see Christ's day of appearing in our nature, and by faith saw it and was glad; so the covenanted seed of the father of the faithful, in the light of prophecy, and by like precious faith, are favored with a view of the certain downfall of mystical Babylon.

8. *And the voice which I heard from heaven spake unto me again, and said, Go and take the little book which is open in the hand of the angel which standeth upon the sea and upon the earth.*
9. *And I went unto the angel, and said unto him, Give me the little book. And he said unto me, Take it, and eat it up; and it shall make thy belly bitter, but it shall be in thy mouth sweet as honey.*
10. *And I took the little book out of the angel's hand, and ate it up; and it was in my mouth sweet as honey; and as soon as I had eaten it, my belly was bitter.*
11. *And he said unto me, Thou must prophesy again before many peoples, and nations, and tongues, and kings.*

Vs. 8-11.—John is next directed by a voice from heaven, or by divine authority,—to take and eat the open book. There is obvious allusion to a similar transaction in Ezekiel iii, 1-3. The prophet was a captive by the river of Chebar in Babylon, under the dominion of the *first* beast of Daniel, as John was in Patmos under that of the *fourth*; and both were favoured and employed by the glorious Head of the church in an eminent part of their ministry. "The word is not bound" when ministers are in confinement.

The "eating of the book" represents the intellectual apprehension of the things which it contained.

"Thy words were found and I did eat them,"(Jer. xv. 16.) A speculative knowledge of the word of God, and especially of those parts that are prophetical, will afford pleasure to the human intellect, even though the mind be unsanctified. (Matt. xiii. 20, 21.) But when the prophet gets a farther insight into the contents as containing "lamentations, and mourning and woe," like Ezekiel's roll;—the pleasure is converted into pain. A foresight of the sorrows and sufferings of Christ's witnesses causes grief to the Christian's sensitive heart. He "weeps with them that weep," by the spontaneous sympathies of a common and renewed nature. "Sweet in the mouth as honey, but in the belly bitter as wormwood and gall."

Upon the apostle's digesting the little book, the Angel interprets the symbolic action by the plain and extensive commission,—"Thou must prophesy again before many peoples, and nations, and tongues, and kings." This commission did not terminate with the ministry of the apostle, although he may be truly said to prophesy by the Apocalypse to all nations till the end of the world. This is equally true, however, of all the inspired penmen of the Holy Scriptures. (Psalm xlv. 17.) But John is to be considered here as the official representative of a living and faithful ministry, on whom devolves the indispensable obligation to open and apply these sacred predictions to the commonwealth of nations, however constituted authorities may be affected by them. And, indeed, these messages will prove unwelcome to the immoral powers of the earth, as in the days of old. (1 Kings xviii. 17.)

CHAPTER XI.

The narrative of prophetic events was broken off at the end of the ninth chapter. The tenth chapter and the greater part of this, from the beginning to the thirteenth verse inclusive, present appearances and actions quite foreign to the events which follow the sounding of the trumpets. Why is this, the thoughtful student of the Apocalypse will naturally ask? Why is the regular series of the trumpets suspended? When the sixth trumpet,—the "second woe,"—has effected its objects, we naturally expect the seventh trumpet to sound; yet we are held in suspense till we come to the fourteenth verse of this chapter. Hitherto we have met with no similar interruption. Let us take a retrospective view:—The seven epistles to the churches followed each other in regular succession. The seals, in like manner, followed successively; and this is true of the vials, (ch. xvi.)

We have seen that the object of the trumpets was the Roman empire, the fourth beast of Daniel's prophecy. The same is the object of the judgments symbolized by the vials. The final subversion and utter destruction of that beastly power, was plainly revealed in the Babylonian monarch's dream. (Dan. ii. 44.) And the same event was afterwards exhibited in vision to Daniel, (ch. vii. 11, 26.) Now the first four trumpets had demolished imperial power in the western or Latin section; and the next two, by the Saracenic locusts and the Euphratean horsemen had subverted the eastern or Greek section. Rome and Constantinople were the capitals of the respective sections or members of the *one* empire. Under the first four trumpets, by the Northern barbarians; and under the first two woes, by the Mahometans, both sections of the empire were overthrown. The question now presses upon our attention, Where shall we find an object for the tremendous judgment to be inflicted by the third and last woe? This question requires a solution. It demands it; and he who succeeds in the application of history to solve this apparent enigma in the Apocalypse, will be able to attain to a satisfactory, a certain, understanding of much that is yet to most readers as if the "sealed book" were to this day in the "right hand of Him that sitteth on the throne." Let us humbly attempt to solve this difficulty.

Daniel's fourth beast, the Roman empire, is to be contemplated in *diverse aspects*, as the varied symbols obviously require. All know that Nebuchadnezzar's "image" is the same as Daniel's "four beasts;" therefore the same thing is presented in different forms or aspects. Of course we are to view that object as presented. We have seen that under the sixth seal, (ch. vi. 12-17,) the Roman empire underwent a revolution; that is, it was destroyed as to its Pagan form. The empire became Christian under Constantine. History proves that Christianity degenerated under the reign of that monarch and his successors. Heresy, idolatry and persecutions characterize the subsequent history of the empire. Then follow the judgments of the trumpets to vindicate the divine government, and alleviate from time to time the sufferings of true Christians. While the two woe-trumpets are demolishing the fabric of idolatry and despotism in the east, the "deadly wound is healed" in the west, which had been inflicted by the first four trumpets. Ten horns are developed upon the beast's head, and another "little horn," by all of which the saints suffer, as had been predicted by Daniel, (ch. vii. 24,) and of which we had intimation after the judgment of the second woe or sixth trumpet, (ch. ix. 20, 21.) All the "plagues," which had been inflicted upon the people of Christendom under this trumpet left them still impenitent,—"worshipping devils," etc. Surely we may now see where the object of the third woe is to be found,—namely in the same Roman empire, now become antichristian more than ever before. To describe this antichristian combination and present the unholy confederacy against the Lord and his Anointed, and so to justify the ways of God; it was necessary to digress from the narrative of the trumpets. We now proceed with our observations on the eleventh chapter.

1. *And there was given me a reed like unto a rod: and the angel stood, saying, Rise, and measure the temple of God, and the altar, and them that worship therein.*
2. *But the court which is without the temple leave out, and measure it not; for it is given unto the Gentiles: and the holy city shall they tread under foot forty and two months.*

Vs. 1, 2.—This chapter, (vs. 1-13,) gives the contents of the "little book" delivered to the apostle; as in the tenth chapter. It contains a brief description and prospective history of the true church of Christ for a period of 1260 years. Her conflicts with Daniel's fourth beast are here epitomized. As the scene is laid in the temple and ministry all along in the Apocalypse, so there is probably a special allusion here to Ezekiel's vision, (ch. xl. 5.) At all times the Christian church is to be organized, and all her ordinances to be administered by divine rule. Accordingly we have here presented the actual condition of Christendom during the whole time mentioned above. The command to John from the Angel, is to be understood as from the Lord Jesus, Zion's only king to the gospel ministry. Long before the time of the transactions here predicted, the apostle John had gone the way of all the earth. The work here enjoined was to be performed by his legitimate successors.

The reed is the symbol of the word of God. It is of the same import as Zechariah's "measuring line." (ch. ii. 1,) and to be used for the same purpose—"to measure Jerusalem," the temple; for both are emblematical of the church of God. The "temple, altar and worshippers," are emblems of the church, her doctrines, worship and membership, tried by the Scriptures—the "reed." There are Gentiles who worship in the outer court, treading under foot both it and the city. These are formal, immoral, idolatrous professors of Christianity. They are rejected by God as reprobate, and by his command to be "cast out" from the fellowship of his people,—authoritatively excommunicated by those to whom Jesus Christ has given the key of discipline.

Here then, at the disclosing of the contents of the little open book, it is manifest that John goes back from the sixth trumpet in the seventeenth century, when the Eastern section of the Roman empire was subverted, by the Othmans, and gives us another view of society in Christendom cotemporaneously with the trumpets. It follows necessarily that the little book does not rank, as some imagine, under any one trumpet; much less does it comprehend all the remaining chapters of the Apocalypse, as others vainly suppose. This matter will receive increasing confirmation as we advance.

Those who worship within the temple and those who worship without, are evidently distinguished from each other. They differ in character tested by the word of God, in fellowship, as authoritatively separated according to the rule of the same word: for whereas the gentile worshippers are so numerous as to crowd both the outer court and the city, the measured worshippers are all included within the confines of the temple, (Song iv. 12.) *Measuring* is equivalent to the *sealing* of the servants of God in the seventh chapter; and imports that they are secured from the sins and plagues of their time. The period of the apostacy from God is fixed to "forty and two months." According to Jewish mode of reckoning, a day for a year, (Num. xiv. 34; Dan. ix. 24,) the whole period is 1260 years. Each month has thirty days. Multiply forty-two by thirty, and we have 1260. The *same* period of time,—not merely an equal period, is otherwise expressed by the prophet Daniel thus: "time, times, and a half." (ch. xii. 7.) That is, 360, the number of days in the Jewish year: times, or 720, the days in two years; and half a time, or 180, the days in half a year. Now, add these three numbers, 360, 720, 180; and the sum is 1260. Now see Daniel iv. 25, where the word "times" means *years*, and then a child may calculate these mystical numbers.

> 3. And I will give power unto my two witnesses, and they shall prophesy a thousand two hundred and threescore days, clothed in sackcloth.

V. 3.—While the nominal church, "the outer court and the holy city," would be "trodden under foot," and the most eminent places would be filled with idolaters, infidels, hypocrites, and mercenary spirits, and true Christians grievously oppressed, the Lord would preserve a faithful few from defiling themselves with the prevailing abominations. These he claims and owns as his "peculiar treasure,"—"my witnesses." These have found that it was "good for them to draw near to God," when the multitude treacherously departed from him. The Lord Christ promises to sustain them in the midst of all their tribulations. The duration of their special work is the very same as that of the treading of the holy city, "a thousand two hundred and three score days,"—1260 years. In attempting to fix the beginning of this period, Daniel and John must be compared; both treat of the same events and dates, and this gives definiteness to the interpretation. Daniel fixes these events to the fourth monarchy *after* it had been *broken in pieces*, and the ten horns had arisen: (ch. vii. 23-25;) so that we have both the geography and chronology determined by the prophets themselves. Hence it follows that we must date the beginning of the 1260 years after the first four trumpets; for by these the western Roman empire was dismembered or broken, that the ten horns might appear. Then the "little horn" of Daniel arose after and among them, (ch. vii. 20, 24.) All reliable expositors agree that the "little horn" is the papacy or the Romish church. This little horn is the special enemy of the "saints of the Most High," and they are to be "given into his hand." (Dan. vii. 25.) The first four trumpets subverted the Roman empire in the west in the latter part of the sixth century. This event made way for the bishop of Rome, in process of time, to acquire a great accession of ecclesiastical power. The civil and ecclesiastical rulers, equally unscrupulous and aspiring, were at this period on terms of comparative intimacy, and occasionally disposed to reciprocate good offices. Phocas, having waded through the blood of the citizens to supreme civil power, in order to secure his position, declared Boniface III., bishop of Rome, head of the universal church. This impious public act took place in the year 606. The pope became also a temporal prince in 756. Now we cannot know *with certainty* which of these events, nor indeed whether *either* of them, marks the period in time when the 1260 years *began*. Hence we must remain at uncertainty as to the exact time when this most interesting period will end. Of all transactions recorded in history, however, that between Phocas and Boniface appears most like "giving the saints into the hand of the little horn." At this juncture in particular, church and state conspire, as never before, to resist the authority of Jesus Christ the Mediator. Paul's "man of sin" has been "revealed in his time." (2 Thess. ii. 6.) Paganism has been abolished by formal edict throughout the Roman empire, and Christianity established as the recognised religion of the commonwealth. That which "letted,"—hindered, that is, the pagan idolatry of the civil state, is "taken out of the way;" and nominal Christianity takes its place. This combination or alliance between church and state will be more clearly made known in the succeeding chapters of this book. Mean while it is the immediate design of the "little open book," to give an epitome or outline of this unholy confederacy in the first thirteen verses of this chapter. The treading under foot of the holy city by the "Gentiles," furnishes occasion for the witnesses to appear publicly against them. These pretended Christians, but real hypocrites, as will appear with increasing evidence as we proceed, have usurped the rights of Messiah's crown, and grievously oppressed his real disciples. Against these outrages on the prerogatives of Christ and the rights of man, these witnesses lift their solemn protest. Their distinctive name, "witnesses," is familiar to every one who searches the Scriptures. (Isa. xliii. 10; Acts i. 8.) But witnesses who love not their lives unto the death are distinguished by the name of *martyrs*. (Rev. ii. 13; Acts xxii. 20.)

God has had his witnesses in all ages since the fall of Adam, in defence of truth and holiness against error and ungodliness; but the specific work *these* witnesses is to oppose the corruption of his two ordinances of church and state during the specified period of 1260 years. The existence of this complex system of civil and ecclesiastical tyranny and heresy, in the holy purpose and sovereign providence of God, calls for the public and uncompromising opposition of the two witnesses. We shall discover the two parties in more visible conflict hereafter; and tracing the struggle to its issue, we shall find, that like the more general and lasting warfare between the seed of the woman and that of the serpent, (Gen. iii. 15,) it is a "war of extermination."

These witnesses are distinguished as a part from the whole. All witnesses are not *martyrs*, but these are such, (v. 7, ch. xx. 4.) And here we are constrained to dissent from the opinion of some expositors, for whose sentiments we entertain profound respect. These "two witnesses" are supposed by these eminent interpreters to "differ as much from the 144,000 sealed ones, (ch. vii. 4,) as Elijah differed from the 7000 in Israel in his time;" whereas, we think the 144,000 and the *two*, are the same identical company. (See chapters vii. 4-8: xiv. 1; xx. 4.) It is evident that they are the same party,—and the *whole* of the party, who are honored to "reign with Christ a thousand years," (ch. xx. 4.)

They are *two* in number, because one witness is not sufficient in law, to establish any matter in controversy. (Num. xxxv. 30; 2 Cor. xiii. 1.) They are a small number compared with their opponents, (ch. xiii. 3.) Again, they are few, but sufficient to confront and confute their two opponents, (ch. xiii. 1, 11.) And, finally, they are *two*, that they may be assimilated to their predecessors.

> 4. *These are the two olive trees, and the two candlesticks standing before the God of the earth.*

5. *And if any man will hurt them, fire proceedeth out of their mouth, and devoureth their enemies: and if any man will hurt them, he must in this manner be killed.*
6. *These have power to shut heaven, that it rain not in the days of their prophecy; and have power over waters to turn them to blood, and to smite the earth with all plagues, as often as they will.*

Vs. 4-6.—"These are the two olive trees, and the two candlesticks," answerable to Joshua and Zerubbabel, the representatives of a gospel ministry and a scriptural magistracy in their day, as seen by the prophet Zechariah, (ch. iv. 14.) The official administrators of the divine ordinances of church and state, require the oil of divine grace to qualify them for the discharge of their responsible duties to God and man. (1 Tim. i. 2; Titus i. 4; Ps. lxxii. 1.) Thus were those public servants of God and of his people qualified who "stood before the God of the earth," as Moses and Aaron in Egypt, Elijah and Elisha in Israel, to whom there is obvious allusion in the special work of these witnesses. (2 Kings i. 10; 1 Kings xvii. 1; Exod. vii. 17.) "Fire proceedeth out of their mouth," when from the scriptures they denounce just judgments upon the impenitent enemies of him whom they represent. They "smite the earth with all plagues," when, in answer to their prayers, vengeance comes upon antichristian communities. (Luke xviii. 7, 8.) They "turn waters into blood," when through their effective agency, the votaries of Antichrist are made the instruments of mutual destruction. And all this is made more clear in the symbolic "vials," (ch. 16.) These witnesses "prophesy," not as being inspired, but because they,—and *they only*, apply existing predictions to their appropriate objects, so far as they receive light from Him who is "the light of the world."

They are "clothed in sack-cloth," because they sigh and cry for all the abominations of their time,—subjected to oppression, and excluded from "kings' palaces,"—places of worldly honor, power and emolument.

But the question is of great importance, and, to themselves in particular, of absorbing interest,—How shall these witnesses be identified among mankind? For however few, humble, despised and persecuted, even unto death; strange as it may seem, there are not wanting many to put forth a claim to be identified with them! Assuming that these mystic witnesses are individual persons, the Papists say, they are Enoch and

Elijah, hereafter to appear on earth! By Protestants, John Huss and Jerome.—Luther and Calvin, have been selected. Others suppose the Old and New Testaments, with many other vague and groundless conjectures. The witnesses die; but the two prophets named "were translated that they should not see death:" and the thought is preposterous that they should be brought again from their glorious state of immortality and subjected to an ignominious death. John Huss and Jerome of Prague did not prophesy 1260 years, nor have we the shadow of a ground to believe that any of the human race shall ever prolong their days on earth to the age of Methuselah. The two Testaments cannot die, for "the word of God liveth and abideth for ever." (1 Pet. i. 23.) But it would be tedious and unprofitable to confute the various chimeras which on this question have been entertained in the minds equally of the learned and the illiterate. The like fanciful and diversified opinions have been, and still are, prevalent in relation to what constitutes "the Antichrist." (1 John ii. 22.) Now, it is evident, even on a cursory perusal of the Apocalypse; that the witnesses and their opponents are the principal parties symbolized in the whole series of the seals, trumpets and vials. How then can any one attain to a rational understanding of the manifold details, who remains "willingly ignorant" of the principal characters in this grandest of all tragico-dramas, presented to man's view on the stage of Jehovah's moral empire, to be contemplated for the whole period of 1260 years? The prevailing ignorance, bewilderment and error, in the minds of most spectators of these moving scenes, we are warranted to expect. (Dan. xii. 10.) For the present we define the witnesses and Antichrist concisely thus:—*The Witnesses are a competent number of Christians, who for 1260 years, insist upon the application of God's word to church and state; and who testify against all communities who rebel against the Lord Christ.* Such communities, in visible organization, constitute THE ANTICHRIST, as will more fully appear in the thirteenth and seventeenth chapters, where the two prominent parties are more formally presented.

Let us never lose sight of the fact, that these witnesses cease not to prophesy,—to apply the scriptures, especially the prophetical parts of them, during the *whole* period of 1260 years; that is, *while they live.* Authentic history supplies abundant evidence that such has been their special work all along since the rise of the antichristian enemy. That enemy is but obscurely mentioned,—*not described* in the "little book," the contents of which we have, as already said, in this chapter, (vs. 1-13.) The character and achievements of the witnesses may be found in the familiar histories of the Culdees and Lollards of Britain, the Waldenses of Piedmont, the Bohemian Brethren; together with the more recent and successful reformers on the continent of Europe and in the British Isles. Is it unnecessary to mention the names of those men of renown,—Zwingle, Luther, Calvin, Knox, Henderson, etc.,—men "mighty in words and in deeds," whose influence on the great "family of nations," their very enemies have reluctantly attested? The testimony of an enemy has ever been deemed weighty. The following is appropriate and decisive from the polished pen of the historian of the "Decline and Fall of the Roman Empire:" "The visible assemblies of the Paulicians, or Albigeois, were extirpated by fire and sword; and the bleeding remnant escaped by flight, concealment, or catholic conformity. But the invincible spirit which they had kindled still lived and breathed in the western world.—In the state, in the church, and even in the cloister, a latent succession was preserved of the disciples of St. Paul, who protested against the tyranny of Rome, embraced the Bible as the rule of faith, and purified their creed from all the visions of the Gnostic theology. The struggles of Wickliff in England, and of Huss in Bohemia, were premature and ineffectual: but the names of Zuinglius, Luther and Calvin, are pronounced with gratitude as the deliverers of nations."[2]

Ever since the time of those eminent witnesses, the same testimony has been maintained. It is not yet finished, the witnesses are yet alive, and the term of 1260 years is not expired.

7. And when they shall have finished their testimony, the beast that ascendeth out of the bottomless pit, shall make war against them, and shall overcome them, and kill them.
8. And their dead bodies shall lie in the street of the great city, which spiritually is called Sodom and Egypt, where also our Lord was crucified.

---

2. Gibbon has unconsciously written a commentary on prophecy!—an involuntary witness, like Josephus!

9. *And they of the people, and kindreds, and tongues, and nations, shall see their dead bodies three days and a half, and shall not suffer their dead bodies to be put in graves.*
10. *And they that dwell upon the earth shall rejoice over them, and make merry, and shall send gifts one to another; because these two prophets tormented them that dwelt on the earth.*

Vs. 7-10.—In these verses we have described the death of the witnesses, as also the agent mentioned, by whom the fatal stroke is given. As future occasion will occur for identifying this bloody tyrant, ascertaining with precision his diabolical origin, here only hinted, his crimes and his awful doom, it is premature to amplify in this place.

If the witnesses cannot be identified, neither can the time of their death be ascertained. We find indeed among expositors as many vague notions relative to the *time* and the *nature* of their death as in relation to their identity. These notions are unworthy of notice; for however they might amuse, they cannot edify.

Four questions are suggested by these verses.—By whom; in what manner, when, and where are the witnesses slain?

The first question is explicitly answered in the sacred text. The "beast," of hellish origin, kills them. But it will afterwards appear that the beast is instigated to this relentless cruelty by another agent of the devil. Again, as to the kind of death, we may in good measure learn this from the kind of life. Now it is obvious that to give testimony, or "prophesy" during the allotted time, constitutes their life. They live, that they may prophesy. Hence it is usual to speak of *silencing*, as equivalent to *slaying* these witnesses. But this is not strictly correct. Why? Because they have been hitherto "killed all the day long." (Ps. xliv. 22; Rom. viii. 36.) Doubtless defection and apostacy do always accompany persecution; and thus the testimony of such is silenced. But the enemy in this case is "drunken with the blood" of these witnesses; and this phrase must be understood literally. Moreover, the enemy gets "blood to drink," because of "shedding blood." (ch. xvi. 6; xvii. 6.) The death of the witnesses is therefore a literal death, of course it will be also moral,—they will cease to prophesy.

Some have supposed the "three years, or days and a half," during which the witnesses lie dead are the same as the 1260 days or years; because if these three and a half days be considered as prophetical, and reduced to literal days, they will amount exactly to 1260. Such an interpretation, however, is preposterous; simply because according to this hypothesis, they *never lived at all!*—The absurdity is evident.

Having ascertained the nature of the death to which the witnesses are appointed by the Lord of life, we now inquire as to the time of this mournful event. The text informs us that their death is connected with the "finishing of their testimony." However the original may be translated,—when they *shall have finished*,—when they *shall be finishing*,—or about to finish, affects not the question as to time. While they live, their work is to prophesy, and their testimony is not completed. Like their Master, to whose example they are conformed, their life and testimony are finished together. These facts, briefly and obscurely hinted here, will be more satisfactorily presented in the next, but especially in the twentieth chapter, (vs. 1-4.) But inasmuch as many, if not most interpreters, have expressed the opinion that the witnesses are already slain, the following arguments in the negative are submitted to the reader.

The 1260 years are not yet terminated, during which,—the whole of which time,—the witnesses are to "prophesy," (v. 3.) Their testimony is yet continued, and sensibly felt by the wicked. They still more or less "torment them that dwell on the earth," (v. 10.) Beyond the usual reproach attached to their names and their work, there has been no general reviling and deriding of them throughout Christendom, to render their memory infamous, (v. 9.)—No opprobrious epithets such as, "These deceivers said, while they were yet alive," (Matt, xxvii. 63,) that so they might be conformed to their Lord in his death. Nor, lastly, have "they that dwell upon the earth" exulted as yet over these hated individuals, as no longer "hurtful to kings and provinces,"—although there have been, often, partial but premature rejoicings by a part of the enemy. But although from time to time, "some of them, have fallen, to try them, and to purge, and to make them white" as predicted, (Dan. xi. 35;) yet the time of "making merry, sending gifts,"—is not yet come.

While we believe, on the grounds adduced,—and much more might have been cited from the context,—that the death of the witnesses is to be understood literally, we do not suppose that every individual will be personally put to death. No, but as in the time of Elijah's banishment, or of our Saviour's lying in the grave, there will be no public body or individual standard-bearer, to bear testimony against the enemies of Jesus Christ, or boldly to assert and press his royal claims upon church and state. In prospect of this dark time,—darker than the "dark ages," we may ask with Joshua,—"What wilt thou do unto thy great name?" But though the witnesses die, the Faithful Witness lives, (ch. i. 18.)

The *place*, where the witnesses lie dead is pointed out by three places well known in sacred history, Egypt, Sodom and Jerusalem. But these are to be understood mystically. The place resembles Egypt for idolatry and cruelty to the people of God; it is like Sodom for literal and spiritual pollution; and Jerusalem, where our Lord was crucified afresh and put to open shame in the persons of his slain witnesses. It follows of course,—that place is to be utterly destroyed; having committed the crimes and contracted the guilt of all those unpardonable criminals. (Ps. lxxiv. 13, 14; Ezek. xxxi. 18; Isa. xiii. 19; Luke xxi. 20.) For similar reasons, Babylon is afterwards mentioned repeatedly as the place of this tragic event, this unpardonable crime,—the slaying of the witnesses, (ch. xviii. 24.) It is to be specially noted here, that in ascertaining the place of the death of these distinguished servants of Christ, our attention is directed by the Holy Spirit to a "street" of the city. At present it is assumed that *streets* of the city and *horns* of the beast substantially harmonize as symbols. Now look over the streets of the great city: contemplate the horns of the beast: ascertain which is most guilty of persecution. In estimating the relative degree of guilt, the degree of heavenly light against which the criminal has rebelled is to be taken into the account. (John xv. 22; Matt. xi. 24.) In view of these scriptural principles, and the actual condition of Christendom as portrayed in authentic history, would the conjecture seem presumptuous, should we venture to designate—Great Britain? There, for centuries, the witnesses have been most numerous, active, and pointed, in testifying against encroachments on the crown-rights of Messiah. There also, lordly prelates, in close alliance with a blasphemous horn of the beast, have often vied with the sworn vassals of the "man of sin," in murdering the saints of God. "Therefore it is no great thing" if, throwing off the mask of Protestantism, English prelacy, combining with Romish Jesuitism, should make common cause with undisguised infidelity, in slaying the witnesses against their heaven-daring rebellion. The signs of the present time, (1870,) render our conjecture not improbable. We give it only as a *conjecture*; for in reference to events yet future,—as we believe that of the death of the witnesses to be,—we may not presume to *prophesy*.—"Three days and a half" is the limited period of their degradation; and this is three natural years and a half: for the word "days" must be taken in the same sense as in v. 3; otherwise we fall into an inextricable labyrinth of endless confusion. From all which it appears that "the triumphing of the wicked is short." If "while the wicked is in power, and we wait upon God." we are called to "join trembling with our mirth;" the pleasing prospect of the speedy and joyful resurrection of "these slain," may inspire us with "a lively hope," and warrant us to join mirth with our trembling.

11. *And after three days and a half, the Spirit of life from God entered into them, and they stood upon their feet; and great fear fell upon them which saw them.*
12. *And they heard a great voice from heaven, saying unto them, Come up hither. And they ascended up to heaven in a cloud; and their enemies beheld them.*

Vs. 11, 12.—In these two verses, as in the preceding, the thoughtful reader will discern a beautiful allusion in the history of these witnesses, to the death and life of our blessed Master. "For if they have been planted together in the likeness of his death, they shall be also in the likeness of his resurrection." Yes, they have communion with him in death and life,—in grace and glory. "Nothing can separate them from the love of God which is in Christ Jesus their Lord."

"The Spirit of life from God entered into them." That is, God will speedily raise up successors, who, maintaining the very same principles, will be gloriously successful in "putting down all rule and authority and power," that had been in hostility to their Lord. (1 Cor. xv. 24, 25. See Ezek. xxxvii. 11-14.) "This is the first resurrection," to be explained by the inspired penman more fully hereafter, (ch. xx. 5.)—As Saul feared David, and Herod John Baptist, because they were "just men and holy;" so were the wicked afraid when these witnesses arose; and, like Shimei, they justly dread the "due reward of their deeds." At the time referred to, "the haters of the Lord will feign submission."—The "great voice from heaven" inviting the witnesses to ascend, and their actual ascent, is another allusion to Christ's exaltation. As when "he was taken up, a cloud received him;" so here, "they ascended up to heaven in a cloud."

It has often been the cry of the antichristian multitude,—"The voice of the people is the voice of God." This cry has been iterated and reiterated, in centuries past, like that of the Ephesian worshippers of Diana; that thereby the testimony of the witnesses might be counteracted and silenced. It has been only too often successful. But where did flattering demagogues and haughty despots find the sentiment? They found it engraved on the moral constitution of man by our beneficent Creator. They found it also transcribed on the pages of objective revelation,—the Bible. But, like other moral and scriptural principles, it has been perverted and misapplied by the perverse ingenuity of wicked men.—This "voice from heaven" is indeed the *people's* voice: and it is legitimate, as coming from the people, because it is first the voice of God. The "heaven" here mentioned is the seat of civil power,—"the ordinance of man." (1 Pet. ii. 13.) In the times here contemplated,—millennial times,—the rights of men will be respected, predicated upon the rights of God, and flowing from them as inseparable. In settling the point of title to civil sovereignty, or the eligibility of any candidate for civil office, the principle enunciated by Hushai the Archite will be found to be alone reliable:—"Whom the Lord and this people choose." (2 Sam. xvi. 18.) Only let the Lord have the first choice of candidates for office in both church and state, and society will be prosperous and happy. (Acts i. 23, 24; vi. 5.) The "great voice" of the 12th verse, comes from "heaven," as the "great voices" of the 15th verse, announcing the millennium.

> 13. And the same hour was there a great earthquake, and the tenth part of the city fell, and in the earthquake were slain of men seven thousand: and the remnant were affrighted, and gave glory to the God of heaven.

V. 13.—"The same hour" that the witnesses mark by their resurrection,—contemporaneously with that joyful event, is "a great earthquake,"—a revolution, (ch. vi. 12.) "The tenth part of the city fell." The city,—"Sodom." "Tenth part of the city,"—a "street," equivalent to "horn." Some one of the "ten kingdoms" will secede from the antichristian confederacy, or imperial dominion; "and the remnant,"—the other nine, dreading the Mediator's vengeance, will reluctantly but speedily submit. (See ch. vi. 16, 17.)—In the "earthquake were slain of men (names, titles,) seven thousand." By "names of men" to be slain,—that is, abolished in reorganized society, we are to understand those "names of blasphemy" mentioned, (ch. xiii. 1,) hereafter to be explained.

We have now taken a very cursory view of the contents of the "little open book." Its place is between the termination of the fourth, and the sounding of the seventh trumpet. In other words, it gives an outline of the contest between the witnesses and Antichrist during 1260 years,—events running parallel in time, at least in part, with the first two woe-trumpets; for it obviously anticipates also, the effects of the third and last woe.

This may be as suitable a place as any other, before proceeding to a consideration of the seventh trumpet, to direct attention to the method which Infinite Wisdom has chosen, by which to reveal to mankind the purposes of God in prophecy. He who alone "knows the end from the beginning,"—who "from ancient times has declared the things that are not yet done," has told us plainly,—"I have multiplied visions, and used similitudes, by the ministry (*hand*,) of the prophets." (Hosea xii. 10.) Now since God has *multiplied* visions, we ought not to think it strange if the same important events in providence be predicted by several, or by many of the prophets; or that one and the same important event be foretold "at sundry times and in diverse manners" by the same prophet. How often, and by how many prophets was the dispersion of the Jews foretold!—the downfall of ancient cities, Babylon, Nineveh, Tyre!—Need we refer to the language of our Lord, addressed to his disciples on the way to Emmaus?—"And beginning at Moses, and all the prophets, he expounded unto them in all the Scriptures the things concerning himself." (Luke xxiv. 27.) We may be sure that the things concerning Christ and the interests of his kingdom in this world, are the theme of inspired prophets in the New Testament as well as in the old. Agreeably to these views, we find Nebuchadnezzar's dream and Daniel's visions relate to the same objects and events. What was more obscurely revealed in the monarch's dream, is rendered more intelligible by various symbols in Daniel's first vision. (Dan. ii. 36-45; vii. 17-27.) But in the next, the eighth chapter, Daniel is favored with still clearer information relative to what he had already seen in vision; and in the eleventh chapter, his attention is called to the most obscure, but most interesting parts of his former visions; and, after all, the "vision is sealed," so that he sees not "the end of these things." (ch. xii. 8, 9.) "I heard, but I understood not," (1 Pet. i. 10, 11.)

In this book, styled Apocalypse, or Revelation, we are told in the first verse, that the Lord Christ "signified,"—made known *by signs*, to his servant John the things that were to come to pass. We have thus far seen that the customary method has been pursued in using signs, symbols or emblems. Henceforth we will find "multiplied visions" employed, more clearly to illustrate events which have already passed under review, but of which we could see little more than a *profile*:—"men, as trees walking."

14. *The second woe is past; and, behold, the third woe cometh quickly.*
15. *And the seventh angel sounded: and there were great voices in heaven, saying, The kingdoms of this world are become the kingdoms of our Lord, and of his Christ; and he shall reign forever and ever.*

Vs. 14, 15.—"The third wo cometh quickly,"—the time elapsing since the end of the second, is not to be so long as that intervening between the first two woes.—The first wo is thought to have begun about the year 612, and continuing by the Saracenic conquests about 150 years, to have terminated in 762. The second woe-trumpet, it is alleged, sounded about 1281, and continuing for 391 years,—the period of the ravages by the Euphratean horsemen, ended about 1672. The destructive influence, however, of these two judgments, may be considered as reaching to the time of the third woe, the one which is to demolish the whole antichristian fabric.

Many eminent expositors,[3] in the early part of the present century, while the first Napoleon was waging successful war with the other powers of Europe, expressed their belief with much confidence, that the seventh angel had begun to sound. They were evidently mistaken.

---

3. "It has been our lot to hear the voice of the third woe," Faber.—"In this I entirely agree with that expositor." M'Leod. The blinding influence of earth's politics upon the minds of pious men, has often occasioned the hearts of their brethren to "sigh for their inconsistency."

Christendom will not fail to hear the voice of the third woe. It may be so that an individual may "not be conscious of having an interest inconsistent with fidelity to the Scriptures," while political "bias" may in fact so influence "sentiments, as to render conviction less dependent upon *evidence* than upon his *wishes*." And we doubt not that misapprehensions and misinterpretation of "the other scriptures," are to be attributed to this cause, insensibly influencing the minds and hearts of learned and godly men, as well as in their expositions of the Apocalypse. Indeed the misapplying of God's word, precept and prophecy, to political and ecclesiastical organizations, has been the principal means of combining and continuing the antichristian apostacy. Thus it is precisely, that the great adversary has been successful, as "an angel of light."

"The little book" has been shown to contain such extensive and important events as to justify the solemnity accompanying its delivery to the apostle.—He now resumes the subject which had been interrupted at the close of the ninth chapter.—The "great voices in heaven" represent the expressions of joy by the saints on hearing the voice of the last of the trumpets, as assuring them of the happy change in the moral condition of the world, which they had been warranted to expect by God's "servants the prophets" from the days of old, (ch. x. 7.) The great, the universal change consists in this:—"The kingdoms of this world are become *the kingdoms* of our Lord and of his Christ." The English supplement,—"the kingdoms," is justified and required, equally by the sense and the laws of syntax: and he is a deceiver, if a scholar, who insists upon any other, to supply the ellipsis. Indeed, the omission of similar supplements, has occasioned needless obscurity to the unlearned in other parts of this book. (See chs. xix. 10; xxii. 9.) The greatest of all revolutions consists in restoring church and state to their scriptural foundation,—transferring both from allegiance to "the god of this world," (Matt. iv. 8; Luke iv. 5, 6;) to their rightful owner,—"the Lord and his Anointed." (Ps. ii. 2, 8.) When this desirable epoch arrives, for which the persecuted witnesses have long and fervently prayed, (ch. vi. 10,) gospel ministers and Christian magistrates will seek to do the will, and aim at the glory of God.—It is painful and pitiable to hear learned and pious men often pray,—"That the kingdoms of this world may soon become the *kingdom* of our Lord and Saviour Jesus Christ." This is to "ask amiss,"—to miss the promise; for no such promise is on record. The groundless conception confounds the revealed distinctions in the Godhead,—the Father with the Mediator; and it would subvert Jehovah's moral empire, annihilating the eternal principle of representative identification! But those good men "mean not so, neither do their hearts think so." They ought, however, to be more careful and diligent in "searching the Scriptures."—If the scriptural significance of this joyful announcement "in heaven" were better understood by gospel ministers generally, a chief barrier would be removed, which now obstructs the advent of the millennium. Would they but cease, their hearers might more readily cease, to "wonder after the beast." But we may not anticipate.

"He, (Christ,) shall reign for ever and ever." When the seventh trumpet, the third woe, shall have accomplished its object, in the utter destruction of immoral power, and the 1260 years shall have come to an end, no other successful combination shall ever again be permitted to assail and harass the city of the Lord:—"of his government there shall be no end." (Dan. vii. 27.) "All dominions shall serve and obey him." The final enterprise of Gog and Magog shall not succeed, (ch. xx. 7-9.)

16. *And the four and twenty elders, which sat before God, on their seats, fell upon their faces, and worshipped God,*
17. *Saying, We give thee thanks, O Lord God Almighty, which art, and wast, and art to come; because thou hast taken to thee thy great power, and hast reigned.*
18. *And the nations were angry, and thy wrath is come, and the time of the dead, that they should be judged, and that thou shouldst give reward unto thy servants the prophets, and to the saints, and them that fear thy name, small and great; and shouldst destroy them which destroy the earth.*

Vs. 16-18.—These verses give us a glimpse of the times following the last woe till the end of the world. The "elders," the representatives,—not of the ministry, as prelates dream, but of the collective body of God's people, now that they are emancipated from a longer and more cruel bondage than that of their fathers in the literal Egypt, "give thanks to God" for the display of his "great power" in their deliverance. Many times had he made bare his holy arm in past ages on behalf of his people: but this is in their eyes the most signal display of his power. "Thou hast taken to thee thy great power."—He now exercises his power over the nations, which was his before; their "anger" in the time of their rebellion is now repressed,—Messiah's "wrath is come," heavier wrath than that which fell upon Rome pagan: (ch. vi. 16, 17.) Then follows an intimation of the final judgment, and suitable "rewards." Our curiosity is excited here, but not gratified; but while left in suspense, we may, with Daniel and the virgin Mary,—"keep these things in our heart." (Dan. vii. 28; Luke ii. 19.) Farther light will be given, (ch. xx. 11-13.)

> 19. And the temple of God was opened in heaven, and there was seen in his temple the ark of his testament: and there were lightnings, and voices, and thunderings, and an earthquake, and great hail.

V. 19.—The inspired books of the Bible were divided into chapters, verses and other parts, for the convenience of reference. But those who performed this useful service were imperfect like ourselves, and therefore we are at liberty to differ from them in our arrangement. Now it seems evident that the 18th verse closes this chapter with a concise account of the ending of the last woe. But the last woe reaches to the final consummation of all things as we have already seen: it follows that the nineteenth verse *must* introduce a new subject. Similar mistakes may be seen in numerous instances elsewhere in our Bibles.

But although a new vision is presented in the twelfth chapter, the two principal parties delineated in the eleventh, engage the apostle's attention. And as preparatory to future scenes, "the temple of God was opened in heaven." "Out of Zion, the perfection of beauty, God hath shined." Before the following scene of warfare, John is favored with a view of the "ark of the testament,"—a symbol of the covenant of grace, which shall continue to be administered in the worst of times; and the opposition to which, in its external dispensation, is emblematically set forth by "lightnings,"—as well as the tokens of Jehovah's presence and avenging judgments: for these awful symbols, taken from fearful convulsions in nature, are usually indicative of the tremendous judgments of God.

CHAPTER XII.

1. *And there appeared a great wonder in heaven: a woman clothed with the sun, and the moon under her feet, and upon her head a crown of twelve stars;*
2. *And she, being with child, cried, travailing in birth, and pained to be delivered.*

Vs. 1, 2.—The Apocalypse, besides the *three* parts into which it is divided by its divine Author, (noticed in ch. i. 19,) is also susceptible of division into *two* parts. With the eleventh chapter terminates the *abridged* prospective history of the church and of the world, emblematically represented under the seals and trumpets. The seventh seal, when opened, disclosed all the contents of the sealed book, and also introduced the seven trumpets. But we have followed the series of the trumpets in order, to the end of the world,—interrupted only by the isolated history of the "little book"; which, treating of events which were matter of history under the first two woe-trumpets, *could not be sealed*. Now at the twelfth chapter, without regard to the seventh, or any other of the trumpets in particular, we are furnished with a second and enlarged edition, as it were, of the most important parts of the first edition. We have observed before, that this is the manner of the prophets on a large scale, especially in predicting "the sufferings of Christ, and the glory that should follow." So it is with John and Paul. What the latter only hints at, when writing to Timothy, (1 Tim. iv. 1-3,) he enlarges upon in addressing the Thessalonians. (2 Thess. ii. 3-12.) The theme is the same as treated by these two apostles; and this coincidence will in due time be more manifest. Next to Christ personal, the prophets have been interested in the destiny of Christ mystical.

Three different views of this twelfth chapter have been taken by the more sober and learned expositors. One considers it as referring to the Roman empire in its heathen state, prior to the time of Constantine. Another understands the first part of this chapter,—(vs. 1-6,)—as relating to Rome pagan, and the rest of the chapter to antichristian Rome. A third conceives that the whole of it applies to apostate imperial Rome *only*. The last is doubtless the correct view.

As the "sealed book" and the "little open book," must be supposed to contain all the prophetical part of the Apocalypse; and as the whole of the little book is comprised in the eleventh chapter, (vs. 1—13,) this twelfth chapter must belong to the sealed book. Being a continuance of the history under the seventh seal, although it may agree in time with some of the trumpets, it cannot go back to a period prior to the seventh seal. But under the sixth seal, paganism was abolished in the Roman empire; therefore this chapter refers to the antichristian empire. Moreover, as the little book was introductory to the seventh trumpet, designating the object of the third woe, so this chapter and the next two, are wholly occupied in describing the object of the vials, (ch. 16.)

We ought to bear in mind continually, that the seals, trumpets and vials, are introduced as symbols, to delineate one character, the impenitent enemy of God and of his saints. But this enemy "beguiles through his subtlety," changing his aspects and instruments, the more successfully to assail the city of the Lord. It is therefore the design of the Holy Spirit in these three chapters to present the foe in his most prominent features, that the two witnesses may be able to identify the enemy, be apprized of their danger, and intelligently choose their commander,—"the Captain of salvation."

"There appeared a great wonder in heaven." The word "wonder" in this verse, and also in verse third, simply means a *sign* or symbol; and the whole structure of the book requires that it be so translated.—"Woman" is here the true church of God. Here most expositors fail to explain the symbol "heaven." Others say "heaven" symbolizes the church. Then we have *two churches*,—a church within a church! This is unquestionably the only correct view of the matter. During most, if not the whole period of the 1260 years, the witnesses are so blended with, or overshadowed by the church catholic or general, that few are able, and fewer still disposed, to distinguish the one from the other. All through the Bible the church is spoken of as a female. She is the "daughter of Zion,—the bride, the Lamb's wife." Any body politic is spoken of in the sacred writings in the same style. "The daughter of Babylon, of Tyre, or even of Egypt,"—These are familiar figures.

This woman is "clothed with the sun." She has "put on the Lord Jesus Christ." (Rom. xiii. 14.) He is "the Lord her righteousness." (Jer. xxiii. 6.) The "moon under her feet," may represent the "beggarly elements" of the Mosaic ritual, sublunary things, or the ordinances which derive all their light from the "Sun of righteousness." The "twelve stars" are the doctrine of the apostles, or rather the apostles' legitimate successors; their *legitimacy* tested by their doctrine and order in opposition to the *imaginary historical line* of papistical and prelatic succession. A faithful gospel ministry are ever her stars and her crown, (ch. i. 20.) The true apostolic church, thus scripturally constituted, (ch. xi. 1,) becomes the joyful mother of a holy seed. (Ps. cxiii. 9; Gal. iv. 26, 27.)

3. And there appeared another wonder in heaven, and, behold, a great red dragon, having seven heads, and ten horns, and seven crowns upon his heads.

4. And his tail drew the third part of the stars of heaven, and did cast them to the earth: and the dragon stood before the woman which was ready to be delivered, for to devour her child as soon as it was born.

5. And she brought forth a man-child, who was to rule all nations with a rod of iron: and her child was caught up unto God, and to his throne.

6. And the woman fled into the wilderness, where she hath a place prepared of God, that they should feed her there a thousand two hundred and threescore days.

Vs. 3-6.—The next "sign in heaven," exciting the apostle's admiration, was "a great red dragon, having seven heads and ten horns,"—The dragon is fully described, v. 9, leaving no place, or even *pretence* for conjecture. He is known from the day that he "beguiled Eve" in the garden of Eden. "That old serpent" still intrudes among the saints, in the garden of the Lord. (Job i. 6; John vi. 70; xiii. 27.) As the devil possessed the serpent to deceive the mother of mankind, so, with the same malevolent design, he possessed himself of the whole political and ecclesiastical power of the Roman empire, thereby to deceive and destroy the "seed of the woman," all true believers. His color is *red*, denoting his character as cruel and blood-thirsty. Sir Isaac Newton considers the dragon as symbolical of the Greek Christian empire of Constantinople.

Scott thinks this symbol represents the pagan Roman empire; while others suppose the British government to answer the symbol, because of the scarlet costume of her officers and soldiers! Thus, inspired symbols may mean any thing suggested to the imaginations of men, not by the text or context, but by their respective and conflicting political prejudices. Surely, if the red color signify any thing besides *cruelty*, it may be discerned with equal clearness in the scarlet cloaks of *Pope* and *Cardinals*. As "heaven" is to be taken in an ecclesiastical sense, so are the "stars," (ch. i. 20,—) "the angels of the churches," ministers of the gospel.—As the Saracenic locusts and the Euphratean horses had stings and hurtful power in their tails, (ch. ix. 10, 19;) so it is with this dragon. The destructive influence of Mahometan delusion and papal idolatry, operated as a fatal poison in the souls of men. The judgments of the past woes left many still in a state of impenitence, (ch. ix. 20, 21.) "The leaders of this people caused them to err," by inculcating submission to existing corrupt civil power. The "little horn" of Daniel, as first rendered visible in the person of the brutal Phocas, began to be addressed in language of most fulsome and degrading flattery, which seems to be copied till the present time. That we may see how mercenary and aspiring ecclesiastics paid court to civil despots from the commencement of the famous 1260 years, let the following instance serve for a sample. Addressing the monster Phocas, Pope Gregory, as the mouth of the clergy and laity,[4] uses this language: "We rejoice that the benignity of *your piety*(!) has reached the pinnacle of imperial power. Let the heavens be glad and the earth rejoice."—Now let us hear the character of Phocas from the pen of an infidel (Gibbon):—"Ignorant of letters, of laws, and even of arms, he indulged in the supreme rank a more ample privilege of lust and drunkenness.—The punishment of the victims of his tyranny was imbittered by the refinements of cruelty: their eyes were pierced, their tongues were torn from the root, their hands and feet were amputated: some expired under the lash, others in the flames, others again were transfixed with arrows: and a simple speedy death was mercy which they could rarely obtain." Thus the dragon's power was in his mouth, issuing bloody edicts to "slay the innocent;" while "his tail drew

---

4. The terms "clergy and laity" are of papal origin, and the unlearned Christian should know that they are contrary to the mind of the Holy Spirit. 1 Pet. v. 3. The body of the people are "God's heritage,"— *clergy*.

the third part of the stars of heaven, and did cast them to the earth." They prostituted their ministry to sustain the policy of the beast. "The ancient and honorable, he is the head; and the prophet that teacheth lies, he is the tail." (Is. ix. 15.) Thus it is that pastors, fond of show and ambitious of worldly distinction, attach themselves to the train of earthly thrones and dignities, and so constitute and perpetuate the antichristian confederacy against the "woman"—the true church. During the first six hundred years of the Christian era the woman had been "travailing" to bring forth a holy progeny. All this time the dragon's "eyes are privily set against the poor." (Ps. x. 8.) The allusion is here to the cruel edict of Pharaoh (Exod. i. 16; Acts vii. 19.) The great city where the witnesses are slain is "spiritually called Egypt." (ch. xi. 8.) By a like form of speech, Pharaoh is called "the great dragon," (Ezek. xxix. 3; Is. li. 9.) It should be noted, that the Roman empire, the beast, in all its heads and horns is actuated by the devil,—before as well as after its dismemberment, from the time of Romulus its founder, till its overthrow by the third woe. At the time referred to in the text, when the empire has "assumed the livery of heaven,"—professedly in the interest of Christ, then it is that the devil bestirs himself. Like his prototype, he dreads the growth and power of the woman's offspring. Under pagan Rome's persecutions, "the more God's people were afflicted, the more they multiplied and grew." Now the adversary shapes his policy accordingly.—"Come on, let us deal wisely with them, lest they multiply."—His avowed object is, to "devour the child as soon as it is born,"—by persecution to prevent ministers from laboring to convert sinners to God; and to destroy all who "as new-born babes, desire the sincere milk of the word."—The woman had still "strength to bring forth."—"She brought forth a man child, who was to rule all nations with a rod of iron."—With united voice papists and prelates declare, this child can be no other than Constantine the first Christian emperor. The very fact that this interpretation comes from such a source, may well suggest suspicion as to its correctness. Two considerations demonstrate the error of this prelatic interpretation, besides the fact that it is *prelatic*. Constantine had gone the way of all the earth some hundreds of years before the birth of this child. And again, the eternal Father never made the promise to Constantine or any other earthly monarch, to which the apostle John here refers. (Ps. ii. 8, 9.) This promise is obviously made to the Lord Christ. But it is objected by those learned expositors,—much like the Pharisees, (John vii. 52,)—"Search and look, for out of Galilee ariseth no prophet." So reason these men. They haughtily and confidently object thus:—"Christ is the son of the *Jewish* church, but this child is the son of the *Christian* church." This argument destroys the unity of the church of God, which is one under all changes of dispensation of his gracious covenant. (Rom. xi. 16-24; Eph. ii. 20.) The Messiah is here represented as in the beginning of the war with the same enemy;—the *seed* of the *woman* shall bruise the serpent's head. Still may the church of God joyfully declare,—"Unto us a *Child* is born, unto us a *Son* is given." (Is. ix. 6.) This *masculine* son, however, is not to be understood of Christ *personal*, but of Christ mystical,—of those who are with him "called, and chosen, and faithful;" whom "he is not ashamed to call his brethren." (ch. xvii. 14; Heb. ii. 11.) The "sealed" company, (ch. vii. 4,) the "two witnesses;" (xi. 3), the "144 thousand," (xiv. 1,) are the "manchild." As many rulers constitute but one "angel," (chs. ii. and iii.,) so the two witnesses are one *manly Son*. The Lord Jesus was *alone* in the work of redemption; but he allows his faithful disciples to share in the honor of his victories, (ch. ii. 26, 27; Ps. cxlix. 9.) From the devouring jaws of the dragon, as it were, the "child is caught up unto God, and to his throne." The leaders in church and state supposed that they had "made sure" of the Saviour, when they had "sealed the stone and set a watch." So thought the enemies of the witnesses while their dead bodies lay unburied.—"He that sitteth in the heavens shall laugh: the Lord shall have them in derision." The Anointed of the Father, the Head of the church, and Prince of the kings of the earth, as the representative of his people, in defiance of the serpent, is caught up to the throne of God, (Eph. ii. 6;) while the church flies to her appointed place in the wilderness during the 1260 years. At the beginning of that gloomy period the woman fled. This flight is not mentioned "by anticipation," as some suppose; for the wilderness condition of the woman, and the sackcloth of the witnesses, are emblematical of the same depressed state of the church, and during the same time. The witnesses prophesy during the whole period of the 1260 years; and the woman is fed in the wilderness during the *same* time. Her flight, sojourn in the wilderness, and feeding there, are allusions to the history of Elijah as before, (ch. xi. 6.) when he fled for his life from the wrath of Jezebel. (1 Kings xix. 1-4.) Jezebel has been already introduced as an enemy to the church, (ch. ii.

20.) There may be allusion also to the miraculous subsistence of the church in the wilderness, till the "cup of the Amorites should be full." During the time of the conflict, to be described in the rest of this chapter, the woman is in a place of safety. In the worst of times there are places of safety provided for God's children. (Isa. xxvi. 20.)

> 7. And there was war in heaven: Michael and his angels fought against the dragon; and the dragon fought, and his angels.
> 8. And prevailed not; neither was their place found any more in heaven,
> 9. And the great dragon was cast out, that old serpent, called the Devil, and Satan, which deceiveth the whole world: he was cast out into the earth, and his angels were cast out with him.
> 10. And I heard a loud voice saying in heaven, Now is come salvation, and strength, and the kingdom of our God, and the power of his Christ; for the accuser of our brethren is cast down, which accused them before our God day and night.
> 11. And they overcame him by the blood of the Lamb, and by the word of their testimony; and they loved not their lives unto the death.

Vs. 7-11.—In this part of the chapter we have three attacks of the dragon upon the friends of true religion. The first is the war in heaven, (vs. 7-12.) The second persecution on the earth, (vs. 12-16.) The third is mentioned in verse 17th: and these three contests cover the whole period of the 1260 years.

The first war is waged in heaven. The allusion is obviously to the rebellion of angels, for which they were cast down from heaven, (2 Pet. ii. 4.) The contest is the same in principle as the first war; but it is conducted in a different form and place. Heaven here, is the church general, and the serpent acts by the authority of the empire. The woman having fled into the wilderness, the dragon's power becomes so great in the symbolical heaven, that he aims at the entire destruction of true religion in the world. The advocates of the true religion at this time were the Waldenses, called by their adversaries in derision *Leonists* and *Cathari*,—citizens of Lyons in France; and Puritans, a term of reproach heaped upon their successors till the present day. These people were deemed the most dangerous enemies to the church of Rome. Yet the reasons for their condemnation by the inquisitors, are their full vindication in the judgment of impartial men. They are three,—"This is the oldest sect; for some say it hath endured,—from the time of the apostles. It is more general; for there is no country in which this sect is not. Because when all other sects beget horror in the hearers, this of the Leonists hath a great show of piety: they live justly before men, and believe all things rightly concerning God; only they blaspheme the church of Rome and the clergy." While the beast by its horns, instigated by an apostate church, and both by the dragon, was "making havoc of the church," represented by the Puritans: there were some even in the Romish cloisters whose hearts God had touched, and who occasionally espoused the cause of a virtuous minority at the hazard of life. This war *in heaven*, conducted with various success by Bernard, Peter Waldo, John Wickliffe and others on the European continent and in Britain, may be pronounced by Gibbon "premature and ineffectual;" but the Captain of salvation and his heroic followers, will give a different verdict. These noble confessors and martyrs, under the conduct of Michael our prince, began the struggle with the dragon, although the war did not come to its height till the early part of the 16th century. Then it was that "Michael and his angels fought against the dragon, and the dragon fought and his angels." Both parties became more visible in the symbolic heaven before the eyes of all Christendom. Michael, (*who is like God?*) is the well known description of Jesus Christ. (Phil. ii. 6; Heb. i. 3.) To Daniel, while contemplating this same contest, he was made known as the "great Prince, that standeth for the children of God's people," and long before Daniel's time, had "contended with the devil." (Jude v. 9.) "Christ and Belial" are therefore the two opposing leaders of the armies. In other words, Christ mystical and the devil incarnate are the belligerents; and we know that "greater is he that is in the saints, than he that is in the world." (1 John iv. 4.) The result of the war is not doubtful. The whole power of Rome, civil and ecclesiastical,—emperors, kings, princes, pope, cardinals and prelates, were baffled; and this too, whether in the use of the sword of the Spirit,—polemic *theses*,—or of the material sword, in literal warfare. When the Lord Jesus "mustered the hosts to the battle," he furnished them "with the whole armour of God to stand in the evil way." When Zuingle, Luther, Calvin, Knox, their compeers and successors, were obliged to wrestle with the hosts of Antichrist,—"against principalities, against powers, against the rulers of the darkness of this world, against spiritual wickedness in high places," (*wicked spirits in heavenly places,*) they found it both lawful and necessary,—"having no sword, to buy one." (Luke xxii. 36.)

The dragon and his angels were defeated and routed,—"They prevailed not,—he was cast out into the earth, and his angels were cast out with him." The thunders of the Vatican thenceforth lost their wonted power to terrify. Ever since, they are but *brutum fulmen,—vox, et praeterea nihel,*—harmless thunder,—unmeaning voice. Papal curses, though annually launched against all heretics, tend only to amuse the popular mind, not to reach or disturb the individual conscience. For centuries the dragon has been unable to rouse any one horn of the beast to deeds of blood.

It is usual for the victors to give outward expression to their joy. "The voice of them that shout for mastery," has been heard since the days of Moses. (Exod. xxxii. 18.) Accordingly, these conquerors congratulate one another on their recent victory, but their joy terminates on the proper object. The "kingdom of their God and the power of his Christ" constitute their theme. His right hand and his holy arm have gotten him the victory. The devil accused Job before God. His accusations in that instance were prosecuted through Job's friends and his wife. (Job ii. 4, 5, 9, 11.)—So it was in the experience of the reformers. They were loaded with infamy by their persecutors; and while they were depressed, God himself seemed to give sentence against them. This was the wormwood and the gall in the cup of their affliction, as it was in holy Job's experience: but in due time God "brought forth their righteousness as the light, and their judgment as the noonday." Their "good conversation put to silence the ignorance of foolish men." The power of the Lord's Christ was made manifest through the instrumentality of his servants, by producing conviction in many hearts that the cause for which they suffered was from God, and thus prevailing with such to join in their fellowship. The hearts of kings and princes of the earth were touched from on high; so that they braved the combinations of imperial and papal power, while extending the shield of their protection to the followers of the Lamb. Frederick the Wise, and especially John his brother, electors of Saxony in Luther's time, were notable bulwarks of defence to the sufferers, against the bloody edicts of Charles fifth, emperor of

Germany. The "good regent" in Scotland and others extended effectual protection to Knox, his coadjutors and followers in the cause of reformation. When the seven thunders uttered their voices, John "was about to write," (ch. x. 4.) He was about to proclaim a final victory! He was too sanguine. "The time was not yet." Just so in the case of his legitimate successors in the work of the Lord. Confident in the power and faithfulness of Michael their Prince, confident in the righteousness of their cause, fondly hoping that at this time their Master is about to restore again the kingdom to Israel, they prematurely exclaim,—"Now is come salvation."—In reaping the first fruits of victory, they anticipate the harvest of final and absolute conquest, (ch. xiv. 8.) Indeed, the salvation of God and the power of his Christ, were experienced by great multitudes during the time of this contest. The saints experienced times of refreshing from the presence of the Lord. Then followed a work of grace, both on the continent of Europe and in the British Isles; Christians entering into solemn covenant bonds with God and with one another, whereby the kingdom of God was rendered more visible among mankind than in the "dark ages." The weapons, with which the saints overcame the dragon, were not carnal, but mighty. These, we are told, were "the blood of the Lamb, and the word of their testimony." They believed and they taught in opposition to the popular doctrine of good works and penances, that the righteousness which the law of God requires of a sinner, is provided by a Surety; that the blood of Christ alone cleanses believers from the guilt of sin, and thus justifies them in the sight of God. No man ever used stronger language than Luther in denouncing the supposed efficacy of works, or in asserting the sovereignty of free grace, in the justification of a sinner. Indeed it was the deep impression which the doctrine of justification made upon the hearts of men, and the firm hold which faith took of it, that enabled and constrained them to forsake the Romish church and to seek and erect a separate fellowship. This was with them "the word of Christ's patience." Other doctrines of grace were, of course, connected with this of justification in the apprehension of the Reformers, but it was the central one. And thus we may learn, that any doctrine of the Bible, when generally opposed, may lawfully become a point of testimony; and when openly opposed and practically denied, it may become a warrantable and imperative ground of separation. In all such cases,—and history supplies multitudes of them,—the declining majority are truly the schismatics and separatists. The malicious, the indolent and credulous, however, in all ages have joined in the cry of schism as attaching to the virtuous minority.

Many of the combatants fell in the conflict, "resisting unto blood, striving against sin." "They loved not their lives unto the death." They could give no stronger evidence of love to Christ and truth. Their faithful contendings constituted their testimony. This testimony is called in the 17th verse, "the testimony of Jesus Christ." Does this mean that it *belongs* to Christ? or that it *treats* of him? The language may probably be taken in either sense, or as embracing both. It is Christ's testimony, as he is "the faithful and true Witness, who before Pontius Pilate witnessed a good confession;" or it may be understood as bearing upon Christ in his person, offices and work. In either sense his faithful disciples enjoy intimate communion with himself, sharing the honour of his victories, (v. 5.) Therefore let the heavens rejoice in prospect of *final* victory, (ch. xviii. 20.)

12. *Therefore rejoice, ye heavens, and ye that dwell in them. Woe to the inhabiters of the earth, and of the seal for the devil is come down unto you, having great wrath, because he knoweth that he hath but a short time.*
13. *And when the dragon saw that he was cast into the earth, he persecuted the woman, which brought forth the manchild.*

Vs. 12, 13.—Here is a note of warning. The dragon, though ejected from the symbolic heaven, the seat of imperial and ecclesiastic power, is not yet bound with the great chain, (ch. xx. 1, 2.) His late defeat has only incensed his rage, "as a bear robbed of her whelps." But the special reason assigned for his "great wrath" is, "because he knoweth that he hath but a short time." How does the devil come to this knowledge? Is he omniscient! No. Was he joint-counsellor with the Most High? No. (Isa. xl. 13, 14; Rom. xi. 34.) He must have derived this knowledge from revelation; and from some instances in Scripture, we might infer that the devil is more skilled in theology, especially in prophecy, than many, if not most modern interpreters. In the time of our Lord's humiliation he quoted and applied to him a prophecy in the 91st psalm, (v. 11, 12.) He also dreaded being tormented,—"before the time." (Matt. viii. 29:) from which it appears that he reasons of the "times and the seasons" as revealed in the Bible. But by the phrase, "a short time," the devil understood,—and we are to understand,—not the time to transpire till the end of the world; but, the time intervening between his ejectment out of heaven, and the overthrow of Antichrist, when he is to be bound. Now, we may learn from the *devil's calculation*, that all those learned and famous divines, especially of the prelatic church of England, "do greatly err, not knowing the Scriptures;" who say, that the dragon was cast out of the symbolic heaven *in the time of Constantine!* The space of duration *from Constantine till the millennium*, cannot be relatively "short," under the New Testament dispensation. The time of the dragon's being cast out of heaven, and the instruments by which this was accomplished, are to be found clearly verified in the authentic histories of the sixteenth century, to which some references have been already made, as elucidating the events of the 11th chapter: for it is to be still remembered that the former part of the 11th chapter *agrees in time* with the 12th, 13th and 14th chapters. At the end of the second woe, which we supposed to be in the latter part of the seventeenth century, about the year 1672, it is declared "the third woe cometh quickly," (ch. xi. 14.) Now here it is said "the devil,—hath but a short time." Taking both expressions as relating to the same period, it follows that we are now living,—not in the time of the third woe, but in the time of the devil's activity among the "inhabiters of the earth and of the sea;" that is, the population of Christendom either in a tranquil or revolutionary state. The enemy makes his *second* attack upon the "woman" in a new and unexpected mode of warfare. So long as permitted, he never ceases to persecute the saints. When defeated in *heaven*, he renews the assault upon the *earth*. If the edicts and bulls of crowned and mitred heads have lost their power to terrify and destroy the souls of men, he will try to effect the same object by other means.

> 14. *And to the woman were given two wings of a great eagle, that she might fly into the wilderness, into her place; where she is nourished for a time, and times, and half a time, from the face of the serpent.*
> 15. *And the serpent cast out of his mouth, water as a flood, after the woman, that he might cause her to be carried away of the flood.*
> 16. *And the earth helped the woman, and the earth opened her mouth, and swallowed up the flood which the dragon cast out of his mouth.*

Vs. 14-16.—To guard against the *second* attack of the dragon, the woman flees a *second* time to the place of safety, which had been mercifully prepared for her preservation before the war began, (v. 6.) And she is in no less peril from her deadly enemy than before.

The "two wings of a great eagle" have furnished occasion to many fertile minds for indulging in fanciful conjectures. To such persons nothing occurs answerable to the symbol but some emblem of imperial power or national sovereignty. And because the eagle was the visible symbol on the military banner of Rome, it is conjectured that "the eastern and western empires afforded protection to the church!" Why, the empire, in both its wings, was the deadly enemy of the church, as we have already seen! (ch. xi. 7.) Alas! what absurdities result from political bias! The unlettered Christian will readily perceive under the emblem in the text, a plain allusion to the gracious interposition of the church's Redeemer in the days of old. "Ye have seen what I did unto the Egyptians, and how I bare you on *eagles' wings*, and brought you unto myself." (Exod. xix. 4.) Thus the Lord delivered his people and brought them into a literal wilderness on their way to the promised land of liberty. And now in a time of equal danger, he will "set his hand again the second time" to deliver his people. He who delivered them from so great a death as Pharaoh threatened, doth still deliver: in whom his saints have ground to trust that he will still deliver them, (2 Cor. i. 10.) The great and beneficial change accomplished among the nations by the reformation in the sixteenth and seventeenth centuries, whereby the dragon was hurled from seats of ecclesiastical and civil power, did not materially change the position of the "two witnesses." The time had not yet come when they were to be called up into the symbolic heaven. They must continue to prophesy till the close of the appointed period of 1260 years. Till the expiration of that definite period the true church of Christ is not to be permanently established in any nation of the earth. The actual condition of the church and of the nations among whom she dwells, is delineated in these verses during the time subsequent to the Protestant Reformation,—consequently in our own time. The "time, times and half a time" of the 14th verse, are an obvious reference to Daniel vii. 25: xii. 7; and are the same period as 42 months, or 1260 days, "a day for a year." During this whole time the woman is nourished in the wilderness "from the face of the serpent." Safety is secured for her only "in her place."

"Water," as a symbol or metaphor, is of frequent occurrence and varied import in Scripture. Among its diversified significations, perhaps that of a destructive element is most common. (Ps. xviii. 4; xxxii. 6.) It is indeed often used to denote gospel blessings, (as Is. lv. 1; John vii. 38; Rev. xxii. 17.) As here used, the "water as a flood," represents something intended by the dragon for the destruction of the woman. If he cannot destroy her by fire, he aims to overwhelm her with water. This water comes out of the dragon's "mouth." So of the "unclean spirits," (ch. xvi. 13.) Soul-destroying errors,—heresies,—are undoubtedly intended. If he cannot devour as a roaring lion, he will endeavour to deceive and seduce as a cunning serpent. We are therefore instructed hereby to look for "damnable heresies" to prevail, accompanied and followed by popular commotions and licentiousness. The age in which we live is remarkably characterized by false systems and impious theories. Speculative atheism caused the French revolution, and led to the erection of the United States government; which, having openly declared independence of England, soon after virtually declared independence of God. France, Germany, England and the United States, have all been pervaded with infidel and atheistical sentiments; and these, whether propagated under the name of *solid science* or *polite literature*, have corrupted the public mind for generations. In the name of science, treating of the material or moral world, the agents of the dragon have been exceedingly successful. Metaphysicians and geologists have constructed systems which would exclude the Almighty from the heavens and the earth. But however active and zealous these laborers in the service of the dragon, they do not reach the popular ear but in part. Those sons of Belial who devise false systems of religion under the name of Christianity, have been still more pernicious to the nations, and dangerous to the church. If the church of Rome cannot prevail with kings as before, to execute her cruel sentences of death upon heretics, she is not less active in disseminating her idolatrous and superstitious dogmas among the nations. By freemasonry, odd-fellowship, temperance associations, and a countless number of affiliated societies,—the offshoots of popery and infidelity, the dragon still assails the woman. Reason, toleration, humanity, charity and liberality are terms which have been selected and abused by the servants of the devil "to deceive the hearts of the simple." These are alike the watchwords of the spiritual seducer and the political agitator. What dogma or heresy so absurd,—what conduct so immoral, as not to find patronage in the journals of the day? or not to find tolerance or protection under the fostering wings of church or state? What is impiously called "free love," as well as avowed infidelity and polygamy, are patronized by constituted authorities in Christendom. When taking a survey of the errors and systems of error, hostile to the honor of Messiah and the free grace of his gospel, how few can be found in the different nations of the earth, who "overcame by the blood of the Lamb!" The religions established by the nations of the world are all more or less tainted with the errors, and disfigured by the ceremonies of the church of Rome. Surely we have before our eyes a constant fulfilment of the prophecy under consideration. To all outward appearance the woman is in the wilderness. She is in fact so obscure that some of her sons begin to question her visibility. They are ready to cry in despondency,—"The witnesses are slain."—They are mistaken. This is their infirmity. The 1260 years are not yet expired, nor the testimony finished. "When the enemy shall come in *like a flood*, the Spirit of the Lord shall lift up a standard against him." (Isa. lix. 19.) The mystic woman is yet in the wilderness, and there she is nourished with the hidden manna "a time, times and half a time," "forty and two months, or twelve hundred and sixty days,"—that is, years; for, as formerly noticed, all these expressions mean the same period of time; the period during which the witnesses prophesy, on the one side, and the gentiles tread the outer court, on the other. The profanation of the holy city,—the church nominal, and the testimony of the witnesses against that conduct, is the same contest which in this chapter is represented under other symbols. The waters of the symbolic flood have spread over all the nations of Christendom, corrupting the very fountains of natural and moral science, literature, politics and religion; so that hardly any principle is accepted by the human mind as settled, but all is thrown into debate. Man's intellect, craving substantial nourishment, and thirsting for refreshment which nothing but the water of life can supply, vibrates between ritualism and skepticism in our day. The flood from the dragon's mouth, consisting of truth and error, a combination of Christianity, refined idolatry and speculative atheism, fails to satisfy the necessary cravings of the immortal soul. "There be many that say, Who will show us any good?" (Ps. iv. 6.)

In this state of the popular mind, there is a general sentiment which discountenances penalties inflicted for mere opinion. The cry of toleration,—"freedom of speech and of the press," resounds in the public ear among most communities since the dragon was cast down from the mystic heaven. This popular sentiment is not an expression of the law of charity, actuating hearts influenced by divine grace; but rather originates from indifference alike to the claims of Messiah and the destinies of mankind. Thus "the earth helps the woman." Indeed, the nations of Christendom, contrary to their former policy, are now much more tolerant of ecclesiastical than of *political* heresies. With few exceptions, the policy of the nations at the present time is to discriminate, not among *churches*, but among *religions*. The popular voice is obviously in favor of dissevering that alliance between church and state, from which mankind have suffered in past generations. While every earthly potentate, usurping the place and prerogatives of the Mediator, assumed to dictate the faith and worship of his subjects, all dissenters and recusants must necessarily be subjected to penalties. Such was the policy of the dragon for centuries, while in the heavens of ecclesiastical and civil power. The nominal church established by the state, *defined heresy*; and the heresy found by the church became rebellion against the civil authority. Of course the saints were then executed as *traitors*. Even a superficial view of the signs of the times will result in the conviction, that a great change has taken place in the policy of nations and churches. The dragon has now prevailed with most politicians and statesmen, as well as with most professing Christians, to demand a total "separation of church and state;" by which demand they do not mean a divorce of the unscriptural and *antichristian* alliance only or chiefly, but a simple and absolute rejection of religion, and especially the *Christian* religion, from any connexion with or influence upon *civil* affairs. This is undeniably the avowed aim and declared desire of the great body of the population of Christendom at the present time, (1870.) And what is this but an open denial of the authority of the Mediator as he is the "Prince of the kings of the earth?" Thus has the dragon, since his ejection from heaven become a terrible "woe to the inhabiters of the earth and of the sea!" And thus has the "earth opened her mouth and swallowed up the flood;" so that the woman remains comparatively safe "from the face of the serpent" in the very obscurity of her position. Some of her sons, from time to time, venturing abroad from their secluded place in the wilderness, becoming weary of sackcloth and aspiring to worldly distinction, have been borne along by the waters of the flood, and *drowned in the general deluge*. Against the force of this strong current of popular errors, nothing will avail the seed of the woman but the "living water" which Jesus imparted to the woman of Samaria. To him who partakes of this water, those of the dragon will be distasteful; for "it shall be in him a well of water springing up into everlasting life." (John iv. 14.) Since the middle of the seventeenth century, when by the reformation in Europe and the British Isles, the dragon was cast down from the symbolic heaven, he has been assailing in "great wrath" all ranks and degrees of men, not, as before, with fire and sword, with scaffolds, gibbets, thumb-screws,—torturing and destroying their mortal bodies, that he might reach their immortal souls: but by bringing them together in *voluntary associations* on principles of the covenant of works, subversive of the covenant of grace, and consequently aiming at the drowning of the mystic woman. This the enemy of all righteousness has been attempting, and with too much success, by public and professed ecclesiastical and Christian associations; such as Jesuits, Socinians and other self-styled Unitarians, Latter-day Saints, Mormons,—or by combinations in secret and sworn confederacies; such as Odd Fellows, Freemasons, Sons and Daughters of Temperance, with other affiliated fellowships innumerable. The special subtlety of the serpent consists in blending these two kinds of communions, so that under the name of reform, moral and spiritual, those who fear God may be unconsciously drawn into the snare. And alas! how many simple ones have been thus carried away by the waters of the flood! And many strong men have been thus cast down from their excellency. We are not to be surprised if we find the witnesses few in our time,—the seed of the woman diminished when the dragon makes his final attack.

> 17. And the dragon was wroth with the woman, and went to make war with the remnant of her seed, which keep the commandments of God, and have the testimony of Jesus Christ.

V. 17.—In this verse we have the last effort of the enemy, to destroy the woman's offspring. It is the *third* attempt, and, as we suppose, is yet future. We cannot therefore, of course, be so exact or certain as to the nature of this contest. Some things, however, are plain enough. The dragon, disappointed in his efforts hitherto against the woman, so far from ceasing the warfare, is only thereby the more exasperated. "The dragon was wroth with the woman." Malice overcomes reason. He knows that he cannot finally prevail,—that "no weapon formed against her shall prosper;" yet he continues to vent his rage. The mode of attack is to be different from what it was in the second struggle. He is said to "make war,"—to resort to open violence, to employ the agency of the civil power, the beast of the bottomless pit, (ch. xi. 7;) for this third and last war, waged by the dragon agrees in time with the *slaying of the witnesses.* This third onset agrees also with the "third woe-trumpet," the "vintage" and the last "vial;" and immediately precedes the introduction of the millennium. "The remnant of the woman's seed" are so called with reference to those of her offspring who had suffered death under pagan and papal Rome, (ch. vi. 9.) Perhaps also we may suppose the number to be comparatively few at the time of the last war with the dragon; as during the whole period of the 1260 years, it was the aim of the dragon, through his instruments, to wear out the saints of the Most High. (Dan. vii. 25.) The character which the Holy Spirit gives of these sufferers proves them to be the woman's seed. They "keep the commandments of God, and have the testimony of Jesus Christ." This is the special ground of the devil's hostility towards them. A more comprehensive and definite description of true believers is not to be found in the whole Bible. In matters of religion they adhere strictly to the commandments of God. They will not introduce, nor permit to be introduced, any corruptions into the doctrines of grace or into the matter of God's worship. The temple, altar and worshippers must stand the measurement of God's word in their fellowship. No human traditions or innovations are to be tolerated. But besides their conscientious care to have all the laws of the house of God duly observed, these remaining witnesses sustain and propagate the testimony of their predecessors, with such additional facts as they may have collected in their own time, for the personal glory, the offices and work of Jesus Christ. This testimony will necessarily bring them into collision with the children of those who killed their fathers in the same quarrel. Like their fathers, "they have the sentence of death in themselves, that they should not trust in themselves, but in God which raiseth the dead,—not accepting deliverance, that they might obtain a better resurrection." (2 Cor. i. 9;

Heb. xi. 35.) For as already hinted, this remnant is to "overcome by the blood of the Lamb and by the word of their testimony," as others did; and in death to gain the final victory over death by vital union to their living Lord, "being made conformable to his death." (Heb. ii. 14, 15.)

CHAPTER XIII.

1. And I stood upon the sand of the sea, and saw a beast rise up out of the sea, having seven heads and ten horns, and upon his horns ten crowns, and upon his heads the name of blasphemy.
2. And the beast which I saw was like unto a leopard, and his feet were as the feet of a bear, and his mouth as the mouth of a lion; and the dragon gave him his power, and his seat, and great authority.
3. And I saw one of his heads as it were wounded to death; and his deadly wound was healed: and all the world wondered after the beast.
4. And they worshipped the dragon which gave power unto the beast: and they worshipped the beast, saying, Who is like unto the beast? Who is able to make war with him?
5. And there was given unto him a mouth speaking great things, and blasphemies; and power was given unto him to continue forty and two months.
6. And he opened his mouth in blasphemy against God, to blaspheme his name, and his tabernacle, and them that dwell in heaven.
7. And it was given unto him to make war with the saints, and to overcome them: and power was given him over all kindreds, and tongues, and nations.
8. And all that dwell upon the earth shall worship him, whose names are not written in the book of life of the Lamb slain from the foundation of the world.
9. If any man have an ear, let him hear.
10. He that leadeth into captivity, shall go into captivity; he that killeth with the sword, must be killed with the sword. Here is the patience and the faith of the saints.

Vs. 1-10.—This chapter may be considered as an explication or commentary upon the seventh chapter of Daniel's prophecy, and a farther elucidation of what is revealed under different symbols in the two preceding chapters; and no one can have an intelligent understanding of its contents without a competent knowledge of the symbols employed in those chapters. Here the Holy Spirit has given a most graphic, intelligible and comprehensive exhibition of the complex power which the dragon employs, to persecute and slay the witnessing servants of Christ. Hitherto the devil has conducted the war against the saints through the agency of the beast of the pit, (ch. xi. 7,) and those allies called "his angels:" (ch. xii. 7:) but there has been a vail of obscurity hanging over these agencies. Who the beast and other allies of the dragon are, it is the very *design* of this chapter to disclose, with greater precision and clearness than heretofore. In a word, we have here the *full portrait* of THE GREAT ANTICHRIST. The distinct features and component parts of this complex and diabolical system of hostility to the Lord and his Anointed, are presented in detail for our inspection. And it is a fact, that by a competent knowledge of this hostile combination, the suffering saints of God have been hitherto enabled to direct their testimony with intelligence and efficacy against their appropriate objects. And although the developments of providence in past centuries, and those transpiring in our own generation, are calculated to shed light upon this and collateral prophecies; yet the gross conceptions of the illiterate in the contemplation of prophetic symbols on the one hand, and the reckless disregard of scripture rules and usage by the learned on the other, have greatly contributed to the present lamentable ignorance and culpable indifference of most Christians. For people cannot feel an interest in that of which they are ignorant. But to be "willingly ignorant" of that which may and ought to be known, is one of the characteristic sins of a generation of impenitent and profane "scoffers." (2 Pet. iii. 3, 5.) On the other hand, all who humbly and earnestly desire to know the mind of God for their direction in faith and holiness, shall assuredly obtain the necessary instruction. (Dan. vii. 16: viii. 15; John xvi. 13; 1 Cor. xiv. 38.)

In these first ten verses are contained the characteristics of that beast whose origin is given, ch. xi. 7. There we had no particular description of this personage; only he was the agent by whom the witnesses were opposed in open warfare, and by whom they were finally killed. Now we have a more full account of his origin, character, achievements and duration. This personage is denominated a "beast." So are designated other characters, who are very different from this, (ch. iv. 6.) In that place we intimated that the authorized version is imperfect; and that either "living creatures" or simply "animals," which latter we prefer, is that which the reader is to understand from the original word.

Not only are the "four animals" different in origin, nature and agency from the "beast;" but in all these respects they are morally opposite. This is a ravenous beast; a beast of prey. Elsewhere the word is translated a "wild beast," a "venomous beast," a "viper." (Acts x. 12; xxviii. 4.) This beast is the same which appeared in vision to the prophet Daniel, (ch. vii. 3.) Of the four great beasts which that prophet saw, this is the last. All the preceding are described by their resemblance to some known animals, but each is ferocious,—"a lion, bear, leopard." The fourth is a *nondescript*; there is no species in the animal kingdom that can represent it; only it was "diverse from all the beasts that were before it," (v. 7.) These four beasts represent "four kings," (v. 17,) that is, "kingdoms," (v. 23,) or *dynasties*. Now all interpreters agree that these four dynasties are the same as those symbolized in Nebuchadnezzar's dream, (ch. ii. 31-43.) The different parts of the "image" answer to the four beasts; and these again are the symbols of the Babylonian, Medo-Persian, Grecian and Roman empires. Thus far, all sober expositors are agreed. Also, there is a like agreement that John's *first* beast identifies with Daniel's *fourth*,—the Roman empire. This is obvious from the general description by both prophets,—"having seven heads and ten horns." (Dan. vii. 7; Rev. xiii. 1.)

The origin of this beast is threefold,—"out of the sea," (v. 1,) "out of the bottomless pit," (ch. xi. 7; xvii. 8,) and "out of the earth." (Dan. vii. 17.) Out of the sea of the commotions arising from the incursions of the northern barbarians, by whom the Roman empire was dismembered. "The ten horns out of this kingdom are ten kings that shall arise." (Dan. vii. 24.) This is the result of revolution,—"the sea." The Roman empire, especially as nominally Christian, is thus characterized as being "earthly, sensual, devilish," a suitable agent of the dragon.

The fact of the ten horns of the beast, *now wearing crowns*, proves that the time to which the prophecy refers, is that which followed the division of the empire into ten kingdoms. The seven heads of the beast have a double significance,—seven different forms of government, and seven mountains, afterwards to be more fully explained, (ch. xvii. 9, 10.) The "name of blasphemy" may indicate "eternal city, mistress of the world."—Of this characteristic of the beast, other examples will be discovered hereafter.

CHAPTER XIII.

Daniel was solicitous to "know the truth (interpretation) of the fourth beast, which was diverse from all the others," (ch. vii. 19.) Although "diverse from all the others" in geographical extent and destructive power, this fourth beast combined in one all the ravenous propensities of the three predecessors, but in *reverse order*. The "leopard, bear and lion of Daniel," by which Grecian, Persian and Chaldean dynasties were symbolized, are all comprised in John's beast of the sea,—the antichristian Roman empire. Since this beast of the sea embodies all the voracious properties of the three persecuting powers which went before it; this may be a suitable place briefly to review the sufferings inflicted by them upon the saints, that we may know what the witnesses were taught to expect at the hands of this monstrous enemy.—"Israel is a scattered sheep, the lions have driven him away: first, the king of Assyria hath devoured him, and last, this Nebuchadnezzar king of Babylon hath broken his bones.—The violence done to me and to my flesh, be upon Babylon, shall the inhabitant of Zion say; and, My blood upon the inhabitants of Chaldea, shall Jerusalem say." (Jer. 1. 17; li. 35.)—"Haman, the son Hammedatha, the Agagite, the Jews' enemy,—thought scorn to lay hands on Mordecai alone."—"If it please the king, let it be written that they (the whole people) may be destroyed; and I will pay ten thousand talents of silver,—to bring it into the king's treasuries."—"Behold also the gallows, fifty cubits high, which Haman had made for Mordecai, who had spoken good for the king, standeth in the house of Haman. Then the king said, Hang him thereon." (Esth. iii. 1, 9; vii. 9.) Such were the crimes and such the punishments of the enemies of God's people in Babylon and Persia, as already matter of inspired history: and had we equally full and authentic records of the punishments as we have of the cruelties of Antiochus and other successors of Alexander the Great, the king of Greece, we would see, as in the other cases, "the just reward of the wicked." Of all these idolatrous, tyrannical and persecuting powers, which the Divine Spirit represented by beasts of prey, it was foretold that they were to be removed in succession and with violence. This fourth beast, "dreadful and terrible and strong exceedingly, was to devour and break in pieces, and stamp the residue with the feet of it." (Dan. vii. 7.) Moreover, while it is predicted of them that "they had their dominion taken away," it is also added,—"yet their lives were prolonged for a season and time," (v. 12.) That is, though their distinct and successive *dominions* were severally swept from the earth, yet their *lives*,—the diabolical principles by which they had been actuated survived; and these passed, by a kind of transmigration, into the body of the fourth beast. This transition of animating principles or imperial policy of inveterate hostility to the kingdom of God, we think, is plainly indicated by the three features of this beast of the sea, the "leopard, bear and lion." If these three "slew their thousands," this monster has "slain his ten thousands" of the saints; and the remnant of the woman's seed are yet to be "slain as they were," (ch. vi. 11.)

"The dragon gave him his power,"—physical force, "his seat" or throne,—his right to reign, "and great authority"—dominion—by the voice of the people. Thus, it is obvious that the seven-headed, ten-horned beast is the first, and the oldest, among the combined enemies of the Christian church; all of whose origin is from the dragon, the abyss or bottomless pit. The writers of the church of Rome, while forced to acknowledge that this beast is emblematical of the Roman empire, still insist that *pagan* Rome is intended. It is sufficient in opposition to this false interpretation to observe, that the beast appears to John with crowns, not upon his *heads*, but upon his *horns*, denoting the actual division of the empire into ten kingdoms: an event which did not transpire till after the empire had become nominally Christian under the reign of Constantine the Great. The reign of this emperor and his successors, by their largesses fostered the luxurious propensities of the Christian ministry, and so contributed to prepare the way for the rise of the next enemy in this antichristian confederacy against the witnesses.—The "head wounded unto death" is the *sixth*. John says expressly, elsewhere, "five are fallen, and one is, and the other is not yet come," (ch. xvii. 10.) The "five fallen" were, kings, consuls, dictators, decemvirs, and military tribunes. All these forms of civil government had passed before the time of the apostle. The one existing in his time, was the sixth head,—the emperors; by one of whom the apostle was now subjected to banishment in the desert isle of Patmos. This wound is supposed by some to be the change from paganism to Christianity in the empire. No; this view is many ways erroneous: but it is enough to remark that the Roman empire, according to both prophets, Daniel and John, is to continue *bestial* under all changes, during the whole period of 1260 years. The deadly wound was inflicted by the northern invaders who overturned the empire, and, for the time, extinguished the very name of emperor in the person of Augustulus. After the division of the western member of the empire had been subdivided among the victorious leaders of the invaders from the north, and the people of that section supposed the beast slain, the throne of Constantinople continued to be occupied by the representative of the empire. In the popular apprehension the imperial head of the beast seemed to be utterly cut off by the sword of Odoacer,—"wounded by a sword:" but the several kingdoms into which the empire was divided, in process of time became united in the bonds of an apostate faith. The imperial name and dignity were revived in the person of the emperor of Germany, Charlemagne, in 800; and by the wars among the horns of the beast, the title of emperor has been claimed alternately by Germany, Austria and France, down to our own time. These dissensions and rivalries among the sovereigns of Europe,—the mystic horns of the beast, were foreshadowed in the Babylonish monarch's dream:—"the kingdom shall be partly strong and partly broken,—they shall not cleave one to another, even as iron is not mixed with clay," (Dan. ii. 42, 43.) And doubtless these internal commotions among the common enemies of the saints of God, have tended, in divine mercy, to divert their attention occasionally from the witnesses. While they have been made the instruments of mutual punishment, the Lord's people have been "hid in the day of his fierce anger." (Zeph. ii. 3.)

At what time the sixth head of the beast disappeared and the seventh became developed, is not clearly marked in the Apocalypse, and it is of comparatively little importance, since the latter is to "continue a short space" (ch. xvii. 10.) The *central fact* is the continuance of the beast a definite time under *all the heads*,—1260 years. Under all the forms of government through which the empire passed, it continued bestial and was the object of popular admiration. "All the world wondered after the beast." The populace made court to, fawned upon, followed in the train, or formed the retinue of the beast. We are to limit the phrase,—"all the world," for not all the inhabitants are to be understood, but such only as professed allegiance to the existing imperial dominion; and among those within the beast's territorial jurisdiction, the witnesses still stood to their protest against his impious claims.—But from admiration and loyalty, the servile multitude break forth into adoration, addressing the dragon and the beast in such language as is proper to God only. (Ps.

lxxxix. 6.) The shouts of the rabble on Herod's birth-day may illustrate the conduct of these votaries of the beast and dragon. (Acts xii. 22.) The poor ignorant and deluded subject, in rendering homage to the beast, did homage to the devil, from whom the power was derived. Such is the degradation to which man is reduced by blind obedience to despotic power, whether civil or ecclesiastical. He glories in the chains which bind him!—And this is the actual and voluntary condition of the great majority of the population of Christendom at the present hour. There has been, indeed, within the current century, an effort by the masses of the people to assert their natural and civil rights, to regain the exercise of the elective franchise; but in selecting candidates to bear rule over them, they generally prefer such as are, like the majority of themselves,—"aliens from the commonwealth of Israel, and strangers from the covenants of promise." Hence, "vile men are exalted, the wicked bear rule, and the people mourn." (Ps. xii. 8; Prov. xxix. 2.)—The "blasphemies" uttered by this beast are all those *royal prerogatives* claimed by the several crowned horns or civil sovereigns who have established idolatry and superstition within their respective dominions. The "blasphemous headship" over the church of Christ, as viewed and designated by his persecuted disciples in the British empire, may tend to illustrate this part of the beast's history. King Henry VIII. of England, upon renouncing the civil and ecclesiastical headship of the Pope, proceeded to usurp an ecclesiastical headship within his own dominions; and all his royal successors till the present day have asserted a similar dominion over the faith of the Lord's people. As an "inherent right of the crown," the sovereign of Britain, male or female, is declared to be "supreme judge in all causes, as well ecclesiastical as civil!" The rest of the horns are no less blasphemous in their haughty pretensions. History attests that the martyrs of Jesus denounced these encroachments on the prerogatives of Christ, and the intrinsic power of his church, as "Erastian supremacies,—blasphemous supremacies." Most expositors tell us that the blasphemies are chargeable to the Pope or to the Romish church. But this interpretation confounds this beast of the sea with the apostate church of Rome; and indeed this confounding of symbols and consequent mistaking of objects in actual history, are the primary errors of expositors in nearly all their attempts at expounding the Apocalypse. This first beast of John, and fourth of Daniel, however, is *wholly secular or civil*; and clearly distinguished by both inspired prophets, from the other agents of the dragon, as we shall find in the subsequent part of this chapter. This beast "blasphemes the name of God" by compelling men to worship idols and images, enacting penal statutes and issuing bloody edicts to force their consciences. He "blasphemes his tabernacle," when stigmatizing the assemblies of God's worshipping people as "traitorous conspiracies, rendevouses of rebellion"—"and them that dwell in heaven," he blasphemes by calling them "incendiaries, fanatics, enthusiasts, rebels and traitors;" for all these terms of reproach are well authenticated in history, as heaped upon the faithful and heroic servants of Christ. Those who suppose that the phrase "them that dwell in heaven," means saints departed and angels as worshipped by papists in obedience to the Romish church, make two mistakes,—the one, that *ecclesiastical* power is here intended, whereas we have already shown that the power is *civil*; the other, that the word "heaven" is to be taken in a literal sense, contrary to the symbolic structure of the whole context. All history, so far as authentic, teaches that the civil powers throughout Christendom, attempt to coerce by penal inflictions the consciences of all who refuse obedience to their commands, no less than the church of Rome. Even *constitutional guarantees of liberty of conscience* have never secured the witnesses from the savage rage of the beast or any of his infuriated horns. Witness the history of the bloody house of the Stuarts of Britain. In vain did the victims of papal and prelatic cruelty plead, in their just defence in the seventeenth century, the constitution and laws of their native land! Those who have done violence to the law of God, will always disregard human enactments which stand in the way of their ambitious schemes. Their own laws will be treated as ropes of sand, as Samson's withs, and the blood of saints as water. Such is persecution.—The seventh verse, expressing the beast's victory over the saints and the extent of his power, is explanatory of ch. xi. 7, 9; and the time of his continuance, (v. 5,) is the same as the treading under foot of the city; (ch. xi. 2:) so that we are assured of the agreement in time between the events here and those of the first part of the eleventh chapter. Also, the parties here presented are the same as in the two preceding chapters, only they are exhibited in different aspects by appropriate symbols.—The worshippers of the beast include all under his dominion except those "whose names were written in the book of life."—This book is different both from the sealed book, (ch. 5;) and also from the open book, (ch. 10.) It is the register, as it were, of the names of all whom the Father gave to the Son, to be by him brought to glory. (John xvii. 2; Heb. ii. 10; Rev. xx. 12, 15.) During the whole reign of the beast, these are preserved, having been "sealed unto the day of redemption." In the seventh chapter we had the angels employed in holding the four winds of the earth, till these servants of God were sealed in their foreheads, before the first alarm should be given by the trumpets. The book of life contained their names from the foundation,—before the foundation of the world. (Eph. i. 4.) They were in time "sealed with that Holy Spirit of promise," so that it was impossible to deceive them, either by lying wonders or the serpent's sophistry. (Eph. i. 13; Matt. xxiv. 24.)—The Lamb may be said to be "slain from the foundation of the world" in the purpose of God, (2 Tim. i. 9;) in sacrifice, (Gen. iv. 4;) in the ceremonial law and prophecy. (Matt. xi. 13;) and in the efficacy of his satisfaction rendered to divine justice, for which the Father gave him credit from the fall of man. (Rom. iii. 25.)—So many erroneous views have been taken, and false interpretations given of this chapter in particular, as of the Apocalypse in general, that the Divine Spirit calls special attention here to the rise, reign and ruin of the beast of the sea. The prophetic description of this beast in an especial manner is of such importance to instruct, and thereby sustain and comfort, the suffering disciples of Christ, that he causes his servant John to pause, as it were, and allow the reader to reflect. Indeed, wherever a note of attention is thus given, we may be sure that something "hid from the wise and prudent" is intended. Accordingly, it were endless to follow the vagaries of even learned men dealing out their "private interpretations" of this chapter. Yet the understanding of its general outlines was at the bottom of the Reformation by Luther, his colleagues and successors. Elsewhere, however, we may take occasion to notice how vague, and inadequate, and bold, were some of their conceptions; all going to show the seasonableness of the solemn admonition,—"If any man have an ear, let him hear."—The beast is to be treated as he dealt with the victims of his cruelty. He is justly doomed to captivity and death. "The beast was taken and—cast alive into a lake of fire burning with brimstone," (ch. xix. 20.) "Tophet is ordained of old." It was used by the prophets as a figure of hell. (Is. xxx. 33.) To this place, whence there is no redemption, this monstrous beast was to be consigned, as predicted by the prophet Daniel, (vii. 11,)—"The beast was slain, and his body destroyed, and given to the burning flame."—In the protracted contest of 1260 years with this imperial power, "the patience and the faith of the saints" were exemplified. Faith and patience would be more severely tried in this case than in any other; as the period of persecution was to be of much longer continuance than any that had preceded since the beginning of the world. (Heb. vi. 12.)

> 11. *And I beheld another beast coming up out of the earth; and he had two horns like a lamb, and he spake as a dragon.*

V. 11.—John "beheld another beast,"—therefore not the *same*, as many expositors strangely suppose. No one can have an intelligent understanding of this chapter unless he views the beast of the sea and the beast of the earth as *perfectly distinct*. As the former arose out of a revolutionary state of society, and was consequently more clearly marked in history, so the latter grew "up out of the earth" more quietly and gradually, like a spear of grass,—we "know not how." As this second beast of the Apocalypse is to act a prominent part in the scenery afterwards presented in vision to the apostle, and a correspondent part in actual history, and as it is called by different names and appears under different aspects, it is necessary that its character be closely inspected, so that its identity may be clearly ascertained. The description here given is very minute. One thing is very obvious,—that this beast of the earth is the confederate, the ally, and the accomplice of the beast of the sea. They act in concert. They had been thus represented in vision to Daniel. In the seventh chapter of that prophecy we have the beast of the sea, as here, with his "ten horns," (v. 7.) While the prophet narrowly "considered the horns, behold, there came up among them another little horn," (v. 8.) It has been already shown that these horns represent the kingdoms into which the Roman empire was divided, (v. 24.) Among these horns, kings, (v. 24,) or kingdoms, "another shall rise after them,"—"among them," yet in the order of time,—"after them." Thus it appears that Daniel's fourth beast had *eleven* horns; but the eleventh is called "another which came up," to distinguish it from the ten, (v. 20.) "He shall be diverse from the first," (v. 24.) It is thus evident that the last horn,—the eleventh, is as really a horn of the beast, as the other ten; and of course this horn,—"little" at its rise, but in time becoming "more stout than his fellows," is the willing accomplice in crime of that beast whose horn it is. "The same horn made war with the saints, and prevailed against them," (v. 21.)—"He had two horns like a lamb." He professed to be gentle and innocent as a lamb,—to be the vicegerent of the "Lamb of God." He claimed only a *spiritual* jurisdiction. As it is natural that a lamb should have only two horns, so the symbol is agreeable to nature. But this lamb "spake as a dragon;" and that was contrary to nature. No two animals in creation are in their respective natures more diverse or opposite than a lamb and a beast of prey. These two antagonistic natures combined, indicate the crafty and cruel policy of this beast of the earth. Daniel mentions the "little horn" of the civil beast; but says nothing of the "two-horned beast." On the other hand, John speaks plainly of this beast of the earth, but omits any mention of the "little horn." But the "beast of the earth" and the "little horn" sustain the same relation to the first beast, the "beast of the sea"—the Roman empire; therefore the "two-horned beast of the earth" and the "little horn" are identical; and this identity is confirmed by the additional name "false prophet," given to the beast of the earth in ch. xix, 20. His alliance and co-operation with the civil beast is precisely the same as in this chapter. He "wrought miracles before him," that is,—in his interest. Some interpreters have mistaken this "false prophet" as a symbol of Mahometanism. The facts of history demonstrate the fallacy of this interpretation; for the delusions of Mahomet never had, and they have not now, any affinity with the idolatries of the Latin Roman empire. But these two beasts of the sea and of the earth are obviously in the closest sympathy, having a common interest.

12. And he exerciseth all the power of the first beast before him, and causeth the earth and them which dwell therein, to worship the first beast, whose deadly wound was healed.

V. 12.—The second beast "exerciseth all the power of the first beast before him,"—in his presence, under his sanction and powerful protection. Thus the state, or empire, lays the church under obligation, and of course expects a reciprocity of kind offices. This is effected by the beast of the earth "causing the earth—to worship the first beast." By force and craft this is accomplished. By his "two horns" of power, the *regular* and *secular* orders of the hierarchy, as from the mouth of a "dragon," he enjoins "submission to the (civil) powers that be." But besides the horns of power, that is, ecclesiastical authority, this beast of the earth, in order more effectually to enforce his commands to worship the first or civil beast, resorts to "great wonders,—miracles," (vs. 13,14,)—"lying wonders;" (2 Thess. ii. 9:) for Paul and John agree in their description of the same diabolical agency. "As Jannes and Jambres withstood Moses,—magicians doing so with their *enchantments*,"—"beguiling unstable souls," so this second beast "maketh fire to come down from heaven on the earth in the sight of (credulous) men." (2 Tim. iii. 8; Exod. vii. 22; Acts viii. 9-11.) The venal ministry of the heathenized church, (ch. xi. 2,) inculcate passive obedience to the beast of the sea, as to the "ordinance of God;"—to "resist" which, subjects the recusant to "damnation." (Rom. xiii. 2.) Here, then, we behold the *counterfeits* of the two great ordinances of church and state, against which it is the special duty and arduous work of the two witnesses to contend for 1260 years. This "false prophet," who "spake as a dragon, and made fire to come down from heaven," to authenticate his divine mission, may represent the bulls, anathemas, interdicts, encyclical letters, which emanate from Rome, together with the less terrifying mandates of her coadjutors,—"daughters."

13. And he doeth great wonders, so that he maketh fire come down from heaven on the earth, in the sight of men,
14. And deceiveth them that dwell on the earth, by the means of those miracles which he had power to do in the sight of the beast; saving to them that dwell on the earth, that they should make an image to the beast which had the wound by a sword, and did live.
15. And he had power to give life unto the image of the beast, that the image of the beast should both speak, and cause that as many as would not worship the image of the beast should be killed.
16. And he caused all, both small and great, rich and poor, free and bond, to receive a mark in their right hand, or in their foreheads:
17. And that no man might buy or sell, save he that had the mark, or the name of the beast, or the number of his name.

Vs. 13-17.—This lamb-like beast of the earth devises another agency, by which to subserve his own diabolical interest, as well as that of the "first beast." He causes to be made "an image" *to* or *of* the beast of the sea. Of images in general, as objects of idolatrous worship, we are warranted to say,—they are *dead* and *dumb* idols; (ch. ix. 20; Jer. x. 14:) but this one is altogether different. And it is surprising to find learned expositors fixing upon the superstitious use of the cross by the papists, as exemplifying this symbol. The Holy Spirit, as if to guard all readers against such misapprehension, declares explicitly, that this image has "life, speaks," and *acts*. The only point in which this image resembles others is, that it is to be *worshipped*: but of all others we are assured that they "cannot do evil," (Jer. x. 5.) This image has such "life," (breath,) and power as to cause the death of such as refuse to worship *itself*. Three agents are to be noticed and clearly distinguished here,—the ten-horned beast of the *sea*, the two-horned *beast* of the *earth*, and the *image* of the beast. At the instance of the second beast, an image is made; not *to* or *of* himself, but *to*, and also *of*, the first beast. Now, as the beasts put forth their power by their horns, so this ecclesiastical beast of the earth makes the image by his horns. In short, history explains the symbols. The Roman clergy,—the horns, the cardinals, create the Pope; and, in their own ceremonial and language,—*quem creant, adorant*, "whom they create, they adore;" like all other idolaters. Thus, the Pope becomes the "man of sin, sitting in the temple of God, showing himself that he is God," (2 Thess. ii. 4.) The Pope is the most perfect image of the Roman emperor; claiming the same universal dominion, the same titles and prerogatives, in the same city: but the Pope and the emperor never identify. They are always distinct. Two authoritative measures are to be specially noticed in this connexion; one by the beast of the earth, the other by the image of the beast of the sea. The image demands worship under pain of death. All *heretics* are judged worthy of death. All are required by the second beast to receive the mark of the first or civil beast. The penalty in this case is privation of civil and political privileges,—to "buy or sell." It is to be noticed here that the "mark" is imposed by the authority of the *ecclesiastical* power, the two-horned beast. As there is liability to mistake as to which of the two beasts the "mark" refers, and as this mistake is in fact generally made by expositors, the apostle John has been directed, as in the case of the image, to be peculiarly explicit, that all may know it to be the mark of the *first* beast. (See chs. xv. 2; xix. 20; xx. 4.) But it will be asked,—What are we to understand by the "mark?" This question is easily answered from history. The heathen idolater gloried in his devotion to his imaginary god; as the ivy leaf was the token of the worshippers of Bacchus: soldiers bore the initials of the names of their commanders; and slaves, of their masters. These *characters* were impressed on the foreheads or other part of the persons of individuals. The general idea suggested by the "mark" was subjection or *property*. In short, the mark of the beast signifies open and avowed allegiance to antichristian or immoral *civil* power, when in the "forehead;" and active co-operation with the same, when in the "hand." It is at once a pitiable and culpable error, to suppose, as many preposterously do, that this "mark of the beast" is *popery!* And as the "mark" is the recognised badge of loyalty to civil rule, of course the prohibition to "buy or sell," must signify civil disabilities,—*disfranchisement*. Men who suffer, necessarily feel. Christ's witnesses, as they only have the *scriptural* conception of the rights of man, have long been familiar with the deprivation of their rights, both civil and ecclesiastical. The moral evils incorporated in the constitutions of church and state, throughout all the streets of mystic Babylon, have effectually excluded the two witnesses, and left them in the "wilderness." Here is their destined "place," and here they are to be "nourished from the face of the serpent" for 1260 years. Christ's promise,—"I will not leave you comfortless," (orphans,) is all along verified in their soul-satisfying experience.—This will appear in the next chapter.

> 18. Here is wisdom. Let him that hath understanding count the number of the beast; for it is the number of a man; and his number is six hundred threescore and six.

V. 18.—"The name of the beast," since the time of Ireneus, the disciple of Polycarp, who was cotemporary with the apostle John, is understood to be *Lateinos*, or *Lateinus*; for it is well known to scholars, that classical usage justifies the orthography of this word. However learned men may indulge their fancy, and sport with this mystic and sacred name and number, no other word fills up all the conditions required by the inspired writer. *Latinus* is the proper name of the "first beast," the *Latin* empire: it is the name common to the whole population of the empire, the *Latins*: it is the name of the *founder* of the empire, *Latinus*; and it contains the *number*, 666. The probability that this word contains the requisite name and number, amounts almost to a certainty. The unlearned reader may be easily taught to understand how to "count the number of the beast." Of course, the apostle John accommodated his expressions to the custom of his own age. Well, even children soon learn to number or count by the use of Roman letters of the alphabet. They know that the letter I, stands for *one*; V. for *five*, etc. Now, in the apostolic age, the Jews, Greeks and Romans, were accustomed to express numbers by the use of the letters of their respective alphabets. This we suppose to be the only rational and probable method of solving the mystery.

In this chapter we have the fullest exhibition of the great antichristian confederacy, spoken of by prophets and apostles, including the "man of sin, to be revealed in his time." The component parts of that complex moral person called "Antichrist," are here graphically portrayed. The three most prominent features are the *two beasts* of the sea and of the earth, with the *image* of the first; or, a tyrannical *empire*, an apostate *church*, and the *Pope*. To suppose that the Antichrist is a power or moral person *distinct from these*,—a "wilful, infidel or atheistical king," is a mere *chimera* framed in a learned brain, disordered by *antichristian* politics. The chief, if not the only ostensible ground of such hypothesis is the language of our apostle, (1 John ii. 22.) "He is Antichrist that denieth the Father and the Son." The *sound* of the words of Scripture is too often mistaken for the *sense*. This is a notable example. From the words of our Divine Redeemer,—"My Father is greater than I", Socinians infer the *essential* inferiority of the Son to the Father. So in the preceding instance. The inference is, that the Antichrist is to be known by a *doctrinal* denial of deity. But the very name of this enemy of all righteousness, *Antichrist*, demonstrates his recognition of the existence and office of our Saviour. For why should he oppose a *nonentity*? All scholars are aware that the primary meaning of *anti*, is substitution. (Matt. xx. 28.) Antichrist usurps Christ's place in church and state, that he may more successfully oppose his interest. There is no mystery to the intelligent Christian in the declaration, that men too often "profess that they know God, but in works deny him." This explains the fact of Antichrist's denying the Father and the Son. Usurping the prerogatives of the Mediator is a practical denial of him,—of his authority, and by consequence, of the Father who sent him. "He that acknowledged the Son," in this sense, "hath the Father also; while it is equally true, in the same sense,—"whosoever denieth the Son, the same hath not the Father." (1

John ii. 23.) Hence it *is not true* that the *Pope* is the *Antichrist* of prophecy, nor the church of Rome, nor both combined; but Daniel's ten-horned beast,—John's seven-headed, ten-horned beast, which are the same: Daniel's little horn and John's beast of the earth, which are the same; together with the image of the first beast: the Saracenic locusts and Euphratean horsemen;—all these go to the composition of the Antichrist, the "eastern and western Antichrist," so identified and *familiarly* designated by the *martyrs* and *witnesses* of Jesus for hundreds of years. The great family of nations, called "the nations of this world," (chap. xi. 15;) in unholy alliance with a *gentile* church; (ch. xi. 2;) *these combined, constitute the Antichrist.* They "will not have this man to reign over them." Against this combination it is the appointed business,—the life of the two witnesses, to prophesy for a definite period of 42 months, 1260 days, time, times and a half; all indicating the same duration, 1260 natural years. All this time the witnesses are alive and active, but in an obscure and depressed condition, wearing sackcloth in the wilderness, "not reckoned, (not *reckoning themselves*,) among the nations." (Num. xxiii. 9; Dan. vii. 22, 27; Rev. xx. 4.) Such is the condition of the saints, and such the powerful combination against them, as symbolically represented in the 11th, 12th and 13th chapters of the Apocalypse. And in this prolonged and eventful conflict we may with Moses, "turn aside and see this great sight, why the bush is not burnt." (Exod. iii. 3.) The Lord was in the bush, and "greater is he that is in them than he that is in the world." (1 John iv. 4.) This will appear in the following chapter.

CHAPTER XIV.

As the 13th chapter contains the most full and graphic description of the great apostacy, so in this chapter we have the other party described which protested against that apostacy. It is a concise history of the two witnesses in holy and happy fellowship with Christ, when he had rejected the heathenized church, because of her unholy league with the beast of the bottomless pit, (ch. xi. 2, 7.) The contrast between the "sealed" ones here, and those who bore the "mark of the beast," is very noticeable. This fact suggests that the parties are *cotemporary*. Besides, it is evident that this company of 144,000 are the legitimate successors of those sealed in ch. vii. 4-8; or rather, from the perpetual identity of the covenant society as a moral person, we may view this company as the same with the sealed ones of the seventh chapter, the two witnesses of the eleventh chapter, and as in the wilderness in the 12th chapter. Political bias caused a learned expositor to interpret the third angel of this chapter as a symbol of the prelatic church of England! and a similar bias, or *modern* charity, induced another to distinguish between the "two witnesses" and the 144,000. To the unbiased and enlightened mind it is obvious that instead of the 144,000 symbolizing the "pious people,—in the different branches of the Christian church"—all true Christians; they are in fact distinguished from *true Christians*, as 144,000 from "a great multitude ... who had washed their robes, and made them white in the blood of the Lamb," (ch. vii. 9, 14.)

As the Antichrist, after his first development in the world, appeared in diverse forms of organization, thereby more effectually to deceive them that dwell on the earth, yet still preserved his moral identity, so the faithful servants of Christ are presented in corresponding attitudes and aspects, to oppose and counteract his diabolical policy and tyranny; yet always preserving their proper identity during the whole period of 1260 years.

The process of "sealing the servants of God in their foreheads," (ch. vii. 4-8,) took place under the *sixth* seal before the opening of the seventh, (ch. viii. 1,) which introduced the trumpets,—the harbingers of the visible organization of Antichrist. For this purpose the "four winds,"—all winds, emblematical of popular commotions, were by four angels restrained from blowing upon the earth etc., during the peaceful reign of Constantine and his successors. Under the patronage of those nominally Christian emperors, as history informs us, multitudes flocked into the church; "the number of immoral and unworthy Christians began so to increase, that the examples of real piety and virtue became extremely rare.... The virtuous few were oppressed and overwhelmed with the superior numbers of the wicked and licentious."[5] Thus the way was prepared for the visible appearing of the "man of sin,"—the papacy. So soon as the confederate hosts of the dragon are completely organized, the two witnesses take their position with the Lamb.

1. And I looked, and, lo, a Lamb stood on Mount Zion, and with him a hundred forty and four thousand, having his Father's name written in their foreheads.

V. 1.—While "all the world wonders after the beast," (xiii. 3,) and the gross senses of the multitude are preoccupied with that object; here is another presented more worthy of our contemplation. Often has the Lord Jesus appeared in vision to John while viewing the grand panorama passing before him in Patmos. Here he appears as the "captain of the Lord's host" at the head of his army; not indeed in active military enterprise, but rather as leader in acts of solemn worship during a temporary recess from sanguinary warfare. He and his associates are on the "Mount Zion." "In Zion is his seat." ... "The Lord hath founded Zion, and the poor of his people shall trust in it." (Is. xiv. 32.) This select company maintain fellowship with Christ, being "really and inseparably united to him as their Head," by the bond of the Spirit, on his part, and faith on theirs. Christ's "Father's name in their foreheads" indicates that they are the *property* and voluntary servants of God in Christ. Of this covenant relation baptism is the visible sign; but while Simon Magus may bear the sign, none but those who are "sealed unto the day of redemption," are honored to "stand with the Lamb on Mount Zion." To him their number is as accurately known, as one hundred and forty-four thousand is to us; and "truly their fellowship is with the Father and with his Son Jesus

---

5. Mosheim.

Christ." The votaries of the beast may either glory in bearing his mark in their foreheads, or conceal the mark in their right hand; but the followers of the Lamb will "confess him and his word before men," at the hazard of all that is dear to men,—even life itself. (Mark viii. 38.)

2. *And I heard a voice from heaven, as the voice of many waters, and as the voice of a great thunder: and I heard the voice of harpers harping with their harps:*
3. *And they sung as it were a new song before the throne, and before the four beasts, and the elders: and no man could learn that song but the hundred and forty and four thousand, which were redeemed from the earth.*

Vs. 2, 3.—"Let the children of Zion be joyful in their King.... Let the high praises of God be in their mouth."—(Ps. cxlix. 2, 6.) Unterrified by the roaring of the beasts of prey, these followers of the Lamb lift their voices in unison; and whether on mountains or in valleys, in dens or in caves of the earth, their songs of praise ascend to the ears of the Lord of Sabaoth. The symphony is heightened by the "voice of harpers, harping with their harps." And if any person be so ignorant as to ground an argument on these words, for the use of instruments in the worship of God, consistency will require him to take his position on the literal Mount Zion with a literal lamb!

The song was *new*. It was not peculiar to the Mosaic economy; that, like it, was to "wax *old* and vanish away."—(Heb. viii. 13.) No, it was indited by the Holy Spirit, "to whom all hearts are known, and all events foreknown." It was a song exactly framed to answer the twofold end of all inspired songs—to display the glories of the Godhead, and delineate the workings of grace and corruption with infallible precision, neither of which can be even successfully imitated by the best of uninspired men; much less by the licentious debauchees—the slaves of Antichrist. Moreover, the *order* of worship, as here exemplified, merits special attention, The 144,000 perform this solemn service "before the four beasts, and the elders." The office-bearers, appointed by the Lamb—the Lord Christ—direct the whole solemnity. Among this joyful and holy company, there is no hint that any part of public worship is left to "a vote of the congregation." This "new song" was unintelligible by the votaries of the beast; nor could they learn it while in that servile vassalage. They only who were "redeemed from the earth," as well as "from among men," were capable of learning it. As this song related to the royal prerogatives of Jesus Christ, and those who "dwelt on the earth" had transferred their allegiance to Antichrist, they became thereby incapacitated for learning that song. Alas! how many complain of the *cloudiness*, the *Jewish peculiarities*, the *unforgiving, revengeful spirit* of the inspired Psalms! In their apprehension, they are "contrary to the spirit of the gospel"—that is, *the Holy Spirit is contrary to Himself!* O, the blasphemy! Can such learn the "new song?" No, indeed, unless they repent and "pray God if perhaps the thought of their heart may be forgiven them."

4. *These are they which were not defiled with women; for they are virgins. These are they which follow the Lamb withersoever he goeth. These were redeemed from among men, being the first fruits unto God and to the Lamb.*
5. *And in their mouth was found no guile: for they are without fault before the throne of God.*

Vs. 4, 5.—These 144,000 worshippers are farther distinguished by their chastity. Betrothed to the Lord Christ from eternity, they were married to him in time. (Hosea ii. 19, 20; Rom. vii. 4; Cor. xi. 2.) Indeed the marriage covenant is employed throughout the Bible, to shadow forth the union between Christ and believers. (See Is. liv. 5; Jer. xxxi. 32; Hos. ii. 2; Rev. xxi. 2) This analogy pervades the 45th Psalm and the Song of Solomon. Idolatry is therefore adultery; and superstition, will-worship and human inventions, as means of grace or of communion with God, are fornication. (Ezek. xxiii. 27.) Accordingly, the "kings of the earth" are charged with this crime, (ch. xviii. 3.) Hence, it is plain that this company with the Lamb are such as do not receive or "teach for doctrines the commandments of men," nor submit to a "voluntary humility and worshipping of angels," (Col. ii. 18,) "for they are virgins." (Ps. xlv. 14.) They are distinguished for "sound doctrine and the power of godliness." "A man that is a heretic, after the first and second admonition," they "reject." (Titus iii. 10.) They cannot be indifferent to truth and error; and they may be known by their love for practical, but *especially doctrinal*, preaching. They frequent the ministry of those who "give attendance to reading, to exhortation, to doctrine." (1 Tim. iv. 13.)

"These follow the Lamb." (John x. 4, 27.) Next after self-denial, taking up the cross, becomes the test of discipleship. (Matt. xvi. 24, 25.) Suffering is the most trying and most difficult part of a Christian's obedience. But mere suffering for one's religion is no evidence that his religion is scriptural. Nor is punishment endured for religion *persecution*; but suffering "for righteousness' sake, or for Christ's sake," is persecution. And this is what is implied in "following the Lamb whithersoever he goeth." Not suffering, but the *cause* for which he suffers, makes a Christian martyr. All these 144,000 are martyrs in principle and intention.

Besides, "these were redeemed (bought) from among men." Purchase supposes contract,—a price fixed and paid. This ransom is both from debt and crime,—from bondage, sin and penalty. The Lamb is their surety. With his blood he "redeemed them to God," (ch. v. 9; 1 Pet. i. 19.) An atonement which *does not reconcile*, a redemption which *does not save*, must be an atonement and a redemption *without a compact*. Hence the covenant of grace, and Christ's engagement as surety in that covenant, determine the *extent* of the atonement; for *without compact no sinner could be saved!* But such is the liberal doctrine of the boasted Roman Catholic Church, and such the sandy foundation of that "general and doubtsome faith" which the witnesses renounce. However numerous these followers of the Lamb may seem to be, they are no more than "the first fruits." But the first fruits are part of the coming harvest, and an assured pledge of a larger ingathering. Their numbers were to be greatly augmented by the Reformation, and still further in the millennial era.

"Godly sincerity" is the last quality of these upright ones. They are "Israelites without guile." Integrity, probity, candor, distinguish them from the "flocks of the companions" by whom they are surrounded. "As they think in their heart, so do they express the truth." (Ps. xv. 2; xii. 2; John i. 47.) They know nothing of the "pious frauds" any more than the "indulgences" and "supererogations" by which the "man of sin" sustains his interest. Their being "without fault before the throne of God," is the highest commendation possible; yet it does not imply sinless perfection. It speaks their justification by the righteousness of Christ, and their Christian sincerity, such as God testifies of Job, (ch. i. 8.) Who would not prefer the society and employments of those who are with the Lamb on Mount Zion, to dwelling in the tents of wickedness? Let our delights be with these excellent ones of the earth.

> 6. And I saw another angel fly in the midst of heaven, having the everlasting gospel to preach unto them that dwell on the earth, and to every nation, and kindred, and tongue, and people,
> 7. Saying with a loud voice, Fear God, and give glory to him; for the hour of his judgment is come: and worship him that made heaven, and earth, and the sea, and the fountains of water.

Vs. 6, 7.—The apostles, Paul and John agree, as already noticed, in delineating a great defection from the purity and power of Christianity in "the last days." Paul calls this event "the Apostacy," (2 Thess. ii. 3.) while John designates it "the Antichrist." (1 John ii, 22.) Both these inspired writers use the Greek article, as may be supposed, to *emphasize* that wicked confederacy of Church and State,—a confederacy of greater extent and longer continuance than any other conspiracy "against the Lord and his Anointed." Against these the saints of God, with Messiah at their head, contend for the allotted period of 1260 years, as we have seen in the three preceding chapters. On their part the warfare is mostly defensive, and their weapons ordinarily spiritual. (2 Cor. vi. 6, 7.)

From the 6th verse to the close of this chapter are presented, under customary and well-defined symbols, three successive stages of successful reformation, showing how the "two witnesses" manage their scriptural and effective testimony against antichristian error and disorder in organized society. Three mystic "angels" successively appear, divinely commissioned to execute their respective and appointed work. These angels have been correctly designated, by judicious expositors, "angels of revival and reform." To the intelligent Christian it will be obvious, that without *reform* there can be no *revival*. The popular idea of our time connected with the term *revival*, is without foundation in the Holy Scriptures. It does not mean the regeneration of a sinner, nor the first work of the Spirit in conviction. It presupposes the existence of the vital principle, and the bringing of that living principle into visible activity, (Rom. vii. 9;) and this is equally true, whether of an individual or moral person. (Ps. lxxxv. 6; Ezek. xxxvii.) Divine truth and external order are characteristics of a genuine revival: for nothing but "sound doctrine" can produce "the power of godliness." The popular commotions and social disorders which accompany modern revivals, render them highly suspicious, if they do not demonstrate them to be spurious. It is true, indeed, that passionate declamation, vociferous assertion of heresy, intensified by theatrical and violent gesticulation, may commove to a higher degree the active powers,—the passions of the sinner; but such appliances can generate only a temporary faith. Such converts, "having no root in themselves, wither away." (Mark iv. 6.) "God is not the author of confusion, but of peace, as in all the churches of the saints." So these angels of reform declare by their ministry.

The first of these angels is the recognized symbol of a gospel ministry, (ch. i. 20; ii. 1, 8, 12, etc.) "Heaven" is the visible church general. "Flying" indicates celerity of motion. This "angel" does not represent any individual, as Luther; but the *collective body* of those who carry the joyful message of "the everlasting gospel." This gospel is *everlasting* as distinguished from "another gospel, which is not another" (Gal. i. 6, 7, 8, 9,)—a spurious, counterfeit, and therefore ephemeral gospel, invented and propagated by the "man of sin," from the flood which issued from the mouth of the dragon, (ch. xii. 15) The gospel preached by this angel is everlasting in its origin and duration. (Tit. i. 2; John iv. 14; Gal. vi. 8.) This angel's commission is as extensive as that of the apostles,—"every nation;" his "loud voice" is expressive of his zeal, energy and authority; the subject matter of his brief sermon indicates very plainly that the object of his teaching is to counteract the heresies of the Romish apostacy. "Fear God and give glory to him,"—not to the Virgin Mary, canonized saints and angels, images of wood and stone, (ch. ix. 20.) All are solemnly warned to "abstain from pollutions of idols," and their attention earnestly directed to their Creator,—to him "who made heaven, and earth, the seas and fountains of waters." This argument of the angel is very short,—that He only is to be worshipped who created the universe; but it is sufficient to "leave all men without excuse who do not glorify him as God." (Rom. i. 20, 21.) And how much more aggravated is the guilt of professing Christians! But the "angel" employs another powerful argument to enforce his teaching,—"The hour of his judgment is come." The final judgment of the last day is often set before us in the Bible, and it is so even in this book; but the last judgment cannot be intended here, for subsequent judgments are to be inflicted according to the messages of the following angels.

That Charlemagne should be mistaken for this flying angel betrays an almost incredible hallucination of the human mind![6] No individual, as already noticed, much less a successful civil or military tyrant, can be intended by the Spirit as the herald of the "everlasting gospel!"

In fact, this "angel" is identical with the "two witnesses," whose special work is to oppose the great apostacy; and this they do in a pre-eminent manner by proclaiming the everlasting gospel. For 500 years those who are known in history by the name of Waldenses, kept the doctrines and order of the apostles, in a state of separation from the Church of Rome. In the latter part of the twelfth century their numbers and influence attracted the notice and brought upon them the wrath of the "man of sin." In the following ages multitudes of them were subjected to all the penalties of confiscation, banishment and death. Like the seed of Abraham in Egypt, however, "the more they were afflicted, the more they multiplied and grew." They revived true religion in the kingdoms of southern Europe, and it is most probable that the good seed sown by them reached even to the island of Britain. John Huss and Jerome, who, by decree of the council of Constance, were committed to the flames for heresy; and Wishart, in England, whose end was similar, together with such as co-operated with them and succeeded them in the same holy warfare, are to be viewed as answering to the mystic angel. These faithful and dauntless men denounced divine judgments against all who worshipped graven images, however enjoined by civil and ecclesiastical authority. For their fidelity to Christ and the souls of men, they were subjected to the heaviest censures of the heathenized church, and the severest penalties of a tyrannical state,—the beast of the earth and the beast of the sea always in unholy alliance and acting in concert. The ministry of this angel is a testimony against papal corruptions, such as the worshipping images of the Creator and creatures, but especially the Pope,—the image of the Roman emperor. It is a mere fancy to suppose this angel symbolizes modern missions. The series of the prophecy forbids such an interpretation. Besides, the idolatry of Rome Christian, is not less real or gross than the idolatry of pagans, and calls for a more earnest testimony; and God has never left himself without witnesses against defection and apostacy. This angel prepares the way for his

---

6. Such is the interpretation of Bishop Newton!

successor, who prosecutes the same work with increasing clearness and confidence.

> 8. *And there followed another angel, saying, Babylon is fallen, is fallen, that great city, because she made all nations drink of the wine of the wrath of her fornication.*

V. 8.—"There followed another angel." Some expositors [7] interpret this angel of Luther, some of Calvin; but no *individual* is sufficiently prominent in history to justify the application to him of so striking a symbol in so concise a prophecy. Such restriction of a symbol to an individual results from *prelatic* habits of thought. In the mind of a prelate the idea of a gospel ministry includes that of a *metropolitan*. This angel is, in fact, as usual, simply the emblem of the ministry, not excluding the social body of which they are the official guides.

This second angel carries forward the reformation effected by his predecessor, reviving that cause when it began to languish under the violence of Antichrist. "While the Roman pontiff," says Mosheim, "slumbered in security at the head of the church, and saw nothing throughout the vast extent of his domain but tranquillity and submission, and while the worthy and pious professors of genuine Christianity almost despaired of seeing that Reformation on which their most ardent desires and expectations were bent, an obscure and inconsiderable person arose on a sudden, in the year 1517, and laid the foundation of the long expected change, by opposing with undaunted resolution his single force to the torrent of papal ambition and despotism." That individual was the heroic Luther, whose praise is in all the churches till the present day. No individual is so famous in the history of that eventful period as Martin Luther, for recovering the doctrine of justification by the righteousness of Christ, to the exclusion of all creature merit. This fundamental principle in the economy of man's salvation he justly denominated *articulus stantis vel cadentis ecclesiae*—"the hinge of a standing or falling church." By the defence and propagation of this doctrine especially, the priestly office of Christ was vindicated against the dogmas of penance, indulgence and supererogation, inculcated by the "Man of Sin;" and by consequence, one of the bulwarks of mystical

---

7. Faber.

Babylon effectually demolished. At the famous Diet of Worms, which, like the Council of Constance, combined the imperial power of Rome, civil and ecclesiastic, that indomitable servant of Christ gave a visible demonstration that "the Spirit of the Father" animated and "spake in him," (Matt. x. 20.) Not less explicit was Luther on the fundamental doctrine of the divine decrees; which, with other Arminian dogmas of creature-merit, had been almost universally propagated and stamped with the pretended infallible authority of Rome. By the translation and circulation of the Holy Scriptures among the people, the idolatries, impositions and profligacy of the priesthood were extensively discovered. And after years of deference to ecclesiastical authority, conditional proposals of submission to the Pope upon conviction of error in his *theses*, or conscientious belief, Luther in time arrived at the conclusion that the church of Rome was irreclaimable, giving publicity to his deep convictions in a treatise *De Captivitate Babylonica*,—"The Captivity of Babylon." In the 18th chapter of this book, he discovered that Babylon is doomed to destruction. He considered the church of Rome as answering to the prophetic symbol, and of course not to be reformed. It was an obvious inference—he ought to obey Christ rather than the Pope,—"Come out of her, my people."—This call was indeed a sufficient warrant to separate from the Church of Rome; and, acting on it, protestant churches have ever since been organized: but the type or symbol, Babylon, was unwarrantably restricted in import, as representing only the Church of Rome. And it is to be deplored that most protestant expositors continue to limit the inspired symbol in the same way till the present time. The literal Babylon, a name common to the ancient city and empire by the river Euphrates, was in no sense a church; and it would be anomalous and incongruous to select either city or empire as an *emblem of a church!* There is, however, in the Apocalypse a combining or blending of symbols in order clearly and fully to represent a complex moral person. This has been already exemplified in ch. xiii. 2, where the prominent features of Daniel's first *three* beasts, (ch. vii. 4-6,) are combined in John's *first* beast of the sea. Just so in this instance. The idolatrous and tyrannical Roman empire, in alliance with an apostate church, constitutes mystical Babylon. History demonstrates the fact of their coalition. The great red dragon, the devil, operates through both during the allotted period of 1260 years against the witnesses of Christ.

Sometimes, indeed, the nominal church is the more active and visible instrument, and at other times the state, in opposing Mediatory authority; and thus Babylon, or one of her streets, which is the equivalent of a horn of the beast, becomes prominent. This second angel confidently proclaims,—"Babylon is fallen, is fallen." So said Isaiah of literal Babylon long before the event; (ch. xxi. 9,) and so said Jeremiah, (ch. li. 8,) to whose predictions John obviously alludes. All these three prophets speak in present time of a future event, simply because of the settled and unalterable purpose of God, acting not formally as a sovereign, but as a judge. The multiplied and aggravated crimes of Babylon, literal or mystical Babylon, are the just grounds of her deserved and awful doom. From ancient times God has declared by his prophets the things that are not yet done. (Isa. xlvi. 10.) His counsel stands and he doeth all his pleasure.

That the mystical Babylon emblematically represented the complex systems of civil and ecclesiastical corruption and despotism organized in Christendom, was in some degree understood by the reformers in Europe; but the work of this second angel was carried on successively by men of piety and learning, who were eminently qualified for systematically arranging the doctrines of grace as deduced from the word of God. Their pious labors we still have in the forms of Bodies of Divinity and Confessions of Faith, in both which the unscriptural and antiscriptural dogmas and heresies of Rome are condemned and solidly confuted by the Scriptures. There is a wonderful "harmony of confessions" framed by those who separated from the fellowship of the Romish church; which harmony can be accounted for only by the fact that those who framed them drew their materials from the Bible. But it was by their public *covenants especially*, that the reformers lifted a testimony against the heresies, immoralities and tyrannies of the church of Rome. And among all the churches of the Reformation, that of Scotland is justly entitled to the pre-eminence. In no nation or state in Christendom did the witnesses of Christ,—the second angel, attain so nearly to a scriptural model of organized society in church and state as in that land, whose mountains and valleys were "flowered with martyrs" for a "Covenanted Work of Reformation." As Zuingle the Swiss-reformer excelled Luther, Calvin and others in Europe in the application of the divine moral law, as revealed in Scriptures, to civil society, so John Knox in Scotland was equally clear, that royal personages are amenable to the body politic, and both to the Mediator.

We are now under the ministry of this *second* "angel." The revival effected by the first angel had greatly declined before the second made his appearance; and all persons of intelligence and spiritual discernment in our day, lament the visible decline in practical godliness, arising from indifference to divine truth. Most professing Christians, including the descendants of the martyrs, are "willingly ignorant" of the attainments and sufferings of their illustrious predecessors. The work of reformation to be accomplished by the second angel, we suppose to have been completed about the middle of the seventeenth century. Since that period his work appears from history to consist in testifying against defection from the reformation which had been reached. The "great city" is to fall "because she made all nations drink of the wine of the wrath of her fornication." She is "spiritually called Sodom and Egypt," neither of which was a church any more than Babylon. These were all heathen communities, never *married* to the Lord; therefore Babylon is not here charged as an adulteress, but with *fornication*. The nations are her paramours. Her wine is intoxicating. It deranges the intellect and stupifies the conscience. Will any reasoning prevail with a drunken man? An active politician is proverbially unscrupulous, and proof against the law of God. There is, however, "wrath" in this cup. Those who refuse to "kiss the Son" must feel the weight of his iron rod. (Ps. ii. 9, 12; lxxv. 8.)

The "little book" introduced at the 10th chapter, is included in the first 13 verses of the 11th chapter, which comprehends a concise history of the 1260 years, as we have seen. At the 15th verse, the seventh and last trumpet is sounded which introduces the millennium and gives a brief outline of events till the end of the world. Then the three following chapters give in detail the events prior to the millennium, a commentary, as it were, on the "little book," but resuming a narrative of the sealed book's contents, which had been suspended at the end of the 9th chapter. There, as we have seen, the first and second woe-trumpets left the population of the Roman church and empire still in rebellion:—"They repented not."—Hence it is apparent that the work of these symbolic angels consists in opposing the antichristian systems of organized society during the period of the fifth and sixth trumpets. This they do partly by declaring the truth as it is in Jesus, and partly by denouncing divine judgments on the impenitent. The first angel, by proclaiming the "everlasting gospel," called upon men to "fear God and give glory to him," and not to idols,—threatening "coming judgment." The great majority of those addressed, however, disregarding alike his loving instructions and faithful warnings, must hear from the second angel that the judgment threatened by his predecessor, is now imminent:—"Babylon is fallen," etc. Notwithstanding the faithful and earnest contendings of the Waldenses, Bohemians and others on the continent of Europe, seconded by the Lollards in England, so far were the votaries of Antichrist from repenting of their idolatry and profligacy, that they became more and more exasperated against those witnesses who tormented them, and attempted to silence their testimony by committing their leaders to the flames. Hence the second angel's ministry consists more in denouncing judgment than in offering mercy to the penitent; and the history of the struggles in Europe and the British Isles between Christ's witnesses and the Roman Antichrist in the 16th and 17th centuries, demonstrates the awful fact that they, with great and wonderful unanimity, judged the church of Rome at least, utterly irreclaimable. Of this united judgment the Confessions of those reformers are at this day a standing evidence. But chief among the churches and nations of Christendom stands Scotland, as well before as after her appearance, by her famous Commissioners, in the Westminster Assembly of Divines. In her full and free Assembly, and by her national representatives, sustained by all their pious constituency, she uttered those memorable words,—"We abhor and detest ... chiefly all kind of Papistry in general and particular heads, even as they are damned (*condemned*) and *confuted* by the word of God and Kirk of Scotland." Perhaps this is the only instance hitherto within the 1260 years, where a *whole church* and *nation*, under the awful sanction of a *solemn oath*, has pronounced a judicial sentence of condemnation upon the church of Rome. Thus with confidence did those noble witnesses pronounce the anticipated doom of the mystic Babylon. But alas! may we not adopt and apply now (1870,) the language of the weeping prophet?—"How is she become a widow! she that was great among the nations, and princess among the provinces!"

As declension among those who had protested against the corruptions of Antichrist, under the ministry of the first angel of reform, together with the continued impenitence of the multitude who still wondered after the beast, called for the appearance of the second angel of revival, so the moral condition of the world called for the work of his successor. In the mean time, living as we now are, within the period allotted in prophecy and in history to the ministry of the second angel of revival and reform, it is but too evident that there is a great and increasing decline among the best reformed churches. Many of the Protestant ministry, especially of the prelatic order, are posting back to Rome; and the growing ritualism, with its gaudy and splendid "attire of a harlot," which characterizes others, plainly indicates their tendency in the same direction. And even those other denominations, which are not yet prepared to adopt that "blasphemous hierarchy," are visibly departing from the soundness in doctrine and purity of gospel worship which constituted the chief glory of the Second Reformation. These are the baleful effects of the dragon's influence "on the earth," (ch. xii. 13, 15.) Besides, nearly all ecclesiastical bodies are yet in cordial alliance with the beast of the sea; and this alliance is the Antichrist. The Pope is now nearly divested of his former civil supremacy, and in this respect become less the express image of the imperial beast of the sea, (ch. xiii. 14;) yet the leaven of the Romish religion pervades all the Christian community, so far as allegiance to the beast or his horns is either enjoined or tolerated. This usurpation of the royal prerogatives of Christ over the churches and nations in the eastern hemisphere by the kings of the earth, and a similar usurpation in the western hemisphere, whether by individual despots or by the body politic, is the *great crime* which fills the measure of the cup of wrath, to be poured out of the "seven vials." While such is the moral condition of society in all lands favored with a revelation of the will of God,—visited with judgments, continuing impenitent and guilt augmenting, what is to be expected but heavier judgments to follow?

> 9. *And the third angel followed them, saying, with a loud voice, If any man worship the beast and his image, and receive his mark in his forehead, or in his hand,*

10. The same shall drink of the wine of the wrath of God, which is poured out without mixture into the cup of his indignation; and he shall be tormented with fire and brimstone in the presence of the holy angels, and in the presence of the Lamb:
11. And the smoke of their torment ascendeth up for ever and ever; and they have no rest day nor night, who worship the beast and his image, and whosoever receiveth the mark of his name.

Vs. 9-11.—"And the third angel followed." The two preceding angels addressed *communities*, calling them to repentance and reformation. Indeed, the language of the second implies little or no hope of their recovery. This third angel, "following" up the scriptural testimony of those who went before, and assuming that church and state,—the essential elements of the antichristian system,—continue irreclaimable, addresses his message to *individuals*. This angel is the last that the Lord Jesus will employ to awaken sinners that "are at ease in Zion." His ministry is yet future, and he will never be succeeded by an angel of mercy until mystical Babylon is overthrown. The special, arduous and perilous work of this angel is, to threaten eternal death against every individual who persists in the hitherto popular idolatry. "If any man worship the beast."—Up to the time of this angel's appearance the beast lives and devours his prey: consequently, his work comes within the period of the 1260 years. During this limited time, there will be found in the Apocalypse *three objects* of popular devotion,—the dragon, (ch. xiii. 4,) the *beast*, and his *image*, (v. 15.) In this place the dragon is omitted, as also in ch. xv. 2; xx. 4. We may ask, why the omission?—Simply because "the things which the *Gentiles* sacrifice, they sacrifice to devils, and not to God," (1 Cor. x. 20;) consequently, these worshippers being *Gentiles*, (ch. xi. 2,) there is no necessity that the dragon (the devil) should be particularized. From the first rise of the beast, he was in alliance with the dragon, (ch. xiii. 2, 3;) therefore both are doomed to perdition, (ch. xx. 10.) Most expositors consider this angel as emblematical of events already past; the reformation effected by Luther, his coadjutors and successors, or the church of England![8] Their error consists in viewing the beast as the symbol of the church of Rome. And it is remarkable, that through the power of local and political bias, those commentators who themselves perceive that the beast of the sea in chapter xiii. 1, symbol-

---

8. This is the opinion of Mr. Faber.

izes the Roman *empire*, lose sight of their *own exposition* when they arrive at the place before us! And of this bias and inconsistency they seem to be wholly unconscious! No, there has never yet appeared in the symbolic heaven a minister or ecclesiastical organization, which has authoritatively denounced everlasting punishment against all who "receive the mark of the beast." It is to be noticed here that the sins charged are *cumulative*, not *distributive*. Guilt is contracted as here charged, by "worshipping the beast and his image, and receiving his mark." If the beast signify immoral civil power, and his image signify the Papacy, as we have seen they do, then it follows that worshipping both, and receiving the mark of the former, constitute the special guilt here charged by the angel: that is, eulogizing, praising, and actively co-operating with civil and ecclesiastical society, at war with the Bible—in organized hostility to the Lord and his Anointed. (Ps. ii. 9.) "Shall the throne of iniquity have fellowship with thee, which frameth mischief by a law?" (Ps. xciv. 20.) But during the 1260 years, the secular imperial beast consists of "kingdoms of this world" in alliance with the beast of the earth, (ch. xiii. 1, 11.) And as both are for their crimes consigned to utter destruction, so in the time of the "third angel," every individual is threatened with everlasting punishment, who identifies with them. "No *temporal* judgments on *collective* bodies can be the fulfilment of this awful denunciation, which evidently relates to *individuals*, and to each individual who is guilty; and if words can convey the idea of eternal punishment, it is here denounced."[9] The words in the original, translated "for ever and ever," (v. 11,) are the strongest in the Greek language to signify eternity, and are not susceptible of any other meaning.

As already intimated, the special mission and awful message of this angel is yet future; but the testimony of his predecessor will have made the tyranny, idolatry, immorality and profligacy of civil despots and mercenary ministers so palpable and glaring, that the vengeance of the Lord proclaimed by the last messenger will appear to be just. In this way the "two witnesses smite the earth with all plagues," (ch. xi. 6;) for they are identical with the "third angel," and have an active agency in the work of judgment to be executed upon the antichristian enemies, (ch. xv. 7.) And "who knows the power of that wrath which is poured out

---

9. Scott.

without mixture into the cup of Jehovah's indignation?" In temporal judgments there may be a mixture of mercy; but there is no such element in the cup of the impenitent votaries of mystic Babylon. "Holy angels" look on without sympathy for her agonies, while the Lamb inflicts the tremendous penalty of her complicated and long-continued crimes. "*He* shall be tormented—*their* torment:"—individuals found guilty of complicity with Babylon, will be bound up into bundles as fuel for that fire and brimstone, whose "smoke ascendeth up for ever and ever." "They have no rest day nor night who worship the beast,"—no mitigation of their sufferings. They are doomed to dwell "with everlasting burnings." (Is. xxxiii. 14.) Such are the denunciations which the "third angel" is commissioned to proclaim in the ears of men, either to bring them to repentance, or to justify the Lamb in punishing their impenitent disobedience. Now "every one who is acquainted with the writings of the reformers and their successors, knows that they generally declared, without hesitation, that popery is a damnable religion."[10] Popery, however, is the religion which has corrupted states and churches throughout the world; and therefore future reformers will not hesitate to join civil states with her in their testimony and prayers, saying,—"The wicked shall be turned into hell, *and all the nations* that forget God. Pour out thy fury upon the heathen that have not known thee, and upon the kingdoms that have not called upon thy name; for they have devoured Jacob and laid waste his dwelling place." (Psa. ix. 17; lxxix. 6, 7.)

12. *Here is the patience of the saints: here are they that keep the commandments of God, and the faith of Jesus.*
13. *And I heard a voice from heaven, saying unto me, Write, Blessed are the dead which die in the Lord, from henceforth: Yea, saith the Spirit, that they may rest from their labours; and their works do follow them.*

Vs. 12, 13.—The faithful and pointed testimony of the "third angel" of reform against the organized enemies of God in church and state, instead of producing repentance, tends only to provoke them to greater rage against those who thus awaken their consciences and disturb their

---

10. Scott.

sinful repose. The fires of persecution are again kindled, and the witnesses are subjected to the anathemas of the church and the sword of the civil magistrate,—the cruelty of the two beasts. It is therefore added,—"Here is the patience of the saints." The events predicted here agree in time with ch. xiii. 10; and the subjects of persecution are the same moral person in their legitimate successors who appeared in ch. xii. 17. They "keep the commandments of God and the faith of Jesus," while the multitude "obey unrighteousness, receiving for doctrines the commandments of men."

To animate these sufferers who are in "jeopardy every hour" and who have the sentence of death as outlaws, pronounced against them by Antichrist, John "heard a voice from heaven," directing him to write,—"Blessed are the dead which die in the Lord, from henceforth."—To "die in the Lord,"—means, in the faith and hope of the gospel, relieved by the "witness of the Spirit" from the overwhelming fears of the pains of *purgatory*. Both negatively and positively, this angel testifies against the antichristian dogma of purgatory. He declares that the torments of the wicked continue "for ever and ever," while the righteous who die in the Lord, "cease from their labours."—No stronger testimony can be conceived against the more gross papal heresy, or the more modern and so called philosophical delusions of Universalists, Socinians and others,—all of whom are the offspring of the "mother of harlots." But besides the voice from heaven, and the concurrent witness of the Spirit, against the papal dogma of purgatory, the "rest" here proclaimed for the comfort of martyred saints, may be also understood as a termination to their sharp conflicts with Antichrist. "*Henceforth* they rest from their labours,"—they shall never again be called to "resist unto blood, striving against sin," as heretofore, by the combined opposition of the "beast and false prophet," organized tyranny and idolatry. The ministry of the "third angel," cotemporary with the "seventh trumpet,"—the third and last "woe," prepares society throughout Christendom for entering into the millennial rest.

> 14. And I looked, and, behold, a white cloud, and upon the cloud one sat like unto the Son of Man, having on his head a golden crown, and in his hand a sharp sickle.

15. *And another came out of the temple, crying with a loud voice to him that sat on the cloud, Thrust in thy sickle, and reap; for the time is come for thee to reap: for the harvest of the earth is ripe.*
16. *And he that sat on the cloud thrust in his sickle on the earth; and the earth was reaped.*

Vs. 14-16.—The gathering in of the harvest is sometimes emblematical of mercy,—as when the believer is gathered to his fathers by death. His sanctification being completed, he is taken home "as a shock of corn ripe in his season." Reaping and threshing, however, are most frequently symbolical of divine judgments, (Jer. li. 33;) and the apostle refers here to the same event which the Lord foretold by the mouth of other prophets. (Joel iii. 13-17; Micah iv. 12, 13.) This harvest is emblematical of divine judgment on the nations of apostate Christendom. He who executes the judgment is one like the Son of man, the Lord Christ. Enthroned on a "white cloud" as his chariot, and having on his royal "head a golden crown," the symbol of sovereignty, at the solicitation, the loud cry of the symbolic angel,—a gospel ministry, he "thrusts in his sharp sickle," the emblem of avenging justice, and with infinite ease, "the earth is reaped." This work of punishing guilty *nations* is not so proper to the ministry, the functions of whose office are of a spiritual nature; yet are they active in a way competent to them, calling upon the "Lord of the harvest" to reap. They judge of the signs of the times. Such is part of their appropriate work. Thus they say,—"The time is come for thee to reap; for the harvest of the earth is ripe." The Lord Jesus appeared in royal majesty to John, as he had appeared to Ezekiel, (ch. i. 26;) and to Daniel, (ch. vii. 13.) The cloud on which he sat had a bright side towards his saints, but to his enemies a dark side, as at the Red Sea. (Ex. xiv. 19, 20.)

The two judgments of the *harvest* and *vintage*, are obviously an allusion to a natural order in the climate of Judea. Not only did the barley and wheat-harvest precede the time of gathering grapes, but some space elapsed between these labors of the husbandman. The usual order is observed here.

17. *And another angel came out of the temple which is in heaven, he also having a sharp sickle.*

18. *And another angel came out from the altar, which had power over fire; and cried with a loud cry to him that had the sharp sickle, saying, Thrust in thy sharp sickle, and gather the clusters of the vine of the earth; for her grapes are fully ripe.*
19. *And the angel thrust in his sickle into the earth, and gathered the vine of the earth, and cast it into the great wine-press of the wrath of God.*
20. *And the wine press was trodden without the city, and blood came out of the wine-press even unto the horse-bridles, by the space of a thousand and six hundred furlongs.*

Vs. 17-20.—As the ministry of the "third angel," (v. 9,) was final, as to pronouncing the deserved doom of all the adherents of the antichristian system, so in the symbols of the *harvest* and *vintage*, we have the execution of that sentence exhibited. The nations of Christendom, having drunk the wine of the mother of harlots, and of her daughters too, and having exhausted the patience of the Lord Jesus, refusing to repent, while he warned them by his servants the three angels of reform,—"rising early and sending them," were at length "ripe" for his sharp sickle. Long had he expostulated with them, saying to them, while addressing his church,—"The nation and kingdom that will not serve thee (O Zion,) shall perish; yea, those nations shall be utterly wasted." (Isa. lx. 12.)—The desolating judgments of the reigning Mediator, having brought those nations to "hate the whore," they become the willing and zealous agents of her destruction, as appears, (ch. xvii. 16.)

The "gathering of the clusters of the vine of the earth,"—is a concise emblematical representation of that tremendous work of punishing the apostate church, to be exhibited in greater detail in the following chapters.

The "angel coming out of the temple,"—represents the gospel ministry as usual. His "having a sharp sickle" may import his more immediate agency in this than in the preceding work of the harvest. Christ himself judged the nations,—had the "sharp sickle;" but in reckoning with impenitent ecclesiastical communities, he will honor his faithful servants. As in "measuring the temple,"—the Mediator held the instrument in his own hand under the Old Testament, (Zech. ii. 1,) but under the New Testament gave it into the hand of John, the representative of a gospel ministry, (ch. xi. 1,) so that transaction may illustrate the symbols here.

The other angel "coming from the altar, who had power over fire," is also symbolical of the ministry. The sickle in the hand of the former angel, is for gathering the grapes; while the connexion of the latter angel with the "altar," imports that a sacrifice is about to be offered, as customary, to appease divine justice.—The "vine of the earth" is plainly contrasted with the true vine. (Ps. lxxx. 1; Jer. ii. 21.) This is a vine of Sodom with clusters of Gomorrah, (ch. xi. 8; Deut. xxxii. 32, 33.) It is the symbol of an apostate church, the chief heresy of which is a practical rejection of the atonement of Christ; for it is certain that vindictive justice is an attribute of God, and that he will demand satisfaction from those impenitent sinners who despise his mercy in the gospel offer, and "tread under foot the blood of the covenant wherewith Christ was sanctified." (Heb. x. 29.) A heavier doom awaits all such than to "die without mercy," which was the penalty for those who "despised Moses' law." No sacrifice is appointed for the man or the church that sins presumptuously. (Num. xv. 30, 31.) To all such, " *our* God is a consuming fire." (Heb. xii. 29.)—The one angel calls upon the other,—encourages his companion, to execute the judgment of God. "Thrust in thy sharp sickle."—Under the superintendence of the Mediator, his servants by their prayers and their sermons have an active part in this work of judgment. From the mouth of the witnesses proceeded fire to devour their enemies, (ch. xi. 5.) This is the last work of judgment in which they will be honoured. Joining their victorious predecessors who overcame the antichristian combinations "by the blood of the Lamb and the word of their testimony," (chs. vi. 9, 10; xii. 11,) these undaunted servants of the Lord are honored by him as instrumental in the infliction of the final judgments symbolized by the seventh trumpet and the seventh vial,—the third and *last woe*.—The "wine-press" is the symbol of the "wrath of God," and its location "without the city," denotes that the churches of the apostacy are excommunicated,—"reprobate silver, because the Lord hath rejected them."

We are not told here by whom the grapes are trodden; but this is the work of the Lord Jesus himself, who in the days of his flesh on earth forewarned his impenitent foes that he would thus deal with them in his wrath. "Those mine enemies, which would not that I should reign over them, bring hither, and slay them before me." (Luke xix. 27; Isa. lxiii. 3; Rev. xix. 15.)—The blood in depth is to the "horse-bridles," and in extent "a thousand and six hundred furlongs,"—200 miles! Although this language is hyperbolical, it is intended to signify "a time of trouble, such as never was since there was a nation even to that same time; and at that same time God's people shall be delivered, every one that shall be found written in the book." (Dan. xii. 1; Rev. xiii. 8.)—Thus it appears that church and state, having combined in the antichristian apostacy, are severally visited with the unmingled wine of the wrath of God. All the saints shall have obeyed the call,—"Come out of her, my people;" and mystic Babylon shall then be utterly destroyed. Whether Palestine, the Pope's patrimony, or some other territory be understood by the "1600 furlongs," is matter of vague conjecture by all expositors, and is to be verified only by the fulfilment of the prediction.

CHAPTER XV.

This chapter introduces the third and last series of symbols under which the prospective history of the church militant is given, to strengthen the faith and animate the hopes of her suffering and heroic children. The warfare of the witnesses for the crown rights of Immanuel, which have been usurped by his enemies, has been symbolized under the seals, (chs. vi.-ix.,) and under the trumpets, (chs. xi. xii.;) and the symbolic narrative is yet under the vials to be greatly amplified, especially their last and greatest conflict, briefly represented in the latter part of the preceding chapter, (vs. 9-18.) Whether or not the vials, to which this fifteenth chapter is introductory, be all comprehended under the *seventh trumpet*, as the trumpets are all comprehended under the *seventh seal*, is a question upon which respectable expositors differ. It is indeed obvious that the breaking of the last seal, lays open the whole of the book, consequently the angels holding the vials would come into view. John, however, is obliged to "write" *consecutively* some visions which he saw as it were at *one view*. Thus he was "about to write what the seven thunders uttered," (ch. x. 4,) but was prohibited. That was not the proper time or place; but it is there intimated, (v. 7,) that "in the days of the voice of the seventh angel," the import of the "seven thunders" would be disclosed. Then would the "mystery of God be finished, as he had declared to his servants the prophets." (Joel iii. 2, 12, 13; Micah iv. 3; Zech. xii. 2-4; 2 Thess. ii. 8.) Some of the most learned and sober divines, who wrote on the Apocalypse during the peninsular war waged by the first Napolean, contemplating the anarchical and bloody scenes of the French Revolution, and the subsequent tyranny and blood connected with the successful wars of the Gallic usurper, thought they heard in the commotions of European nations the sound of the seventh trumpet, and saw the plagues inflicted as symbolized by the vials. And thus it is that local events, which excite the political feelings, the prejudices and partialities of even good men, are hastily interpreted as a fulfilment of prophecy. It does not appear, however, that those events were either of sufficient magnitude or geographical extent to answer the tremendous symbols of either *harvest* or *vintage*. Did the French revolution, the American revolution, or the wars of Napolean First, influence the civilized world or affect the church of God, as Popery and Mahometanism have done? No, the comparison is preposterous. Hence it is most probable that Christendom has not yet heard the alarming sound of the seventh trumpet.

> 1. And I saw another sign in heaven, great and marvellous, seven angels having the seven last plagues; for in them is filled up the wrath of God.

V. 1.—"Another sign in heaven."—All the visions were seen by the apostle in the same place, (ch. i. 1; xii. 1.) The word translated "sign" here is the same as "wonder" in the twelfth chapter, which for greater clearness to the English reader ought to have been rendered by the same word.—The symbol or sign consists of "seven angels having the seven last plagues,"—the *last* to be inflicted on the Antichrist, but not absolutely the last penal inflictions on the enemies of God; for "Gog and Magog" are in like manner to be destroyed, and there is *eternal* wrath.

Upon the "Lamb's taking the book," and before he had opened the first seal, songs of joy burst forth from saints and angels, (ch. v. 8, 9.) So it is here. Before the angels proceed to execute their commission, the redeemed of the Lord, anticipating the effects of these judgments, give expression to their joy.

> 2. And I saw as it were a sea of glass mingled with fire; and them that had gotten the victory over the beast, and over his image, and over his mark, and over the number of his name, stand on the sea of glass, having the harps of God.
> 3. And they sing the song of Moses the servant of God, and the song of the Lamb, saying, Great and marvellous are thy works, Lord God Almighty, just and true are thy ways, thou King of saints!
> 4. Who shall not fear thee, O Lord, and glorify thy name? for thou only art holy: for all nations shall come and worship before thee; for thy judgments are made manifest.

Vs. 2-4.—The "sea of glass," or transparent sea, (as in ch. iv. 6,) refers us to the brazen sea before the throne of God in the temple. In this sea the priests were to wash themselves, (Exod. xxx. 18, 19,) and in water drawn from it the sacrifices were to be washed also. (Lev. i. 9, 13.)

As the brazen sea typified the blood of Christ, that "fountain opened for sin and for uncleanness," (Zech. xiii. 1,) so this "sea of glass" is the symbol of the same thing; for the Lord washes away the filth of the daughters of Zion, and purges the blood of Jerusalem from the midst thereof by the spirit of judgment, and by the spirit of burning. (Isa. iv. 4.) This happy company were victorious by the blood of the Lamb, "over the beast, his image, his name and number;" having clean escaped from them who live in error, both in civil and ecclesiastical relations. Holding the eucharistic "harps of God," they are the same company as those on Mount Zion with the Lamb, (ch. xiv. 1, 2.) There, their song was called *new*; here it is more fully described. There it was said, "no man could learn that song" but themselves, here we have the matter of the song epitomised. It is constructed of two parts, "the song of Moses and the song of the Lamb." As the children of Israel at the Red Sea celebrated the praises of God's justice in the overthrow of their enemies the Egyptians, so do these with united voice express their admiration and praise in anticipation of the final and awful end of these cruel, idolatrous and persecuting mystical Egyptians, (ch. xi. 8,) "saying, Great and marvellous are thy works, Lord God Almighty; just and true are thy ways, thou King of saints." They do also declare their faith in the universal dominion of their King; that "all nations shall come and worship before him." And to this day none but the witnesses are prepared either with intelligence or affection to "learn" or use this song. We have the subject matter of both parts of this triumphant song, framed by the Holy Spirit and incorporated in the Book of Psalms, (as Ps. ii. 8; xviii. 37-45; xlv. 3-6; cx. 1, etc.) The fortunes of God's covenant people till the ingathering of the Jews, with the fulness of the Gentiles, may be found in Moses' song, (Deut. xxxii. 1-43,) and the "song of the Lamb" is found in chapter v. 9-13.

5. *And after that I looked, and behold, the temple of the tabernacle of the testimony in heaven was opened:*
6. *And the seven angels came out of the temple, having the seven plagues, clothed in pure and white linen, and having their breasts girded with golden girdles.*

Vs. 5, 6.—John looked again, and saw the "temple opened," that the seven angels might have egress to enter upon their heavenly mission. Their clothing resembled the garments of the priests under the law, "white linen and golden girdles," representing the holiness or moral purity of their work. They shed the blood of the victim, so to speak, without soiling their garments; but the Lord Jesus, whose work of judgment this is, "stains all his raiment," (Isa. lxiii. 3,) "for the day of vengeance is in his heart," (v. 4.)

> 7. And one of the four beasts gave unto the seven angels seven golden vials full of the wrath of God, who liveth for ever and ever.

V. 7.—"One of the four beasts,"— *animals*, the symbol of the gospel ministry, as we found, (ch. iv. 6.) Not all the ministry were employed in this action, but *one* only. That is, some few, a fractional part, possessing more insight into the "sure word of prophecy," and endowed with larger measure of heroic spirit by the Lord Jesus, co-operated with holy angels in this work of judgment. "He gave the vials into the hand of the angels." By their preaching, their prayers and their example, faithful ministers, unseduced by the blandishments of corrupt power, and undismayed by the bloody edicts of the beast,—"in nothing terrified by their adversaries," denounce the judgments represented by these vials, upon the impenitent enemies of the Lord and his Anointed. For an illustration of this symbolic action of giving the vials of divine wrath to the appointed agents, reference may be had to Jer. xxv. 15-26; li. 7.

> 8. And the temple was filled with smoke from the glory of God, and from his power, and no man was able to enter into the temple, till the seven plagues of the seven angels were fulfilled.

V. 8.—"The temple filled with smoke," represents the darkness of these dispensations, the horror and dismay which seizes upon the votaries of Antichrist. But during the time of executing these judgments, the progress of the gospel will be retarded,—"no man being able to enter into the temple." It is intimated, moreover, that these judgments will, as it were, clear away the "smoke," and render the temple once more luminous. So we may conclude by comparing the 4th and 8th verses. In the 4th verse the witnesses declare their faith thus,—"All nations shall come and worship before thee." But this is a description of the millennial state of the world. (Ps. lxxii. 11.)

CHAPTER XVI.

All preliminaries being now arranged, the seven angels receive their commission by a "great voice out of the temple." It is the "voice of the Lord, full of majesty." (Ps. xxix. 4.)—As the *seals* and *trumpets* were not coincident, but successive, so it is doubtless with the *vials*. No two begin to be poured out at the same time. One follows another in orderly succession.

Several questions of difficult solution, arise in the minds of devout and humble students of the Apocalypse, respecting the series of the vials. Are the vials cotemporary with the trumpets? Seeing that the seventh seal included all the trumpets, does analogy require that all the vials be comprehended under the seventh or last trumpet? Or, do the seven vials come under the last three trumpets, distinguished as they are by the character of woe-trumpets? (ch. viii. 13.) Other questions may here be propounded; but these seem to be the most obvious and important, in fixing the time of the events predicted.

The breaking of the seventh seal unquestionably laid open the whole of the book, including all the trumpets and vials,—all future events till the end of the world; but it does not follow, for instance, that the awful scene of the final judgment is to be cotemporary with any of the trumpets, (ch. xx. 11, 12.) The seventh seal, therefore, discloses important events, which are to come to pass subsequently to both trumpets and vials. The fact that both trumpets and vials are disclosed by the opening of the last seal, admits of their being cotemporaneous.

From the striking resemblance between the effects of the trumpets and those of the vials, (ch. viii. 7-12; xvi. 2-12,) they might seem to be cotemporary. This, however, is not the case, for the objects of the judgments are different, that of the trumpets being more formally the civil empire, while that of the vials is the ecclesiastical empire; each, however, greatly affecting the other, because of their unholy union against the cause of Christ. Perhaps it may be most consonant to the mind of the Spirit to view the vials as agreeing in time with the three woe-trumpets. Keeping in view the definite period of Antichrist's domination in church and state, 1260 years, and the probability of its drawing to a close, the remaining part would seem too short for the period of the vials. As the series of the vials, like those which in vision preceded them, is successive, the application of them all to the French Revolution is simply preposterous.[11] That event answered not to the symbol either in extent or duration. Nor indeed is there satisfactory evidence in the actual condition of the Christian world, notwithstanding the fond imagination of learned and good men, that the voice of the seventh angel has yet been heard by Christendom.

> 1. And I heard a great voice out of the temple, saying to the seven angels, Go your ways, and pour out the vials of the wrath of God upon the earth.

V. 1.—"Earth" has here the usual meaning,—the whole territory and population of the Roman empire, those only and always exempted, who are true to the cause of Immanuel. The angels of destruction cannot hurt those who are under the protection of his blood. (Exod. xii. 23.) They may not "come near any man upon whom is the mark." (Ezek. ix. 6; Rev. xiv. 1.)

> 2. And the first went, and poured out his vial upon the earth; and there fell a noisome and grievous sore upon the men which had the mark of the beast, and upon them which worshipped his image.
> 3. And the second angel poured out his vial upon the sea; and it became as the blood of a dead man: and every living soul died in the sea.
> 4. And the third angel poured out his vial upon the rivers and fountains of waters; and they became blood.
> 5. And I heard the angel of the waters say, Thou art righteous, O Lord, which art, and wast, and shalt be, because thou hast judged thus:
> 6. For they have shed the blood of saints and prophets, and thou hast given them blood to drink; for they are worthy.
> 7. And I heard another out of altar say, Even so, Lord God Almighty, true and righteous are thy judgments.

Vs. 2-7.—"And the first went."—However disagreeable the service, as we are ready to suppose, this holy agent at once obeys the divine

---

11. So Mr. Faber imagined.

command. The best of men hesitate and remonstrate when called to difficult and disagreeable work. So it was with Moses, and with Jeremiah. (Exod. iv. 10; Jer. i. 6.) But all these heavenly messengers in succession, execute their respective tasks without gainsaying. It is the will of our common Lord that his disciples should emulate their example, that they should "know, obey and submit to his will in all things as the angels do in heaven." (Ps. ciii. 20, 21.)—The judgments upon the antichristian enemies which have been briefly represented in the close of the 14th chapter by a *harvest* and *vintage*, are in this chapter more extensively exhibited by the seven vials. A resemblance to the first four trumpets may be observed in the effects of the first four vials, and besides, these plagues resemble those inflicted on Egypt. If by her crimes, especially by idolatry and cruelty to the people of God papal Rome has copied the manners of Egypt and Babylon, it is but just that she should be visited with like punishment.—The first vial selects as victims those who "had the mark of the beast and worshipped his image;" and this is true of the succeeding plagues, although the fact be not repeated. The object of this vial is the "earth" in a more restricted sense than in the first verse. The "earth" in the first verse comprises all the parts of a system, "earth, sea, fountains, sun and air," mentioned in the following verses.—The "noisome and grievous sore," refers to one of the plagues of Egypt. (Exod. ix. 9-11.) The *earth* was the object affected also by the first trumpet; (ch. viii. 7;) but as Antichrist had not then arisen, this plague cannot agree in time with the first trumpet, though it might with the fifth or sixth trumpet; for while these trumpets were demolishing the eastern member of the Roman empire, making way for the development of Mahomet's imposture, the "little horn" of Daniel, and Paul's "man of sin," was revealed in the west. But the "two witnesses" were coincident in origin with Antichrist, and were empowered by the Lord Christ "to smite the earth with all plagues as often as they would," (ch. xi. 6.) The "grievous sore" is to be understood metaphorically, not literally; for so the construction of the Apocalypse requires. It may import the festering of unmortified corruption among the votaries of Antichrist, intensified by the faithful application of the divine law by the witnesses.—The object of the second vial is the "sea," the same as that of the second trumpet, (ch. viii. 8, 9.) The allusion is to Exod. vii. 20, 21. Intestine commotions, with war, blood and death, seem to be symbolized. The horns of the beast were often turned against one another; for the bestial kingdom was "partly broken." The toes in Nebuchadnezzar's image did not "cleave one to another." (Dan. ii. 42, 43.)—The object of the third vial is the "rivers and fountains of waters," (ch. viii. 10; Exodus vii. 19.) These symbols may signify the several kingdoms of the empire, tributary by their wealth and traffic to the great city. And as the witnesses continued to prophesy, giving increased point and publicity to their testimony, and as the Turks were making encroachments upon the territories of nominal Christian princes in the west, extensive wars and great slaughter were the results. These awful judgments are followed by the plaudits of two angels. The eternal Jehovah is recognized as the Author of these judgments. The Mediator may here be understood, (ch. i. 8; John v. 22, 27.) The "angel of the waters" may be the same who poured out the vial. He gives to the Lord the glory of his justice:—"Thou art righteous." He also approves the "law of retaliation:"—"For they are worthy." The other angel "out of the altar" speaks on behalf of the martyrs, (ch. vi. 9, 10,) recognizing the faithfulness of God:—"True and righteous are thy judgments."

8. And the fourth angel poured out his vial upon the sun; and power was given unto him to scorch men with fire.
9. And men were scorched with great heat, and blasphemed the name of God, which hath power over these plagues; and they repented not to give him glory.

Vs. 8, 9.—The object of the fourth vial is the "sun," (ch. viii. 12.) "Power was given him,"—the angel. The two witnesses are represented as armed with "fire, which proceedeth out of their mouth, devouring their enemies," (ch. xi. 5.) As the formal object of all the vials is the ecclesiastical, rather than the civil empire, and the sun is the symbol of the chief dignitary, perhaps this vial strikes more directly upon the "man of sin." The expression in the introduction to the vials, (ch. xv. 4,)—"thou only art holy," seems to be a testimony against the antichristian "name of blasphemy,"—"His Holiness." By the Reformation, symbolized by successive angels of the fourteenth chapter, those valiant men tormented the Pope and his vassals, so that they raged and blasphemed more and more, but "repented not to give God the glory." So it was at the sounding of the sixth trumpet, (ch. ix. 20, 21.)

> 10. And the fifth angel poured out his vial upon the seat of the beast; and his kingdom was full of darkness; and they gnawed their tongues for pain,
> 11. And blasphemed the God of heaven, because of their pains and their sores, and repented not of their deeds.

Vs. 10, 11.—"The seat of the beast" is the object of the fifth vial. The "beast" is all along from chapter xi. 7, the Roman empire. The "image of the beast," we have found to be the papacy, (ch. xiii. 14, 15.) Now the "seat (throne) of the beast," would seem to point to the metropolis, where the Pope, as a kind of imperial, politico-ecclesiastical head, keeps his court, and whence decrees are issued. This plague is like the ninth inflicted upon Egypt, (Exod. x. 21.) It was the last but one, and left Pharaoh still impenitent. Just so here; although this vial is the last but one to be poured out on the western limb of the great antichristian conspiracy: the population of the spiritual empire repress their complaints before men,—"they gnawed their tongues for pain;" while they in their hearts "curse their king and their God, and look upward." (Is. viii. 21.) This may be understood to be the actual condition of the Pope and his retainers at the present time, and especially since the year 1848, when he was forced to flee from Rome. *Darkness* is the emblem of distress, of mental despair, (Ps. xxxv. 8; Is. viii. 22;) and the actual relation of European powers to the see of Rome,—Austria, France, Spain, and the Italian states, is not calculated to mitigate, but rather to augment and irritate the "pains and the sores" inflicted by this and former vials.

We can, however, offer only conjectures here, and dare not be too confident; for learned and pious expositors are of the opinion that all the vials are comprehended under the seventh trumpet; that the seventh trumpet has not yet begun to sound; and consequently, that the vials are all future. On the other hand, equally learned and godly interpreters of these Apocalyptic hieroglyphics, are very confident that the *sixth* vial is in process of pouring out in our present time; and that in fact its effects are obviously traceable in providence. Already we have indicated our humble opinion, that all the vials are not necessarily comprehended under the seventh trumpet; inasmuch as the opening of the last seal disclosed equally trumpets and vials: yet doubtless it is requisite that the series of the trumpets should precede that of the vials, while nothing hinders that of both series should cotemporate. We may conceive that as the first four trumpets demolished the western member of the Roman empire, and the next two the eastern limb, so the vials may be distributed in a manner somewhat similar. The second woe, or sixth trumpet, has not yet finished its appropriate work in the final subversion of the Turkish empire, which still exists; and during the time of its last echoes, the vials may be supposed to be accomplishing their appropriate work upon the western empire, as being "wholly given to idolatry." While the first five vials are consuming the Antichrist in the west, the sixth is operating in the east.

> 12. And the sixth angel poured out his vial upon the great river Euphrates; and the water thereof was dried up, that the way of the kings of the east might be prepared.
> 13. And I saw three unclean spirits like frogs come out of the mouth of the dragon, and out of the mouth of the beast, and out of the mouth of the false prophet.
> 14. For they are the spirits of devils, working miracles, which go forth unto the kings of the earth and of the whole world, to gather them to the battle of that great day of God Almighty.
> 15. Behold, I come as a thief. Blessed is he that watcheth and keepeth his garments, lest he walk naked, and they see his shame.
> 16. And he gathered them together into a place called in the Hebrew tongue Armageddon.

Vs. 12-16.—"The great river Euphrates" is the object of the sixth vial. By the very general consent of expositors the Turkish empire is intended by this symbol; and they seem to be equally agreed that the sixth vial in now in process of pouring out. The object of the sixth trumpet is the same, (ch. ix. 14.) There is, besides, an obvious allusion to the ancient literal Babylon; and to the manner of its overthrow by Cyrus the king of Persia. (Jer. l. 38; li. 36; Dan. v. 26-28; Is. xliv. 27, 28.)—This monarch, as historians relate, changed the current of the Euphrates, and by this means took possession of the city, while Belshazzar and his nobles were engaged in a drunken festival. (Dan. v. 1-30.)—The waters of this river are to be taken as representing the population of the Ottoman empire, (ch. xvii. 15.) By the "kings of the east" may be understood the Jews, agreeably to the symbolical nature of this book; (Is. xli. 2, 3;) yet as the

Turkish empire and Mahometan imposture constitute barriers to the extension of Christ's kingdom among the populous nations of the east, as Popish despotism and idolatry, obstruct the gospel in the west, we may give this symbol of the "kings of the east" a more extensive interpretation. Probably a larger proportion of the natural seed of Abraham are to be found on the west than even on the east of the Turkish empire. The dynasty of the Turk is in process of visible exhaustion, and nothing but what is termed among antichristian nations "the balance of power," prolongs its existence or hinders its extinction. "Drying up," evaporation, is a gradual process, and with singular precision describes the waning light of the once proud Crescent,—the expiring breath of what has been termed by a bold figure, "the sick man."[12] —Under this vial, however, and likewise as the termination of the second woe, a general, final and desperate alliance is to be found to resist the aggressive forces of the "Lord of Hosts."—This confederacy is headed by the dragon, and is identical with the war, (ch. xii. 17,) against the "remnant of the woman's seed."—These "unclean spirits like frogs" are called "spirits of devils." They "come out of the mouth" of all the agents, the dragon, (ch. xii. 3, 9,) the beast, (ch. xiii. 1,) and the false prophet,—the same as the two-horned beast, (v. 11,) and (ch. xix. 20.) These "unclean spirits" succeed in gathering the kings of the earth, by "working miracles," "lying wonders." (2 Thess. ii. 9; 1 Tim. iv. 1, 2.) They are the agents of antichristian Rome, spiritual wickedness in high places," (Eph. vi. 12;)—"like frogs," living in moral filth; garrulous and impudent, stealthily gaining access into the bedchambers of the kings, "after the manner of Egypt." (Exod. viii. 3.)—Surely the policy of Rome is here portrayed, her cardinals, archbishops, Jesuits, etc., gaining entrance into the councils and cabinets of princes, inciting them to debauchery, tyranny and blood. Hellish hosts are thus "gathered to the battle of that great day of God Almighty,"—the day of the seventh vial, of the "vintage," (ch. xiv. 18-20,) and of the seventh trumpet, (ch. xi. 15;) for all these agree in point of time.—This will be an "hour of temptation," as intimated in the 15th verse, which is a parenthesis, interrupting a little the narrative of the effects of the vial. There is danger of apostacy, of "falling away to these Chaldeans," of temporizing with the enemy in order to escape suffering. Thus Christian soldiers of the cross, losing "the armour of righteous-

---

12. So designated by Nicholas, late emperor of Russia.

ness," would be exposed to "shame." But "blessed is he that watcheth," that looks to the Captain of Salvation, to his cause, as elucidated by his providence,—the signs of the times; for so shall he "keep his garments," when others are "found naked."—"And he gathered them" or rather "*they* gathered," (for the singular verb agrees with its nominative plural neuter as usual,)—the "unclean spirits gathered the kings of the earth" to the destined place. This hinders not but that these antichristian enemies of the church are brought together by the Almighty. Just so he sent the king of Assyria against "a hypocritical nation." (Is. x. 5-7.) And doubtless the prophet Joel prophesied of this great and decisive battle, (ch. iii. 11-14.) "Thither cause thy mighty ones to come down, O Lord." Compare vs. 1, 2. The place is called "Armageddon," the *mountain of destruction*, suggesting the issue of the battle in the final overthrow of Antichrist; for it is not necessary to suppose that any *place* is literally pointed out; but as this is a compound word in the "Hebrew tongue," allusion may be made to the slaughter of Sisera's army, (Judges v. 19;) or to the mournful death of Josiah, (2 Chron. xxxv. 22.)

17. And the seventh angel poured out his vial into the air; and there came a great voice out of the temple of heaven, from the throne, saying, It is done.
18. And there were voices, and thunders, and lightnings; and there was a great earthquake, such as was not since men were upon the earth, so mighty an earthquake, and so great.
19. And the great city was divided into three parts, and the cities of the nations fell; and great Babylon came in remembrance before God, to give unto her the cup of the wine of the fierceness of his wrath.
20. And every island fled away, and the mountains were not found.
21. And there fell upon men a great hail out of heaven, every stone about the weight of a talent; and men blasphemed God, because of the plague of the hail; for the plague thereof was exceeding great.

Vs. 17-21.—"The seventh angel poured out his vial into the air."—The devil is emphatically styled "the prince of the power of the air." (Eph. ii. 2.) All the preceding vials fell upon their respective and successive objects, the several parts of the symbolic system; but this "vial of consummation" affects the whole of that system at once. The dragon, the beast, and his image, together with the false prophet,—all the "kingdoms of this world and the glory of them," which the god of this world claimed as his own, and offered to our Lord Jesus Christ in the days of his humiliation, (Luke iv. 6, 7;)—all will be destroyed for ever. He who gave commission by a "great voice," (v. 1,) to these angels, now that they have fulfilled his pleasure, solemnly declares his approbation,—"It is done." The Lord Christ had solemnly sworn that "in the days of the voice of the seventh angel, when he should begin to sound, the mystery of God should be *finished*," (ch. x. 6, 7.) He is faithful to his oath,—*It is done*. Hence, it is undeniably evident that the seventh trumpet agrees in time with the seventh vial; and it is equally evident that the events which they represent are yet future. What was obscurely intimated as following the sounding of the seventh trumpet,—"the nations were angry,—and thy wrath is come," (ch. xi. 18,) is here amplified; for the "voices, thunders and lightnings," are the visible and sensible tokens of the wrath of God. (Exod. xix. 16; Heb. xii. 21.) Next follows an "earthquake," the usual symbol of revolution; but this one is without parallel. An earthquake followed the opening of the sixth seal, (ch. vi. 12;) when paganism was overthrown in the Roman empire by Constantine, and another earthquake marked the close of the second woe, (ch. xi. 13,) when "the tenth part of the city fell:" but this *concussion* is "so mighty and so great" as to "divide the great city into three parts," or rival factions: next, "the cities of the nations fell,"—revolted from their wonted allegiance, and "great Babylon came in remembrance before God," who seemed to have forgotten both her and his saints whom she had so long and so cruelly persecuted. At the fall of Rome *pagan*, mountains and islands were only "moved out of their places," (ch. vi. 14;) but at the fall of Rome *papal*, "every island fled away, and the mountains were not found;"—the former indicating *transition*, the latter utter *destruction*.—The "fall of hail" is to be viewed as accompanying, not following, the fall of cities, flight of islands and mountains. As hailstones are symbolical of divine judgments, and as there may be allusion here to another of the plagues of Egypt, (Exod. ix. 18;) so more especially may the facts of history supply the figurative language with which the judgments of the vials terminate. If any escaped the destroying sword in the battle of Armageddon, they are overtaken by these ponderous hailstones out of heaven; even as "the Lord cast down great stones from heaven" upon the five kings of the Amorites; so that "more died with hailstones than they whom the children of Israel slew with the sword." (Jos. x. 11.)—The result is as before; the survivors remain impenitent. As history supplies no instance of literal hail-stones of a talent weight, (sixty pounds, or as others, a hundred,) so the symbol represents this as the most tremendous of all the judgments of God, (ch. xiv. 20.)

Thus, we have seen that the last trumpet and the last vial combine, in the final perdition of Babylon the great.

CHAPTER XVII.

This chapter may be considered introductory to the eighteenth, or as a digression in the narrative, to explain more fully the integral parts of that complex, mystical moral person so often called "great Babylon," whose destruction was so awfully presented in the foregoing chapter.

> 1. And there came one of the seven angels, which had the seven vials, and talked with me, saying unto me, Come hither; I will show unto thee the judgment of the great whore, that sitteth upon many waters;
> 2. With whom the kings of the earth have committed fornication, and the inhabitants of the earth have been made drunk with the wine of her fornication.

Vs. 1, 2.—The angel that "talked with the apostle" was probably the seventh. "The great whore" is the symbol of the idolatrous church of Rome, which broke her marriage covenant with Christ. Idolatry is spiritual whoredom. (Hosea vi. 10.) Her "sitting upon many waters" is explained, verse 15. "The kings of the earth" are her paramours, and their subjects are partakers in the crime,—"made drunk."

> 3. So he carried me away in the spirit into the wilderness; and I saw a woman sit upon a scarlet-coloured beast, full of names of blasphemy, having seven heads, and ten horns.
> 4. And the woman was arrayed in purple and scarlet-colour, and decked with gold, and precious stones, and pearls, having a golden cup in her hand, full of abominations, and filthiness of her fornication.
> 5. And upon her forehead was a name written, MYSTERY, BABYLON THE GREAT, THE MOTHER OF HARLOTS, AND ABOMINATIONS OF THE EARTH.

Vs. 3-5.—The "scarlet-coloured beast" is the Roman empire professing the Christian religion, modelled by the Romish church; for the "woman sits upon the beast," guiding and controlling all its motions. (James iii. 3.) The raiment of both is at once *imperial and bloody*,—"purple and scarlet."—The raiment of this "woman" is decked with precious metal, stones and pearls, after the usual "attire of a harlot." (Ezek. xvi. 17.) The "cup" alludes to the practice of harlots giving love-potions to their paramours, very expressive of the indulgences, absolutions, preferments, etc., by which the church of Rome attracts disciples to her idolatry. "The nations have drunken of her wine; therefore the nations are mad." (Jer. li. 7.)—The inscription "upon her forehead" is after the manner of shameless prostitutes, avowing Rome's whoredoms of idolatry, monasticism, indulgences to sin, as essential to religion, a "mystery of iniquity," by which the "man of sin thinks to change times and laws." (Dan. vii. 24, 25; xi. 36, 37.)

6. *And I saw the woman drunken with the blood of the saints, and with the blood of the martyrs of Jesus: and when I saw her, I wondered with great admiration.*

V. 6.—This "woman,"— *Christian church,*—was "drunken with the blood of saints and martyrs." Of course, such a sight would give rise to the apostle's astonishment. The attempt of popish writers to apply this to *pagan* Rome's persecutions is demonstrably false; for John could not "wonder" at the persecution of the church when he was himself an actual victim in Patmos, (ch. i. 9.)

7. *And the angel said unto me, Wherefore didst thou marvel? I will tell thee the mystery of the woman, and of the beast that carrieth her, which hath the seven heads and ten horns.*
8. *The beast that thou sawest, was, and is not; and shall ascend out of the bottomless pit, and go into perdition: and they that dwell on the earth shall wonder (whose names were not written in the book of life from the foundation of the world,) when they behold the beast that was, and is not, and yet is.*
9. *And here is the mind which hath wisdom. The seven heads are seven mountains, on which the woman sitteth.*
10. *And there are seven kings: five have fallen, and one is, and the other is not yet come; and when he cometh, he must continue a short space.*
11. *And the beast that was, and is not, even he is the eighth, and is of the seven, and goeth into perdition.*

Vs. 7-11.—The angel explains the "mystery of the woman and of the beast that carrieth her." The beast, the civil power, carrieth, sustains the woman, the church; as the church controls the state, (v. 3; ch. xiii. 1, 11, 16.) The "beast that was, and is not, and yet is," is a mysterious personage as well as the woman; therefore all who "dwell upon the earth,"—not in "heaven, wonder," (ch. xiii. 3-6;)—that is, all the vassals of Antichrist, distinguished from those whose "names are in the book of life,"—the two witnesses.—"The seven heads" of the beast signify seven mountains, on which Rome literally stands, namely, Capitoline, Palatine, Aventine, Esquiline, Coelian, Viminal and Quirinal. Here the woman and Rome are manifestly identical,—the spiritual empire. But the heads of the beast have a double meaning; for they also signify "seven kings" or successive forms of civil government. At the time when John wrote, "five had fallen;" they had passed into actual history. One was then existing, namely, the emperor, in the person of Domitian, as is supposed. This is the imperial head, whose "deadly wound was healed," (ch. xiii. 3.)—The "seventh head was not come" in the apostles' time, but on his appearance, he was to "continue a short space." The papacy is not the seventh head. *He* is a horn. (Dan. vii. 8, 20.) But a *horn* of the beast cannot identify with the *beast himself.* It is otherwise with a head, which is the form of government over the *whole empire.* The *patriciate* succeeded the imperial, being the seventh head, and only of *short* duration, about fifty years. Charlemagne was crowned emperor of the Romans in the year eight hundred; and so the patriciate terminated. This is the *eighth*, which "is of the seven;" and goeth into perdition. This septimo-octave head is so variable, sometimes acknowledged as residing in Austria, then in France, etc., that for hundreds of years, the great republic of the nations,—all *bestial,*—are at a loss to identify the visible head in whom resides the precedency: hence the "balance of power" is so perplexing and difficult to adjust. Were there an acknowledged imperial and despotic head, this obvious difficulty could not exist. But the beast is not. Nevertheless the arbitrary power of the horns of the beast is sensibly felt in every part of the Roman empire.—The beast is, and will continue till "the time of the end;" (Dan. xii. 9;) for the Roman empire must be equal in duration with the life and actings of the two witnesses, 1260 years.

12. And the ten horns which thou sawest are ten kings, which have received no kingdom as yet; but receive power as kings one hour with the beast.
13. These have one mind, and shall give their power and strength unto the beast.
14. These shall make war with the Lamb, and the Lamb shall overcome them; for he is Lord of lords, and King of kings; and they that are with him are called, and chosen, and faithful.

Vs. 12-14.—"The ten horns" signify "ten kings" or regal or civil sovereignties, into which the empire was to be partitioned after John's time, and which we have seen was effected by the first four trumpets, (ch. viii. 7-12.)—These "received power *one hour* with the beast,"—rather, at *one time*, or cotemporaneously with the beast; for they are his horns, and are of "one mind, giving their power and strength," all their resources, to him. These shall make war with the Lamb," the Mediator, headed by the dragon, and instigated by the beast and his image, (ch. xii. 7; xiii. 7.)

15. And he saith unto me, The waters which thou sawest, where the whore sitteth, are peoples, and multitudes, and nations, and tongues.

V. 15.—"The waters," controlled by "the whore," are the multitudes whom the apostate church of Rome commands to volunteer in the wars of the kings against the Lamb.

16. And the ten horns which thou sawest upon the beast, these shall hate the whore, and shall make her desolate and naked, and shall eat her flesh, and burn her with fire.

V. 16.—What a surprising change! yet how natural! (2 Sam. xiii. 15.) The punishment is that which was adjudged in the case of a priest's daughter. (Lev. xxi. 9.)—The "ten horns," here, are to be understood generally, not universally, (ch. xviii. 9; xix. 19.) Some of those princes that have contributed most to the aggrandizement of the Romish church, and been most devoted to her religion, as the ruler of France, "the eldest son of the church," their "catholic majesties" of Austria, Spain, Portugal,—may be among the first in executing divine judgments on Babylon.—"Make her desolate and naked, eat her flesh;" that is, withdraw the lands, endowments, etc., which enriched her monasteries and fattened her bishops, priests, etc.

> 17. *For God hath put in their hearts to fulfil his will, and to agree, and give their kingdom unto the beast, until the words of God shall be fulfilled.*

V. 17.—Here we are led into the secret cause of the wonderful change in the policy of the horns: "God hath put into their hearts." They just do to the "great whore, whatsoever God's hand and counsel determined before to be done." (Acts iv. 28. See also Exod. vii. 3; Gen. xiv. 8; l. 20; Ps. cv. 25.)

> 18. *And the woman which thou sawest is that great city, which reigneth over the kings of the earth.*

V. 18.—This "woman is the great city;" not literally the city of Rome; but the imperial ecclesiastical jurisdiction, to whose authority intoxicated kings and their subjects bowed in slavish submission; and whose bloody decrees they had executed for 1260 years upon many of their best subjects and fellow-creatures.

CHAPTER XVIII.

1. And after these things I saw another angel come down from heaven, having great power; and the earth was lightened, with his glory.
2. And he cried mightily with a strong voice, saying, Babylon the great is fallen, is fallen, and is become the habitation of devils, and the hold of every foul spirit, and a cage of every unclean and hateful bird.
3. For all nations have drunk of the wine of the wrath of her fornication, and the kings of the earth have committed fornication with her, and the merchants of the earth are waxed rich through the abundance of her delicacies.

Vs. 1-3.—After the apostle had described Babylon in the preceding chapter, he "saw another angel." This seems to be the Lord Christ, the same as in ch. x. 1. He "confirmeth the word of his servants," (ch. xiv. 8;) that "Babylon the great has fallen," and is adequately punished for her crimes, which are enumerated, v. 3.

4. And I heard another voice from heaven, saying, Come out of her, my people, that ye be not partakers of her sins, and that ye receive not of her plagues.

V. 4.—The phrase, "my people" indicates that the speaker is not a created angel whose warning is here given with a "voice from heaven." This call of the Lord Jesus has been addressed to his elect, ever since the revelation of the "man of sin." It has been obeyed but partially hitherto: but upon the sounding of the seventh trumpet, his Holy Spirit will give the call unusual efficacy.

5. For her sins have reached unto heaven, and God hath remembered her iniquities.
6. Reward her even as she rewarded you, and double unto her double, according to her works: in the cup which he hath filled, fill to her double.
7. How much she hath glorified herself, and lived deliciously, so much torment and sorrow give her: for she saith in her heart. I sit a queen; and am no widow, and shall see no sorrow.

8. Therefore shall her plagues come in one day, death, and mourning, and famine; and she shall be utterly burnt with fire; for strong is the Lord God who judgeth her.

Vs. 5-8.—"Her sins have reached unto heaven," and now she is to be visited with condign punishment; although it seemed both to her and God's own people long delayed. "God hath remembered her iniquities." There is reference to ancient Babylon's punishment, and the law of retaliation. (Jer. l. 15; Ps. cxxxvii. 8; Is. xlvii. 1-8.) Her punishment is destruction from the Almighty": "strong is the Lord God who judgeth her."

9. And the kings of the earth who have committed fornication and lived deliciously with her, shall bewail her, and lament for her, when they shall see the smoke of her burning.
10. Standing afar off, for the fear of her torment, saying, Alas, alas, that great city Babylon, that mighty city! for in one hour is thy judgment come.
11. And the merchants of the earth shall weep and mourn over her; for no man buyeth their merchandise any more.
12. The merchandise of gold, and silver, and precious stones, and of pearls, and fine linen, and purple, and silk, and scarlet and all thyine wood, and all manner of vessels of ivory, and all manner vessels of most precious wood, and of brass, and iron, and marble.
13. And cinnamon, and odours, and ointments, and frankincense, and wine, and oil, and fine flour, and wheat, and beasts, and sheep, and horses, and chariots, and slaves, and souls of men.
14. And the fruits that thy soul lusted after are departed from thee, and all things which were dainty and goodly are departed from thee, and thou shalt find them no more at all.
15. The merchants of these things, which were made rich by her, shall stand afar off, for the fear of her torment, weeping and wailing,
16. And saying, Alas, alas! that great city, that was clothed in fine linen, and purple, and scarlet, and decked with gold, and precious stones, and pearls!
17. For in one hour so great riches is come to naught. And every ship master, and all the company in ships, and sailors, and as many as trade by sea, stood afar off,

18. And cried, when they saw the smoke of her burning, saying, What city is like unto this great city?
19. And they cast dust on their heads, and cried, weeping and wailing, saying, Alas, alas! that great city, wherein were made rich all that had ships in the sea, by reason of her costliness! for in one hour is she made desolate.

Vs. 9-19.—At the fall of Babylon some of the kings who had been her supporters, will lament for her while utterly unable to protect her, and afraid of partaking of her plagues. It may be proper to remark, that the word translated "alas," and repeated in this chapter, is the same in the Greek text as that which is rendered, "woe" in ch. viii. 13; from which fact we are to infer that the fall of mystical Babylon described in this chapter comes under the last three, or probably the seventh trumpet. That the Turkish empire is to be overthrown by the sixth trumpet or second woe, and gradually exhausted by the sixth vial, hardly admits of a doubt: but it does not necessarily follow, that said trumpet and vial are to terminate when that judgment ends. Each trumpet and vial may continue its effects for some time after the following one commences.—Kings, merchants and shipmasters are mentioned as chief mourners, while they are helpless spectators of this judgment. In all this narrative there is plain allusion to the language of Old Testament prophets who predicted the destruction of the enemies of God's people; as Babylon, Tyre, Egypt. All these powerful kingdoms have been made desolate for their idolatry and cruelty; and thus history comes in aid of prophecy to confirm the faith of the saints. The moral government of the Most High is uniform, and he will execute vengeance upon his and Zion's impenitent enemies. The merchandise and lamentations are borrowed from Ezek. xxvii. In ver. 13 there is mention made of "the persons of men" as part of the wares in the markets of Tyre, and we find "slaves (*bodies*) and souls of men," among the commodities for sale in modern Babylon. How can we, in view of historic facts, exempt the United States of North America from complicity in the crimes of mystic Babylon as one of her dependencies? While earthly politicians, sustained by eminent divines, proclaimed to the world in gushing oratory that "America was an asylum for the oppressed of all nations,"—"the land of the free, and the home of the brave;" perhaps there never was a more effectual refutation of this popular sentiment, accompanied with a more biting sarcasm, than that which was uttered in derisive song by the sable, coffled chain-gang in the streets of the national capital,—"Hail! Columbia, happy land!"—All who are acquainted with the internal and political history of the United States, know that the adherents of the "Man of Sin" always gave their suffrages for the support and continuance of that cursed traffic.

The great variety of the articles of merchandise here enumerated, is calculated to impress the reader with the idea of the wealth, luxury, splendor, and self-indulgence of the metropolis of the idolatrous Roman empire, the "mother and mistress of all churches."—The prophetic declaration, however,—"with feigned words shall they make merchandise of you," (2 Pet. ii. 3,) is not confined to the Romish communion. This traffic, in *souls*, pervades all the streets of symbolic Babylon.—The overthrow is sudden and unexpected,—"in one hour." This is thrice repeated, (vs. 10, 17, 19.) In v. 18 this "spiritual Sodom" is compared to her prototype in her fearful end. "They saw the smoke of her burning." (Gen. xix. 28.)

> 20. *Rejoice over her, thou heaven, and ye holy apostles and prophets; for God hath avenged you on her.*

V. 20.—Judgments on the impenitent enemies of God and of the saints, are mercies to the church. (Ps. cxxxvi. 15-20;) and consequently, while the former are lamenting for the fall of the great city, the latter are exhorted to rejoice in her ruin,—all the members of the church in general, and "holy apostles and prophets" in particular. The apostles are daily worshipped at Rome in their supposed likenesses, the work of the "cunning artificer"; but here they are mentioned as rejoicing in the destruction of the idolatrous sinners who so greatly *dishonoured* them, and detracted from the glory of God.—As "there is joy in heaven over one sinner that repenteth," so is there over the destruction of the impenitent. (Jer. li. 48.) "So let all thine enemies perish, O Lord." (Judges v. 31.)

> 21. *And a mighty angel took up a stone like a great millstone, and cast it into the sea, saying, Thus with violence shall that great city Babylon be thrown down, and shall be found no more at all.*

22. And the voice of harpers, and musicians, and of pipers, and trumpeters, shall be heard no more at all in thee; and no craftsman, of whatsoever craft he be, shall be found any more in thee; and the sound of a millstone shall be heard no more at all in thee;
23. And the light of a candle shall shine no more at all in thee; and the voice of the bridegroom and of the bride shall be heard no more at all in thee: for thy merchants were the great men of the earth; for by thy sorceries were all nations deceived.

Vs. 21-23.—The emblem of "a great millstone cast into the sea," is a very striking indication of the sudden and irretrievable ruin of mystic Babylon, and contains an allusion to Jer. li. 63, 64.—The removal of "musicians, craftsmen, candles, etc.," from this devoted city, as they plainly point to the statuary, music and paintings which have attracted multitudes to the idolatry, superstition and harlotry of antichristian Rome, emphatically proclaims the utter and perpetual desolation of papal Rome. The language is borrowed from Isa. xxiv. 8; Jer. xxv. 10; Ezek. xxvi. 13.—Her merchants being the "great men of the earth," and the "sorceries" by "which the nations were deceived, very plainly indicate the successful traffic of the "mother of harlots,"—the church of Rome.

24. And in her was found the blood of prophets and of saints, and of all that were slain upon the earth.

V. 24.—When the Lord "maketh inquisition for blood," the "blood of all that were slain upon the earth,"—*for Christ's sake*, will be found in the skirts of this Jezebel. Papal Rome has shed more innocent blood than pagan Rome; than Babylon, Tyre and Egypt; and by her relentless cruelty to "prophets and saints," ministers and members of the witnessing church, she has endorsed all the murderous persecutions from Abel down to the present day. (Luke xi. 50, 51; Acts vii. 52.)—Now when we contemplate in the light of prophecy, confirmed by authentic history, the numberless, aggravated and long-continued crimes of Babylon the great, her pride, (v. 7,) her cruelty, (v. 3,) her luxury, her tyranny, her idolatry, her fornication, her impenitence in all,—can we hesitate to acquiesce in the righteousness of her final doom, or to join in the plaudits of the saints in the next chapter?

CHAPTER XIX.

1. *And after these things, I heard a great voice of much people in heaven, saying, Alleluia; Salvation, and glory, and honour, and power, unto the Lord our God:*
2. *For true and righteous are his judgments: for he hath judged the great whore, which did corrupt the earth with her fornication, and hath avenged the blood of his servants at her hand.*
3. *And again they said, Alleluia. And her smoke rose up for ever and ever.*
4. *And the four and twenty elders and the four beasts fell down and worshipped God that sat on the throne, saying, Amen; Alleluia.*

Vs. 1-4.—The frequent repetition of the Hebrew word "Alleluia" in this chapter, may perhaps be an intimation of something which specially relates to the Jews. The perpetuity of the covenant made with Abraham, renewed to Isaac, and confirmed to Jacob, (Ps. cv. 9, 10,) is clearly taught in the Scriptures. (Gen. xvii. 7; Acts ii. 39; Rom. iv. 13; Gal. iii. 14, 29.)

It has been already intimated, (ch. xi. 15,) that at the sounding of the seventh trumpet, "there were great voices in heaven, saying, The kingdoms of this world are become *the kingdoms* of our Lord and of his Christ; and he (Christ,) shall reign for ever and ever." Beholding the overthrow of Babylon, all the people of God were invited, (ch. xviii. 20,) to "rejoice over her," for her downfall was effected under the last trumpet and vial. With that invitation the saints here joyfully comply. "*Much people* in heaven," implies a great augmentation of their number, and as "heaven" signifies the church on earth, we are warranted to expect a rapid increase of her membership as the consequence of the sounding of the seventh trumpet.—At the pouring out of the third vial, (ch. xvi. 7,) the angel of the altar said, "True and righteous are thy judgments." The very same sentiment is repeated here by the "much people,"—all the saints. Thus they recognise the faithfulness and justice of God, as he heard and answered the cry of the "souls under the altar;" (ch. vi. 9, 10,) for he had now "avenged their blood" and that of their "brethren that had been killed as they were," upon them that dwell on the earth,—the population of mystic Babylon. (Ps. cxxxvii. 8, 9.) "And again they said, Alleluia; and her smoke rose up for ever and ever," like that of Sodom. In all this, the ministry and members of the whole church cordially join, adding their hearty and solemn "Amen!"

For this protracted joy and exulting praise, two causes seem to be in operation, God's judgment on Babylon, and his mercy on Zion. Both are matter of praise. (Ps. ci. 1.)

5. *And a voice came out of the throne, saying, Praise our God, all ye his servants, and ye that fear him, both small and great.*
6. *And I heard as it were the voice of a great multitude, and as the voice of many waters, and as the voice of mighty thunderings, saying, Alleluia: for the Lord God Omnipotent reigneth.*
7. *Let us be glad and rejoice, and give honour to him; for the marriage of the Lamb is come, and his wife hath made herself ready.*
8. *And to her was granted, that she should be arrayed in fine linen, clean and white; for the fine linen is the righteousness of saints.*
9. *And he saith unto me, Write, Blessed are they which are called unto the marriage supper of the Lamb. And he saith unto me, These are the true sayings of God.*

Vs. 5-9.—This happy company are called upon to renew their song. The call seems to come from some one who is authorized to speak with authority, "out of the throne." All the servants of God are invited, and all appear to respond, "a great multitude." This is the most animated of all the examples of praise recorded in this book. It is compared to the rushing of waters down a cataract, as the roaring of the sea, or the rolling of thunder in the heavens. It is indeed the "voice of them that shout for mastery,"—and "all the people shout with a great shout, for the Lord hath given them the city,"—"Alleluia, *praise ye the Lord*, for the Lord God omnipotent reigneth." "Thou wilt perform the truth to Jacob, and the mercy to Abraham, which thou hast sworn unto our fathers from the days of old."—These joyful victors encourage each other to prolong their acclamations:—"Let us be glad and rejoice," ... "for the marriage of the Lamb is come:" and what can that be, but the recalling of the Jews? This is the day of our New Testament Solomon's espousals, and the day of the gladness of his heart. (Song iii. 11.)—Not only the Jews, but the great majority of professing Christians during the 1260 years of Antichrist's usurpations, have refused to "submit themselves to the righteousness of God." (Rom. x. 3.) The kings of the earth also have fostered the pride and profligacy of the great whore, instead of the bride of the Lamb. The lewd woman, and the woman in the wilderness hitherto, are now to be distinguished. As their character and conduct are different, so is their raiment. The gaudy and splendid attire of the former, is in striking contrast with that of the latter; which is that of a "woman professing godliness," (ch. xvii. 4; 1 Tim. ii. 10.)—"To her was granted,"—Precious words; for the "Lamb's wife of herself was utterly destitute," (ch. iii. 17.) The Jews, in the day of their Messiah's power, (Psa. cx. 3,) convinced of the law as transgressors, will be brought to adopt the language of their own prophet, (Is. lxi. 10;) "he hath clothed me with the garments of salvation, he hath covered me with the robe of righteousness." The righteousness of Christ imputed for justification, and the Spirit of Christ imparted for sanctification, together with good works, the visible evidence of both, will constitute the "fine linen, clean and white, which is the righteousness of saints." This is, after all, a more *costly*, as well as more comely attire, than that of the mother of harlots. (Ps. xlv. 13, 14.)—"And he saith."—That is, say some, the angel, (ch. xvii. 1, 7; or ch. xviii. 1;) but we are rather to view him as the same who brings all these messages from Christ to the apostle, (ch. i. 1.) The angel pronounces those "blessed who are called to the marriage supper of the Lamb."—In the beginning of the New Testament dispensation, the invitation was to a *dinner*. (Matt. xxii. 4.) The day will have been far spent at the sounding of the seventh trumpet, when Jews and Gentiles are called to this supper. It will be the last *great feast* of the church militant. But who shall live to partake of the banquet? The angel gives his solemn attestation to "these sayings."

> 10. And I fell at his feet to worship him. And he said unto me, See thou do it not; I am thy fellow-servant, and of thy brethren that have the testimony of Jesus. Worship God: for the testimony of Jesus is the spirit of prophecy.

V. 10.—This is a surprising incident,—an aged, experienced and holy man, an apostle, "falling down to worship the angel!" And we are told that he relapsed into the same sin, (ch. xxii. 8, 9.) Like Peter on the mount, who "wist not what to say;" or Paul in the "third heaven ...

whether in the body or out of the body, he could not tell." (Mark ix. 6; 2 Cor. xii. 3.) John had become overpowered by the visions and transported by the high praises which he saw and heard. The like effects were experienced by Daniel, (viii. 18; x. 8, 17.)—This sin of idolatry by the apostle was doubtless permitted by the Lord, in order to furnish occasion for a testimony from the angel, against the "voluntary humility and worshipping of angels," (Col. ii. 18;) practised by the Papists, and to leave them without excuse.—The abrupt language of the angel in this and a subsequent case, is strongly expressive of resentment:—"See—not." Such is the *curt, sententious* utterance in the Greek text. He assigns the best reason and strongest argument against idolatry:—"I am thy fellow-servant," a creature as well as yourself: we are servants of one Lord, who alone is the object of our devotion, "Worship God." This is the best counsel, enforced by the most cogent reasoning,—"For the testimony of Jesus is the Spirit of prophecy." This sentence may be read,—"The Spirit of prophecy is the testimony of Jesus;" and it will be equally true. "To him give all the prophets witness," (Acts x. 43;) for "the Spirit of Christ was in them;" (1 Pet. i. 11;) and this fact is well known to holy angels. (Eph. iii. 10; 1 Pet. i. 12.) So this angel plainly declares.

11. And I saw heaven opened, and, behold, a white horse: and he that sat upon him was called Faithful and True: and in righteousness he doth judge and make war.
12. His eyes were as a flame of fire, and on his head were many crowns: and he had a name written, that no man knew but he himself.
13. And he was clothed with a vesture dipped in blood: and his name is called The Word of God.
14. And the armies which were in heaven followed him upon white horses, clothed in fine linen, white and clean.
15. And out of his mouth goeth a sharp sword, that with it he should smite the nations, and he shall rule them with a rod of iron: and he treadeth the wine-press of the fierceness and wrath of Almighty God.
16. And he hath on his vesture, and on his thigh a name written, KING OF KINGS, AND LORD OF LORDS.

Vs. 11-16.—"Heaven opened" once more, allows the apostle to look upon Messiah the Prince going forth to fresh conquests. As he began, (ch. vi. 2,) so he continues, "in righteousness to judge and make war;"

not as the ambitious tyrants who "destroy the earth," (ch. xi. 18.) He has here three names,—"Faithful and True, The Word of God, king of kings and Lord of lords; yet he has a "name written which no man knoweth but he himself."—His infinite essence and eternal generation are incomprehensible by angels and men.—He is, however, known by his mediatorial titles,—"faithful and true" to all covenant engagements; as the prophet of the church, he "declares the Father," making known the "word of God;" and his lordship is at once a warning to his enemies and security to his friends.—"On his head were many crowns," emblematical of his numerous victories over the princes of the earth, especially the "ten kings," (ch. xvii. 14.)—"His eyes as a flame of fire," going though the whole earth "in every place," (Prov. xv. 3;) render it impossible for his enemies to elude discovery. (Jer. xxiii. 24.)—His "vesture dipped in blood," refers to his victories over all his malicious and impenitent foes. (Is. lxiii. 1-3; Rev. xiv. 20.)—His "armies on white horses, clothed in fine linen, white and clean," are uniformed like their leader, (ch. xii. 7;) for "they that are with him are called, and chosen, and faithful," (ch. xvii. 14.)—The weapon with which he "smites the nations" that oppose him, is the "sharp sword," an emblem of his ruinous and avenging justice; for he "tradeth the wine-press of the fierceness and wrath of Almighty God."—"On his thigh," where he wears his sword, there is a legible inscription, indicating his universal and rightful authority.

17. And I saw an angel standing in the sun; and he cried with a loud voice, saying to all the fowls that fly in the midst of heaven, Come and gather yourselves together unto the supper of the great God;
18. That ye may eat the flesh of kings, and the flesh of captains, and the flesh of mighty men, and the flesh of horses and of them that sit on them, and the flesh of all men, both free and bond, both small and great.
19. And I saw the beast, and the kings of the earth, and their armies, gathered together to make war against him that sat on the horse, and against his army.
20. And the beast was taken, and with him the false prophet that wrought miracles before him, with which he deceived them that had received the mark of the beast, and them that worshipped his image. These both were cast alive into a lake of fire, burning with brimstone.

21. *And the remnant were slain with the sword of him that sat upon the horse, which sword proceeded out of his mouth: and all the fowls were filled with their flesh.*

Vs. 17-21.—The position of the "angel standing in the sun," and "crying with a loud voice;" represents, that Messiah's judgments would be visible to all the world; and the extent of the invitation to the "fowls," indicates the vast slaughter of his enemies. Babylon being "utterly burned with fire," (ch. xvii. 16, xviii. 8,) as a suitable punishment of an apostate church; the "flesh of kings, of captains, of mighty men," etc., as a sacrifice to divine justice, is given as a feast to the fowls of heaven. The allusion here is to the destruction of "Gog and Magog." (Ezek. xxxix. 17-20.) These enemies of the saints are to appear and be overthrown before the millennium; and although John borrows the names of these enemies, (ch. xx. 8,) they are not the same as those of Ezekiel; the one appearing *before*, the other *after* the thousand years. We have often found the enemies of the church called in the Apocalypse by the names of persecutors under the Old Testament;—Babylon, Egypt, etc.—We may consider the "fowls," the birds of prey, as symbolizing the kings who retaliate upon Babylon; (as in ch. xvii. 16;) or rather, as the Lord's people reclaiming their own, of which they had been unjustly and long deprived,—"spoiling the Egyptians." (Exod. xii. 36.)

Some suppose that the confederacy of the "kings of the earth" with the beast, (v. 19,) is a distinct attack from that mentioned in chapter seventeenth; (v. 14;) but perhaps it is safer to consider it as the same, only more distinctly and fully exhibited here. Indeed it seems, from the agency of the "false prophet," to be the same event as that under the sixth vial, (ch. xvi. 14;) preparing to the battle of Armageddon. The Lord Jesus as "captain of the Lord's hosts," and the army of heaven following him, all of them on white horses, appear to be on the one side; and the beast with the kings of the earth, instigated by the false prophet, on the other. The rank and file like their leaders are described as having "received the mark of the beast and worshiped his image." But the beast of the earth, (ch. iii. 11,) causes all ranks to receive the mark, and worship the image of the beast, (vs. 15, 16) The beast of the earth, the woman, and the false prophet, all mean the same thing; and that is, an apostate church in alliance with tyrannical civil powers, (ch. xvii. 3.) Now, if the great city Babylon, a symbol which comprises the whole antichristian confederacy, has been utterly destroyed, as appears in the eighteenth chapter, whence come these enemies bearing the same characters? The only solution of this apparent difficulty is by supposing as we have done, that this is a re-exhibition of what has been more obscurely symbolized, (ch. xiv. 20; xvi. 17; xvii. 16; xviii. 2, 8, 20,) in order more distinctly to point out the end of two principal leaders,—the "beast and the false prophet," the empire and church of Rome. "These both were cast alive into a lake of fire burning with brimstone."—"The remnant were slain." When the leaders were discomfited, the ranks were soon broken, and the whole army melted away. They were slain with Messiah's sword, the emblem of his justice, (ch. i. 16.)

Thus "Babylon is fallen, to rise no more at all:" all the visible enemies of the Lord and his Anointed are cut off from the face of the earth: and it remains only that he who originated the rebellious conspiracy be put under necessary restraint.

CHAPTER XX.

1. And I saw an angel come down from heaven, having the key of the bottomless pit and a great chain in his hand.
2. And he laid hold on the dragon, that old serpent, which is the devil, and Satan, and bound him a thousand years.
3. And cast him into the bottomless pit, and shut him up, and set a seal upon him, that he should deceive the nations no more, till the thousand years should be fulfilled: and after that, he must be loosed a little season.

Vs. 1-3.—"And I saw an angel." This angel is the Lord Christ, (ch. x. 1.) The key is the symbol of authority. (Is. xxii. 22; chs. i. 18; iii. 7.) The dragon had been previously cast down from heaven, (ch. xii. 9;) by the Reformation, and during the "short time" of his liberty, he persecuted the woman and the remnant of her seed, on the earth. Now, however, his career is arrested. "Seizing, binding, casting into the abyss, shutting up, and setting a seal upon that old serpent," (ch. xii. 9,) are strong figurative expressions, by which his secure confinement is signified. Thus is the devil to be restrained from deceiving the nations for a "thousand years." That this period is to be taken in a proper, and not in a mystical sense, appears thus. If we multiply one thousand by three hundred and sixty, as some fancifully do, the resulting number of years, three hundred and sixty thousand, would be out of all proportion to the past duration of the world, as well as the well-defined period of 1260 years. Add to this, that when by Daniel and John definite duration is symbolically mentioned, it is by "months, days; time, times and a half a time," or "the dividing of time,"—never by "years."

At the expiration of the thousand years, Satan will be loosed a "little season,"—*little*, as compared with the thousand years; so little, as not to be deemed worth estimating.

4. *And I saw thrones, and they sat upon them, and judgment was given unto them: and I saw the souls of them that were beheaded for the witness of Jesus, and for the word of God, and which had not worshipped the beast, neither his image, neither had received his mark upon their foreheads, or in their hands: and they lived and reigned with Christ a thousand years.*

V. 4.—"And I saw thrones." Here there is no mention of *heaven being opened*. Nothing henceforth obstructs John's vision. "The darkness is past, and the true light now shineth."—"At evening time it shall be light." (Zech. xiv. 7.)—"And they sat on them." Who?—There is here what may be termed a remarkable chasm in the language of the text. There is no visible or proximate antecedent. Who are they who "sit on thrones?" Did Millenarians only put this question, and patiently search for the solution in the context, agreeably to the *allegorical texture* of this whole book, all their hallucinations might be easily and happily obviated. The inspired writer assumes, of course, that the reader will readily identify these persons, who are thus promoted to honour, now that Antichrist is no more, and society is to be reorganized.—Daniel furnishes a satisfactory answer to our question. "I beheld till the thrones were cast down." (Dan. vii. 9.) The Roman imperial thrones of *civil despotism* were subverted. Again,—"But the judgment shall sit, and they shall take away his dominion, to consume and to destroy it unto the end." (v. 26.) The Roman imperial *throne* of ecclesiastical domination shall be destroyed. Then when Messiah "shall have put down all rule, and all authority and power," of both sorts of tyranny, "the kingdom and dominion, and the greatness of the kingdom under the whole heaven, shall be given to the people of the saints of the Most High, whose kingdom is an everlasting kingdom, and all dominions, (*rulers*) shall serve and obey him," (v. 27.) The "saints of the Most High," according to Daniel, are to be exalted to civil rule, and these are the same whom John saw "sitting on thrones." Now, the effect of the seventh trumpet becomes a fact in history.—"The kingdoms of this world," which had been controlled by the beast, and bewitched by the sorceries of the lewd woman, "are become the kingdoms of our Lord and of his Christ."—For in the millennial state of the world, there will be a *plurality of kingdoms.*—Hence a very common petition of pious but ignorant people,—"That the kingdoms of this world may soon become the kingdom of our Lord and Saviour Jesus Christ," neither will, nor ever can be answered.—Under the righteous and benign administration of the saints, "kings shall be nursing-fathers, and their queens nursing-mothers to the church:" for "the nations and kingdoms that would not *serve her*, have perished; yea, those nations have been utterly wasted." (Is. xlix. 23; lx. 12.)—The souls which the apostle saw under the altar, whose cry for vengeance he heard, and who were directed to rest for a little season, till the roll of their martyred brethren should be completed, are here presented in quite a new position, "sitting on thrones," (ch. vi. 9.) Although they are not the same identical persons *physically*, they are the same *morally*; for the life of the two witnesses is commensurate with the reign of Antichrist,—twelve hundred and sixty years. These "lived and reigned with Christ a thousand years; that is, in their successive generations: for otherwise they would over-live the age of Methuselah!—Souls are here evidently persons, and not souls as distinct from bodies, as some needlessly argue against Millenarians: for "foreheads" and "hands" are attributed to them: but foreheads cannot be literally ascribed to those who had been "beheaded." Their living is to be understood of their succeeding to the same scriptural position occupied by their predecessors, as well as succeeding them in the order of natural generation. The Holy Spirit says, "Levi, who receiveth tithes, paid tithes in Abraham." (Heb. vii. 9, 10.) Elijah reappeared in the person of John the Baptist. (Matt. xi. 14.) Jezebel and Balaam were recognised in their wicked successors, (ch. ii. 14, 20.) But this is the very structure of the Apocalypse, being composed of hieroglyphics, that the free agency of the wicked might be left untrammelled, and the diligence of God's people might be tested in "searching the Scriptures."

> 5. But the rest of the dead lived not again until the thousand years were finished. This is the first resurrection.

V. 5.—"The rest of the dead" supposes two classes of the dead. These are the witnesses, who died a violent and cruel death, and the wicked, who died a natural death,—there "were no bands in their death." As there are *two kinds* of death, so are there two kinds of resurrection,—a *first* and *second* of each. Those who had been "beheaded for the witness of Jesus," etc., lived in their successors,—sat on thrones, reigned with Christ a thousand years. Of course those who were slain by Christ and his army at the battle of Armageddon, and whose flesh was given to the fowls of heaven, "lived not again" in their successors, "until the thousand years were finished." Consequently, "this is the first resurrection," with which the true disciples of Christ shall be honoured. They must, however, die as all others, and await the *second* resurrection: but "on them the second death shall have no power."

> 6. *Blessed and holy is he that hath part in the first resurrection; on such the second death hath no power; but they shall be priests of God and of Christ, and shall reign with him a thousand years.*

V. 6.—"Blessed and holy,"—and blessed, because *holy*; for sin is the procuring cause of misery. This is a summary description of the millennial period. The dragon being bound by the almighty power of Christ, and not permitted to deceive the nations, wars shall cease unto the ends of all the earth: the population of the globe must be rapidly and greatly multiplied beyond all precedent. (Ps. xlvi. 9; lxxii. 16,) the life of man will be prolonged; (Isa. lxv. 20-25,) holiness, righteousness and praise shall spring forth before all the nations, (lxi. 11.)

That condition of our globe, which divines call the *millennium*,—a state of holiness and happiness, second only to the enjoyment of heavenly felicity, is as clearly and frequently promised to God's people, as the promise of the Messiah was under the former economy. But as many were "in expectation that the kingdom of God should immediately appear," who then entertained unwarrantable and carnal conceptions of the Messiah's person and reign, just such groundless and gross expectations and aspirations are cherished now. A literal resurrection of *all* the righteous, who shall have died before the millennium is supposed to take place at the personal appearance of Christ; and this, too, before the general judgment. By *personal*, they mean *corporeal*: for the Lord Christ promised his gracious *personal* presence with his people *all days*, when he was about to disappear from their bodily vision. (Matt. xxviii. 20.) "To them that look for him shall he appear the *second* time, (not a *third*,) without sin unto salvation." (Heb. ix. 28; Rev. i. 7.) Besides, is it for a moment supposable that saints who have passed into glory, are to be brought upon earth to conflict once more with enemies, when Gog and Magog shall surround the "camp of the saints?" Such is a specimen of questions suggested by the *Millenarian system*, which have failed of either scriptural or rational solution by all the learning and ingenuity of its fanciful advocates.

The whole series of the Apocalypse proves that the *two witnesses* live and prophesy throughout the 1260 years of Antichrist's reign. Their lives and their testimony end together, (ch. xi. 7.) But the beast that slays them is himself with his ally, the false prophet, at the close of the contest, cast alive into the lake of fire, (ch. xix. 20.)

After three and a half prophetical days, the witnesses are raised, and ascend up to heaven, (ch. xi. 12;) and this is the identical fact which is more fully presented here in the 20th chapter. The resurrection of the witnesses in the 11th chapter is a spiritual and mystical resurrection in the persons of their successors; the heaven to which they were exalted is a mystical heaven: and just so of those beheaded and advanced, after their resurrection, to positions of civil and ecclesiastic power as in this 20th chapter. Thus exalted, and ruling in the fear of God, they become a terror to evil doers, and a praise to them that do well. (Rom. xiii. 3.) Then shall be realized the glorious predictions of Isaiah and the Sweet Psalmist of Israel. (Isa. xi. 1-9; Ps. lxxii. 1)

7. *And when the thousand years are expired, Satan shall be loosed out of his prison.*
8. *And shall go out to deceive the nations which are in the four quarters of the earth, Gog and Magog, to gather them together to battle: the number of whom is as the sand of the sea.*
9. *And they went up on the breadth of the earth, and compassed the camp of the saints about, and the beloved city: and fire came down from God out of heaven, and devoured them.*

Vs. 7-9.—"Satan shall be loosed out of his prison."—The Lord Christ will remove the restraint which had repressed the chief enemy during the thousand years, that the Faithful and True Witness may give a final testimony to the moral universe, that neither the philosophy of proud man, nor the law of Moses,—no, nor the ordinances of the gospel, will ever change the nature of a sinner:—That neither judgments nor mercies have any efficacy to subdue the stubborn will, or renew the desperately wicked heart of man; and that it is a righteous thing with God to render tribulation to them that trouble his saints and insult his Majesty.

Thus released "for a little season," the prime enemy goes out as before to "deceive the nations." He is successful. "The rest of the dead," who lived not again during the 1000 years, at once re-appear in the persons of their genuine successors. They are the children of them that killed the witnesses;—the seed of the serpent aiming a last fatal stroke at the seed of the woman.—They are called "Gog and Magog;" and because of the identity of names, many have supposed them to be the same as those enemies of the people of God described by Ezekiel, (chs. xxxviii., xxxix.) This view is, however, without sanction in the Scriptures. The characters are mystical according to the uniform structure of the Apocalypse. Ezekiel's Gog and Magog come from the "north quarters;" those of John from the "four quarters or corners of the earth." It is also probable, if not absolutely certain, that the enemies predicted by Ezekiel are to appear before, while those of John are to arise after the millennium. The overthrow of Gog and Magog, foretold by Ezekiel, is evidently connected with the conversion of the Jews, (ch. xxxix. 22, 29;) but that event must precede the millennial period. (Rom. xi. 26.)—Magog is reckoned with Meshech and Tubal among the sons of Japheth, (Gen. x. 2;) and those nations called in history Scythians and Tartars, in the "north quarters" of Europe and Asia, as well as the "isles of the Gentiles," are supposed to be their descendants. By the "three unclean spirits," (ch. xvi. 13,) a confederacy was effected under the sixth vial to the battle of Armageddon; and the same is again presented in ch. xix. 20, as the final attempt against the saints previously to the millennium, when two of the prime instigators, the beast and the false prophet, are cast into the lake of fire. Thus we may suppose *eastern* and *western* Antichrist finally destroyed.

Ezekiel's Gog and Magog being slain in the battle of Armageddon, how or where shall we find those of John? They are to be found precisely on the same principle on which we find the witnesses of Christ in this chapter. Satan is loosed "a little season,"— *little* as compared with the thousand years of Messiah's reign; or rather, as compared with the 1260 years of the dragon's successful enterprises against the saints through the beast and false prophet as agents. These being now cast into the lake of fire, Satan is for ever deprived of their agency. During the millennial period people will be born in sin as at other times; and at the close of that happy period, Almighty God will display his sovereignty by withholding his grace, that a last demonstration may be given to all the world of the necessity and efficacy of that grace in changing the heart of a sinner. Without the intervention of the beast or the false prophet, Satan will prevail by more direct temptations to gather together to battle a multitude of the *same spirit* as Ezekiel's Gog and Magog displayed against the saints before the millennium. These are the "rest of the dead that lived not again till the one thousand years were finished." As the "deadly wound" of the civil beast "was healed," and he received a new life, to the astonishment of spectators, (ch. xiii. 3,) as the witnesses received "the Spirit of life from God," to the dismay of their enemies; (chs. xi. 11; xx. 4,) so Gog and Magog re-appear in the persons and bloody cruelties of their genuine successors. And in language similar to that in the context we may warrantably say,—this is the *second resurrection*; for when it is declared that the "rest of the dead lived not again," it is manifest that two classes of dead are intended. All are said to be dead; the witnesses, slain by the beast; their enemies, slain by the Lord. The witnesses rise, and "this is the first resurrection." A *first* implies a *second of the same kind*. Well, "the rest lived not again till the thousand years were finished." What then? Why, simply this,—that the other remaining class of the dead *lived again*; and this appears to be the obvious scope and meaning of these terms, so vexing to many critics.

By deception Satan prevails to assemble the nations in vast multitudes, "as the sand of the sea,"—a proverbial form of expression applied to Abraham's seed. (Gen. xxii. 17.) "They went up on the breadth of the earth." Coming from the "four quarters of the earth," they "compassed the camp of the saints." The allusion here is twofold: to Israel in the wilderness, in the time of Moses; and to the holy city Jerusalem, in the days of David; (Ps. cxviii. 10-12,) for often did the enemy with "joint heart" attempt to "cut off the name of Israel." (Ps. lxxxiii. 4-8.) Never was Pharaoh or Sennacherib more confident of a sure and easy victory over the saints. (Exod. xv. 9; Isa. xxxvi. 20.) As in the days of Noah, most of the generation of the righteous had been taken home to glory before the ungodly were destroyed by the deluge, so we may suppose the "camp of the saints" to be but a "little flock," when assailed for the last time, while they are in a militant state.—The issue in this case, however, will be more decisive and glorious than any other battle with the powers of darkness. We may adopt and apply the words of the prophet to God's people in the time of Jehoshaphat:—"Thus saith the Lord,—Be not afraid nor dismayed by reason of this great multitude; for the battle is not yours, but God's. Ye shall not need to fight in this battle." (2 Chron. xx. 15, 17.)—"Fire came down from God out of heaven, and devoured" this great multitude. This most dreadful of all elements in the material universe, is that which is commonly employed to represent the wrath of God. By it Sodom and Gomorrah were destroyed, Corah and his rebellious company, the captains and their fifties; fire proceeded out of the mouth of the two witnesses and devoured their enemies; Gog and Magog are consumed by this element; the heavens and the earth which are now, are reserved unto fire; the Lord Jesus shall be revealed from heaven ... in flaming fire, taking vengeance on them that know not God, and that obey not the gospel,—most probably *these very enemies*; and all such are to be consigned to "the fire that never shall be quenched." Awful thought! Tremendous destiny! Who would not fear thee, O Lord; who art a consuming fire to all thy impenitent enemies?

> 10. *And the devil that deceived them was cast into the lake of fire and brimstone, where the beast and the false prophet are, and shall be tormented day and night for ever and ever.*

V. 10.—The *first* rebel against the righteous authority of the Lord and his Anointed, and the ceaseless instigator of all rebellions of individual and social man, is the *last* to be consigned to adequate punishment. When the Lord first called sinners to account, the same order is noticeable: First, Adam, then Eve, and last the serpent. The beast and the false prophet are already in the lake of fire; (ch. xix. 20;) and now, Satan, who is here called the devil, is dismissed after them, that they may all be tormented "for ever and ever,"—words, as already noticed, which are the strongest in the Greek language, to convey to the human mind the idea of *endless duration*.

> 11. *And I saw a great white throne, and him that sat on it, from whose face the earth and the heaven fled away; and there was found no place for them.*
> 12. *And I saw the dead, small and great, stand before God: and the books were opened; and another book was opened, which is the book of life: and the dead were judged out of those things which were written in the books according to their works.*

13. And the sea gave up the dead which were in it; and death and hell delivered up the dead which were in them: and they were judged every man according to their works.
14. And death and hell were cast into the lake of fire. This is the second death.
15. And whosoever was not found written in the book of life was cast into the lake of fire.

Vs. 11-15.—Nothing now remains to bring to a close the moral administration of Messiah, but the raising of the dead and pronouncing final sentence on all the subjects of his government. There is no intimation that any events shall intervene between the casting of the devil into the burning lake, and the appearing of the Judge.

The "great white throne" is suitable to the majesty and holiness of the Judge. He is not at first called by any name, for "every eye shall see," and seeing, recognise his divine dignity. In the next verse he is styled God, not to identify him, but as a matter of course in the narrative.—No sooner did the Judge take his seat, than "the earth and the heaven fled away." The simplicity and sublimity of this language are inimitable by human genius; and rarely if at all equalled, even by those who spake as they were moved by the Holy Ghost. The first inspired writer uses language very similar. (Gen. i. 3.) We are frequently and sufficiently taught that the Lord Christ in person is to be the judge of quick and dead. (Acts xvii. 31.) "All must appear before the judgment seat of Christ." (2 Cor. v. 10.) No person is competent to this work of judgment but one who is omniscient and omnipotent, not to speak of other divine perfections. The "Judge of all the earth" is a divine person, possessed of all the attributes of deity; and as there is not *now* among apostate angels, so there will not *then* be a child of Adam, to *deny the supreme deity of Jesus Christ.* (Matt. viii. 29.) Of this he gave intimation at the beginning of the Apocalypse:—"Every eye shall see him, and they also which pierced him," (ch. i. 7;) yes, they pierced him for *blasphemy,* "because that he, being a man, made himself God." (John x. 33.) Here the Judge on the throne demonstrates to an assembled universe, the scriptural warrant for the language of the Reformers when they say he is "very God, and very man." "God is judge himself," (Ps. l. 6,) in the person of the Father; but "he hath appointed a day in the which *he* will judge the world in righteousness, by that *man* whom he hath ordained."—(Acts xvii. 31.)

CHAPTER XX.

Before the righteous Judge "shall be gathered all nations," (Matt. xxv. 32,) all that have ever lived upon the earth, from the creation till the end of time, all ranks and degrees, however diversified by sex, age, or social position; righteous and wicked, Jews and Gentiles, Herod and Pontius Pilate, Cain and Abel, Judas, etc.

In order to this general assize, "the dead shall hear the voice of the Son of God," (John v. 25, 28, 29;) "and many of them that sleep in the dust of the earth shall awake, some to everlasting life, and some to shame and everlasting contempt." (Dan. xii. 2.) The "sea, death and hell," or the grave, (or rather, the place of souls as separated by death from their bodies,) which are thus awfully, but beautifully personified, shall surrender their respective tenants, that they may stand before the Son of man in judgment.—Only such as have died are mentioned here: but some will not die, but "remain alive unto the coming of the Lord," the judge; and these, it is probable, will be the "camp of the saints" which have been miraculously delivered from the rage of Gog and Magog, (vs. 8, 9.) There is a beautiful order in the final resurrection. "The dead in Christ shall rise first." (1 Thess. iv. 16; 1 Cor. xv. 23.) Next will be raised the wicked; for "like sheep they are laid in the grave; death shall feed on them, and the upright shall have dominion over them in the morning." (Ps. xlix. 14.) The dead, being all raised, those who shall be alive will undergo a change equivalent to death,—"in a moment, in the twinkling of an eye;" for these "shall not prevent (anticipate) them which were asleep;" that is, they will not be *changed* until their companions are called from the grave, etc. All being now "before the judgment seat of Christ,"—the "books are opened!" Oh, what emotions will swell and heave the bosoms of the righteous!—"joy unspeakable and full of glory:" for before the sentence of acquittal is publicly pronounced, their position on the Judge's right hand indicates the sentence. And next what terror insupportable will now seize the wicked! What "fearful looking-for of judgment and fiery indignation," when in breathless suspense, they await the just sentence,—"Depart from me, ye cursed, into everlasting fire, prepared for the devil and his angels!" (Matt. xxv. 41; Heb. x. 27.) The righteousness of this sentence will be attested by the "opened books,"—of the divine omniscience, the human conscience, and in the case of gospel-rejecters, the Bible. (2 Thess. i. 7, 8.) And the like condemnation would pass upon the righteous, but that "another book is opened," in which are inscribed the names of all the objects of God's electing love: and this will be the key-note in their songs of praise to all eternity. (Jer. xxxi. 3; Rev. i. 5.) All are "judged according to their works," as these are witnessed by the books,—for "their works do follow them," (ch. xiv. 13.)

"Death and hell were cast into the lake of fire." Death, or the grave; hell, or the separate state, will never again be needed, as prisons to keep their inmates for trial. "The lake of fire" is the place of ceaseless and endless torment for all who are not "found written in the book of life;" and this place seems to be distinct from the "bottomless pit," Satan's "prison," out of which he had been loosed, (v. 7.)—Of the beast it was said, he "ascendeth out of the bottomless pit," but not that he was remanded thither again: he is said to "go into perdition," which must be "the lake of fire." (Compare ch. xvii. 8, with xix. 20; and xx. 1-3 with v. 10.)—The plain and obvious meaning of these closing verses of the 20th chapter, as delineated in its general import by appropriate and familiar symbols and intelligible words, for ever excludes, and emphatically condemns the conscience-stupifying heresies and blasphemies of Unitarians and Universalists. The God-man Mediator, seated upon the "throne of his glory," before whose face the "earth and the heaven fled away," is thus evidenced to be the Son of God, Jehovah's Fellow. And we may here adopt the assertion and caution of the "beloved disciple,"—"This is the true God and eternal life.—Little children, keep yourselves from idols." (1 John v. 20, 21.)—Moreover, these verses reveal a place or state, more to be dreaded than the "killing of the body,"—"the lake of fire, which is the second death," "where their worm dieth not, and the fire is not quenched." (Matt. x. 28; 2 Thess. i. 8-10; Heb. x. 26-31.)

With the 20th chapter of the Apocalypse terminate the events of time, in which the divine Author demonstrates, that "known unto him are all his works, from the beginning of the world." (Acts xv. 18.) Many, indeed, of the learned and pious have supposed the remaining chapters of the Apocalypse, to be a description of the church on earth during the millennial period. But besides the series, coherence and dependence of the several parts of the book, precluding such *retrogression*, this interpretation overthrows the scriptural distinction between the militant and triumphant state of the church. And it is not to be thought out of place, that the inspired prophet should describe, by suitable emblems, the outline of the heavenly state; for this he has done briefly already in a number of instances. (See chs. ii. and iii., also ch. vii. 15, 17.)—Those who consider the last two chapters as a delineation of the church on earth, have first formed in their minds ideas of a corporeal or bodily presence of Christ, and of a literal and visible reign on the earth. Such views we have already shown to be without scripture warrant, yea against plain declarations of the Holy Spirit, (as Acts iii. 21; Matt. xvii. 11, 12; Heb. ix. 28.) Hence we shall contemplate the symbols of the following chapters,—except as incidents or allusions may render this incompatible,—as shadowing forth the glories of the church's heavenly state.

CHAPTER XXI.

1. And I saw a new heaven and a new earth: for the first heaven and the first earth were passed away; and there was no more sea.
2. And I John saw the holy city, new Jerusalem, coming down from God out of heaven, prepared as a bride adorned for her husband.
3. And I heard a great voice out of heaven, saying, Behold, the tabernacle of God is with men, and he will dwell with them, and they shall be his people, and God himself shall be with them, and be their God.
4. And God shall wipe away all tears from their eyes: and there shall be no more death, neither sorrow nor crying, neither shall there be any more pain: for the former things are passed away.
5. And he that sat upon the throne, said, Behold, I make all things new. And he said unto me, Write: for these words are true and faithful.
6. And he said unto me, It is done. I am Alpha and Omega, the beginning and the end: I will give unto him that is athirst, of the fountain of the water of life freely.
7. He that overcometh shall inherit all things: and I will be his God, and he shall be my son.

Vs. 1-7.—It is unquestionable that the phrase "new heavens and a new earth" is to be understood sometimes as descriptive of moral renovation in the world. As the moral change affected by grace in the character of an individual sinner is called a new creation, and is in truth no less, so in respect to a community. The analogy in this case is the same as between a revolution and an earthquake. Thus, we must understand Is. lxv. 17, lxvi. 22, of that great moral change which will characterize the millennium. But the "new heaven and the new earth" are here contrasted with the "first heaven and the first earth which were passed away," (ch. xx. 11.) The apostle Peter describes the very same grand and glorious change. Mingling the important facts of authentic history with the future facts of prophecy, he tells us that the "heavens and the earth which are now, ... are reserved unto fire."—He speaks obviously of the visible heavens and earth. These "heavens shall pass away ... and "the earth also, ... shall be burnt up." He adds,—"We look for new heavens and a new earth, wherein dwelleth righteousness." (2 Pet. iii. 7,

13.)—"There was no more sea," no more disorderly passions, animosities, arising from human depravity, to interrupt the delightful harmony and fellowship of saints in glory. It is estimated that about two thirds of this world are occupied by water. In that happy place occupied by the people of God, there is no sea; consequently, "yet there is room," many mansions, room enough for all the redeemed. "The holy city," compared to a "bride," two very incongruous emblems, shows the poverty of symbols, their inadequacy to represent the church triumphant: how then shall created objects furnish suitable emblems of the glorious and glorified Bridegroom? In vision the city seemed to the apostle as if suspended in the air on the same plane with himself; for now he stood neither on "the sand of the sea," (ch. xiii. 1,) for "there was no more sea," nor upon the earth, for it was "passed away." No intervening object could obstruct his view.—He heard a voice from heaven, saying, "Behold, the tabernacle of God is with men, and he will dwell with them," as his reconciled and beloved people. As a tender Father, he will "wipe away all tears from their eyes." "There shall be no more death," either of themselves or their beloved friends, to open the fountain of tears any more for ever. But death is the last enemy to be destroyed; (1 Cor. xv. 26;) how then can these words apply to any state short of immortality in heaven? "Neither sorrow nor crying,"—for sin or suffering; "neither shall there be any more pain," causing tears or cries: and what is this but heaven? Yes, "the former things are passed away." Now "he that hath the bride is the bridegroom," and she shall never be false to her marriage covenant any more.—"He that sat on the throne," denotes the Father most frequently in this book, as he is distinguished from the Son; but the Son "is set down with his Father in his throne," (ch. iii. 21;) and the Son is to be viewed as the person on the throne here, as the following words, compared with the twentieth chapter, verse eleventh, make evident.—He it is who "makes all things new." He left his disciples as to his bodily presence, and went to "prepare a place for them," (John xiv. 2;) and now he has come again and received them to himself, in fulfilment of his promise. Having sent the Holy Spirit to create them anew and to carry on to completion their sanctification, he now sees of the travail of his soul, the Father has given him his heart's desire, and hath not withholden the request of his lips. Now, all his ransomed ones are with him, in answer to his prayer, and also their own prayers, that they may behold his glory which the Father gave him. (Ps. xxi. 2; John xvii. 24; Phil. i. 23.)—The Lord Christ said to John,—"Write; for these words are true and faithful." And what has sustained the spirits, animated the hopes, and filled with exulting joy, the confessors, witnesses and martyrs of Jesus, but faith's realizing views of the King in his beauty, and the glories of Immanuel's land? For this peculiarity the disciples of Christ have been as speckled birds, men wondered at, in all generations.—"It is done," so he said at the pouring out of the seventh vial, (ch. xvi. 17;) when the final stroke was given to the antichristian enemies: but now these words import the completion of the whole counsel of the will of God, as carried into effect by the Captain of salvation, in bringing the beloved and adopted sons and daughters of the Father home to glory. (Heb. ii. 10.) He who is the "Alpha and Omega," is the "author and finisher of their faith."—Although the Lord Jesus has made of sinners "new creatures," prepared them as "vessels of mercy unto glory," and introduced them into heaven, they are *creatures* still, and necessarily dependent. They thirst for refreshment suited to their holy nature; and accordingly he gives of the "*fountain* of the water of life freely," for the *streams* of which they thirsted, "as the heart panteth for the water brooks," while they sojourned in a dry and parched land, far from their Father's house. Man's sin consisted in forsaking this "Fountain of living waters," and his recovery and felicity must arise from his returning from his own "broken cisterns" to the original spring.—The water of life was purchased at infinite cost by Christ; but he offers it to the thirsty without price, (Is. lxv. 1, 2.)—Those who are refreshed by the streams of the water of life, have many enemies to encounter in their militant state, but all who overcome are encouraged in their warfare by the animating promise, that they shall "inherit all things." (1 Cor. iii. 21.)—"He shall be my son," and "if a son, then an heir of God, and joint heir with Christ."

> 8. But the fearful and unbelieving, and the abominable, and murderers, and whoremongers, and sorcerers, and idolaters, and all liars, shall have their part in the lake which burneth with fire and brimstone; which is the second death.

V. 8.—"But the fearful," who dread suffering or reproach for the cause of Christ,—not the self-diffident who loves his Captain, but the coward or deserter, who "turns back in the day of battle," who fears the enemy more than his Captain:—"and unbelieving," not the misbelieving, as Thomas; nor the *weak* in faith, but such as have *no* faith,—*infidels*;—"the abominable," defiling the flesh as Sodomites:—"murderers," suicides, duelists, assassins, burglars, etc., "whoremongers," adulterers, fornicators:—"sorcerers," necromancers, spiritualists, who are the devil's prophets, pretending to new revelations, "and all liars," perjured persons, deceivers, hypocrites, false teachers, who handle the word of the Lord deceitfully, for filthy lucre's sake,—all such shall have their part in the lake, with the devil, the beast, and the false prophet. (1 Cor. vi. 9, 10; Gal. v. 19-21; Eph. v. 5, 6; 2 Cor. xi. 13.)

> 9. *And there came unto me one of the seven angels which had the seven vials full of the seven last plagues, and talked with me, saying, Come hither, I will show thee the bride, the Lamb's wife.*
> 10. *And he carried me away in the spirit to a great and high mountain, and showed me that great city, the holy Jerusalem, descending out of heaven from God,*
> 11. *Having the glory of God: and her light was like unto a stone most precious, even like a jasper-stone, clear as crystal;*
> 12. *And had a wall great and high, and had twelve gates, and at the gates twelve angels, and names written thereon, which are the names of the twelve tribes of the children of Israel.*
> 13. *On the east, three gates; on the north, three gates; on the south, three gates; and on the west, three gates.*
> 14. *And the wall of the city had twelve foundations, and in them the names of the twelve apostles of the Lamb.*

Vs. 9-14.—This "angel" is probably the same who had shown John the mystic Babylon and her destruction, (ch. xvii. 1;) and who now proposes to show him the "bride of the Lamb" by way of contrast.—Under the influence of the Spirit, who has access to the soul without the use of the bodily organs, (2 Cor. xii. 2,)—John was "carried to a great and high mountain," where the prospect might be sufficiently enlarged. When the angel proposed to show him the "scarlet whore," he "carried him into the wilderness," intimating that such is the *only position* in which the "mystery of the woman, and of the beast that carrieth her," can be clearly seen or perfectly understood. (2 Pet. i. 9.) Great indeed is the contrast. Both objects are complex, and the combination of symbols, wholly incongruous in nature, admonishes the sober interpreter to beware of indulging his vain fancy by attempting to trace analogies in detail, where none are intended by the Holy Spirit. The true church of Christ is compared to a virtuous and fruitful woman, (ch. xii. 5;) and the apostate church is symbolized by a fruitful but profligate woman, (ch. xvii. 5.) Then both are also represented by two cities, which are equally contrasted. As the women differ in their outward adornment, (chs. xix. 8, xvii. 4,) so do the cities in the quality of population, commerce and employment, (ch. xviii. 4; xxii. 14.)—The nuptials being consummated between the Lamb and his bride, and she being now "made perfect in holiness;" under the emblem of a city, she is illuminated with "the glory of God," made "comely through his comeliness put upon her," rendered beautiful and illustrious beyond conception or expression: for the happiness of heaven results from conformity to the God-man, communion with him and communications from him. (1 John iii. 2.)—"Her light" resembled the "jasper, clear as crystal." The knowledge of saints in heaven will be intuitive: they will no longer "see through a glass darkly," by word and sacraments; nor shall the glorious Bridegroom show himself as formerly "through the lattice;" (Song ii. 9;) but they "shall see him as he is." (1 John iii. 2.)—"A wall great and high" denotes the security of this city, which can never be scaled by an enemy. The "twelve gates" are to admit the twelve tribes of God's spiritual Israel,—the sealed ones, (ch. vii. 5-8;) who "shall come from the east, and from the west, and from the north, and from the south, and shall sit down in the kingdom of God." (Luke xiii. 29.)—At the gates were "twelve angels," as guards and porters. The "foundations" of the wall, named after the "twelve apostles," denote that all who enter the city, gained admission by "belief of the truth" as taught by the apostles,—had "continued steadfast in the apostles' doctrine and fellowship," in the face of reproach, persecution and apostasy. They were "built upon the foundation of the apostles and prophets,"—Old and New Testament believers saved by the blood of the Lamb: for the twelve tribes, multiplied by the twelve apostles, make a hundred and forty-four; and these again, multiplied by a thousand, make the whole number who appeared with the Lamb on Mount Zion, (ch. xiv. 1;) *the public witnesses* of Christ, in the *church militant* during the great apostasy.

15. And he that talked with me had a golden reed to measure the city, and the gates thereof, and the wall thereof.
16. And the city lieth four square, and the length is as large as the breadth. And he measured the city with the reed, twelve thousand furlongs: the length, and the breadth, and the height of it are equal.
17. And he measured the wall thereof, a hundred and forty and four cubits, according to the measure of a man, that is, of the angel.

Vs. 15-17.—The apostle borrows the symbols and language of preceding prophets, especially those of Ezek. (xl. 3,) and Zech. (ii. 1.) The "furlongs" measured by the "reed," indicate a city of vast dimensions; and being "four square," each side would be about fifteen hundred miles! And as the "length and breadth and height of it are equal," we are hereby taught that no gross conceptions are to be formed in our imaginations, since a city fifteen hundred miles high, is utterly inconceivable. The instruction intended to be conveyed to us by the vast dimensions, and precious materials of this city may be, the incomprehensible nature and transcendent glory of heaven. (1 Cor. ii. 9.) A cubit, as the word signifies, "is the measure of a man" from his elbow to the end of his middle finger. The measure of the wall, in height or breadth, was a hundred and forty-four cubits, or the twelve tribes, as before, multiplied by the twelve apostles; for the idea of a cube, as the most perfect symbol of symmetrical form, seems to be intended.

18. And the building of the wall of it was of jasper: and the city was pure gold, like unto clear glass:
19. And the foundations of the wall of the city were garnished with all manner of precious stones. The first foundation was jasper; the second, sapphire; the third chalcedony; the fourth, an emerald;
20. The fifth, sardonyx; the sixth, sardius; the seventh, chrysolite; the eighth, beryl; the ninth, a topaz; the tenth, a chrysoprasus; the eleventh, a jacinth; the twelfth, an amethyst.
21. And the twelve gates were twelve pearls: every several gate was of one pearl: and the street of the city was pure gold, as it were transparent glass.

Vs. 18-21.—The "jasper, gold and glass," are here all combined; though their natural properties and chemical elements are so different. Glass is clear, transparent, but brittle; gold is solid and shining, but opaque. In heaven, the saints shall *know* more than we can now *imagine*. The glass will be all gold. As the eye sees an object through glass at a glance, so the saints in heaven will perceive truth without the tedious process of comparison and reasoning. The gold will be all glass. All these symbols are intended to show to the devout reader, that the antichristian harlot is incomparably eclipsed by the glory of the Lamb's bride,—having "no glory, by reason of the glory that excelleth."—The twelve "precious stones" which "garnished the foundations of the wall of the city," are an allusion to those of Aaron's breastplate of judgment. (Exod. xxviii. 17-20;) indicating that the *Urim* and *Thummim*, the *light* and *perfection* of glory, shall be there, superseding the oracle and Shekinah: for one thing is peculiar to this city by which it is distinguished from the old Jerusalem,—no temple.

22. And I saw no temple therein: for the Lord God Almighty, and the Lamb, are the temple of it.
23. And the city had no need of the sun, neither of the moon, to shine in it; for the glory of God did lighten it, and the Lamb is the light thereof.
24. And the nations of them which are saved shall walk in the light of it, and the kings of the earth do bring their glory and honour into it.
25. And the gates of it shall not be shut at all by day; for there shall be no night there.
26. And they shall bring the glory and honour of the nations into it.
27. And there shall in no wise enter into it any thing that defileth, neither whatsoever worketh abomination, or maketh a lie; but they which are written in the Lamb's book of life.

Vs. 22-27.—There was "no temple therein." As there *was a temple* in the city which Ezekiel saw in vision, (ch. xli. 1,) and this fact determines the point, that his prophecy relates to the church *militant*; so, the absence of even the semblance of such a structure here, proves that this is a description of the church *triumphant*. In heaven there is no need of external, material, visible symbols of God's presence. As the ceremonial "law had a shadow of good things to come," but "vanished away" when Christ appeared, (Heb. x. 1,) so will it be in heaven; no ordinances will be used to act upon either sense or faith, these having issued in vision.

The glorious presence of "the Lord God Almighty and the Lamb," having superseded the necessity of a temple; the light of the sun and moon shall be no longer needed. "God is light, and in him is no darkness at all," (1 John i. 5;) and "as long as Christ was in the world, he was the light of the world." (John ix. 5.) We have seen that other suns and moons which were *symbolical,* have been darkened or blotted out of existence by the omnipotent Mediator; but now these natural luminaries are totally and for ever obscured by the ineffable effulgence of uncreated light,—the manifested and immediate presence of the Father and the Son.—All the redeemed shall "walk in the light of the Lord;" and all the glory of "the kings of the earth," concentrated in one place, would bear no comparison with the splendor of this "holy city." The gates are not to be shut during the "day" of *eternity*; and since the "excellent ones of the earth" shall all enter the twelve open gates from every part of the world, it may be truly said "they bring the glory and honor of the nations into it." What a delightful scene of a holy, happy, safe and harmonious fellowship!—It is observable that the apostle altogether drops *personalities* here. He seizes only upon properties or qualities,—"any thing,"—so holy is the place, and so holy the inhabitants; yea, so safe and secure, that no creature,—no "beast of the field which the Lord God has made," shall ever gain an entrance into this heavenly Paradise: but only those whose names are "written in the Lamb's book of life;" who, despite of the Serpent, brings all his spiritual seed safe to glory.

CHAPTER XXII.

1. *And he showed me a pure river of water of life, clear as crystal, proceeding out of the throne of God and of the Lamb.*
2. *In the midst of the street of it, and on either side of the river, was there the tree of life, which bare twelve manner of fruits, and yielded her fruit every month: and the leaves of the tree were for the healing of the nations.*
3. *And there shall be no more curse: but the throne of God and of the Lamb shall be in it; and his servants shall serve him.*
4. *And they shall see his face; and his name shall be in their foreheads.*
5. *And there shall be no night there: and they need no candle, neither light of the sun: for the Lord God giveth them light: and they shall reign for ever and ever.*

Vs. 1-5.—These verses, being a continuance of the description of the "holy city," naturally belong to the preceding chapter.—The angel proceeds to show John the source and current from which emanate all heavenly blessings. The allusion is to Ezekiel, xlvii. 1-12; but both he and John call our attention to man's primeval state, when our first parents dwelt in Eden. This abode of the blessed is beautified and enriched with all the products, delights and attractions which are adapted to the refined senses of holy creatures,—"pleasant to the eyes, and good for food." It is Paradise restored, by the "doing and dying" of the second Adam. It is also Paradise *improved*, having not only the "tree of life," as the first had, but also, in addition, the "water of life." The "tree of life" was to sinless Adam a symbol and pledge of immortality to himself and all his posterity whom he represented in the Covenant of Works. Now that heaven is procured for all believers by the second Adam, it is emblematically represented to our weak apprehension by directing our attention to the primitive and earthly Paradise. This is repeatedly done in Scripture. The Lord Jesus, before he expired upon the cross, said to the penitent thief,—"To day shalt thou be with me in Paradise. (Luke xxiii. 43.) Paul was "caught up" thither, (2 Cor. xii. 4;) and he calls the place "heaven," (v. 2;) and in this book, (ch. ii. 7,) the Lord promises,—"I will give to him that overcometh to eat of the tree of life, which is in the midst of the paradise of God." The "tree" is an emblem of Christ, (Song ii. 3;) the "river of the water of life" symbolizes the Holy Spirit, (John vii. 38, 39;) for as the Son and the Holy Ghost proceed from the Father, the former by generation, the latter by emanation from eternity,—so "that eternal life which was with the Father" in the person of the Son, and purchased by the Son, is communicated by the Holy Ghost to all the redeemed by regeneration. (2 Cor. iii. 6; Rom. viii. 2.)—Thus, the eternal duration of life in glory "proceeds out of the throne of God and the Lamb." On each side of the river "the tree of life" is accessible by the inhabitants; and the fruits of the tree, ripe in all months of the year, and adapted to every taste, each one may "put forth his hand" as he passes, "and take ... and eat, and live for ever." (Gen. iii. 22.) Or, "the people that are therein" may "sit down under its shadow, and its fruit will be sweet to their taste."—"The leaves of the tree" are for medicine, being preventive of all disease, so that "the inhabitant shall not say, I am sick: the people that dwell therein are forgiven their iniquities." (Is. xxxiii. 24.) "There shall be no more curse." Satan gained entrance into the garden of Eden, and succeeded in entailing the "curse" upon man, and upon beast, and upon the fruits of the ground; but he shall never be loosed again, or emerge from "the lake of fire," to disturb the repose of that blessed society in heaven, (ch. xxi. 27.)—As the "throne of God and the Lamb" is *one,* (ch. iii. 21;) so it is remarkable that the distinction of persons is omitted, as though the Father and the Son were but one person. True, Christ said, "I and my Father are one," (John x. 30;) but he referred to *unity* of *nature* and purpose, not of *personality;* for, in consistency with this, he said also,—"My Father is greater than I;" an assertion which must consist with the former, and which plainly involves personal distinction, (ch. xiv. 28.)—"His name shall be in their foreheads."—Which of them? We have found Christ's Father's name "written in the foreheads" of a hundred and forty-four thousand saints *militant,* (ch. xiv. 1.) While in conflict, "the world knew them not," and the adherents of Antichrist "cast out their names as evil," branding them as *heretics*; but now they are known to the whole universe, as the *covenant property* of both the Father and the Son, (ch. iii. 12.)—"Behold, I and the children which God hath given me;" (Heb. ii. 13.) "I have manifested thy name unto the men which thou gavest me cut of the world. Thine they were, and thou gavest them me; and they have kept thy word. ... All mine are thine, and thine are mine; and I am glorified in them." (John xvii. 6,10.)—There will be no intermission or interruption of service, "no night there,"—no hidings of God's countenance, no desertions; for "they shall see his face" in the "express image of the Father's person," be assured of his love;—"need no candle," nor any earthly accommodation; "for the Lord God giveth them light; and they shall reign for ever and ever," in fulness of joy and unalloyed pleasures for evermore. (Ps. xvi. 11.) How different is this heaven from the Mahometan paradise, which, if real, could gratify only carnal and sensual sinners! yet the imaginations of many, and their aspirations too, with the Bible in their hands, are little better than those of Mahometans or pagans. All speculations of heathen philosophers about the "chief good," or the enjoyments of their imaginary gods, are so gross and brutish as to demonstrate the all-important truth, that "except a man be born again, *he cannot* see the kingdom of God." (John iii. 3.) And it is too evident that some modern philosophers are as little acquainted as Nicodemus with the humbling doctrines of the gospel. The society of learned men, making perpetual advance in natural science, especially in astronomy,—would seem to be the highest conception of happiness which too many modern philosophers can reach. They know not some of the elementary teachings of the Holy Scriptures; such as,—"Without holiness no man shall see the Lord;" and that this indispensable preparation for heavenly felicity consists in "the washing of regeneration, and the renewing of the Holy Ghost."

The hundreds of diverse and conflicting opinions of learned writers on the *summum bonum,* or chief good, proves to demonstration, that without supernatural revelation and regeneration, man cannot conceive in what happiness consists. Thus far is the description of the heavenly state; and how little can we know, or even conceive of the glory and felicity of the upper sanctuary! We must still say with the prophet Isaiah and the apostle Paul,—"Eye hath not seen, nor ear heard, neither have entered into the heart of man, the things which God hath prepared for them that love him." (Isa. lxiv. 4; 1 Cor. ii. 9.)

> 6. *And he said unto me, These sayings are faithful and true: and the Lord God of the holy prophets sent his angel to show unto his servants the things which must shortly be done.*

7. *Behold, I come quickly, blessed is he that keepeth the sayings of the prophecy of this book.*

Vs. 6, 7.—The angel assures the apostle and all who read, that "these sayings are faithful and true," however sublime and incomprehensible; however, incredible to infidels; however contradicted and misinterpreted by antichristian apostates and enthusiasts. They are all from "the Lord God of the holy prophets,"—from Jesus Christ and God the Father, (ch. i. 1.)—All prophets who wrote *any part* of the Bible, were "holy men of God." (2 Pet. i. 21.)—Of "these things" some were "shortly to be done;" and all in regular series would be accomplished in due time.—"Behold I come quickly." Christ is the speaker here, and declares that each one is "blessed who keepeth the sayings ... of this book." This benediction was pronounced on such at the beginning of this Revelation, (ch. i. 3,) and it is repeated by its immediate divine Author, to encourage all to study it. This blessing is not to be expected by any who merely *read* or *hear*, but by those only who *keep* the "sayings of this prophecy." Its Author foreknew its enemies and corrupters.

8. *And I John saw these things, and heard them. And when I had heard and seen, I fell down to worship before the feet of the angel, which showed me these things.*
9. *Then saith he unto me, See thou do it not: for I am thy fellow-servant, and of thy brethren the prophets, and of them which keep the sayings of this book: worship God.*

Vs. 8, 9.—A *second* time, John attempts an act of idolatry! While we may wonder at this, let us not fail to admire the wonderful wisdom of God in permitting his servant to fall, as he did in the case of our first father Adam, that he might take occasion more fully to display his glory in "bringing good out of evil." The Apocalypse is directed chiefly against that primary feature of the great Antichrist, *idolatry*. This was part of "the mystery of inquity "which did already work" in the time of the apostles, (Col. ii. 18,) and was to be fully developed afterwards. (2 Thess. ii. 4.) This second rebuke of an apostle, by one of the most exalted of creatures, for ever answers all arguments of Papists or others, who plead for, or palliate the "worshipping of angels" or souls of men. Idolaters worship angels and souls *when absent*, as though they were omniscient, omnipresent and omnipotent; thus giving the glory to creatures of these divine perfections: whereas this heavenly messenger, *when present*, keenly resents this indignity to his and the apostle's adorable Creator and Lord. Once more the angel directs John and all men to join him and all the heavenly host in observing "the first and great commandment,"—"Worship God," (ch. v. 11-14.) This angelic rebuke, leaves Papists for ever without excuse; and consequently all others who deny the *supreme deity* of our Lord and Saviour Jesus Christ, and yet worship him.

10. And he saith unto me, Seal not the sayings of the prophecy of this book; for the time is at hand.
11. He that is unjust, let him be unjust still; and he which is filthy, let him be filthy still; and he that is righteous, let him be righteous still; and he that is holy, let him be holy still.
12. And, behold, I come quickly; and my reward is with me, to give every man according as his work shall be.

Vs. 10-12.—Christ himself addresses John in person. He had done so at the beginning of these glorious scenes of the future, (ch. i. 8.) Now he appears again in glory, though not described as before, that he may thus authenticate and close the vision.—"Seal not the sayings of the prophecy of this book." Why is this? The reason is assigned, because "the time is at hand" when they shall begin to be verified in actual history. The case was different in Daniel's time, who was inspired by the same omniscient Spirit to predict the same events. "O Daniel, shut up the words, and seal the vision, even to the time of the end." (Dan. xii. 4.) If the vision of the empires of Persia and Greece was to be "for many days," (ch. viii. 26,) then the rise, reign and overthrow of the Roman empire, were still more remote. No wonder that Daniel, with becoming humility but intense interest inquired, "O, my Lord, what shall be the end of these things?" Such was the subdued anxiety of other prophets. (1 Pet. i. 10.) And here we may once for all notice the *three distinct* periods mentioned by Daniel, as measuring the duration of the Roman empire, the Romish apostasy, and as they bear upon the promised and desirable millennium. The two prophets, Daniel and John, agree in fixing and limiting the domination of the Antichrist to 1260 years. This agreement has been already pointed out. The Lord, however, to allay the laudable anxiety of his "greatly beloved" servant Daniel, makes mention of two other periods of time,

1290 and 1335 days or years, (ch. xii. 11, 12.) Now, when we have manifold assurances that the great apostacy shall terminate with the close of the 1260 years, we may venture humbly to suppose, that the next thirty years may be occupied in the conversion of the Jews, and the remaining forty-five in the effectual calling of the residue of the gentile nations; so as to bring the kingdoms of the earth and the church of Christ to perfect organization and visible harmony, and the whole population of the globe into voluntary and avowed subjection to the Lord and his Anointed,—to perfect millennial splendor, the nearest approximation to heaven. (Rom. xi. 25, 26; Ps. cii. 15, 16.) But "who shall live when God doeth this?" (Num. xxiv. 23.)—The divine Author of this book, having given to mankind a complete and sufficient revelation of his will, containing invitations and warnings, at this juncture gives intimation that obstinate sinners shall at length be left to the consequences of their own free and perverse choice, "unjust and filthy still;" no further means to be employed for their conviction; but those who have embraced the offer of the gospel, shall be confirmed for ever in holiness and happiness,—"righteous and holy still."—He also repeats the assurances of his sudden appearance to reward "every man according as his work shall be." The recompense which he brings will be of debt or justice to the impenitent unbeliever; but wholly of free grace to the believer; for the works of each class shall follow them, as decisive evidence of their respective characters, (ch. xiv. 13.)

> 13. I am Alpha and Omega, the beginning and the end, the first and the last.

V. 13.—The Lord Christ here declares and asserts the eternity of his personal subsistence and official standing, as an all-sufficient guarantee of his ability and authority to deal with the righteous and the wicked, as also to bring to pass all events by his providence which are here predicted. The same guarantee he had given at the beginning of the Apocalypse, (ch. i. 8.)

> 14. Blessed are they that do his commandments, that they may have right to the tree of life, and may enter in through the gates into the city.

V. 14.—Those who "do his commandments," are believers, (John xiv.

15,) and no others can obtain a "right to the tree of life"—all the blessings of Christ's purchase: for "without faith it is impossible to please God," (Heb. xi. 6;) and "this is the love of God, that we keep his commandments." (1 John v. 3.) "By the deeds of the law,"—keeping the commandments, whether moral or ceremonial, "shall no flesh be justified in the sight of God," or *merit* a "right to the tree of life," or to "enter in through the gates into the city." This right, power, or privilege, is confined to those, and to those only, who "receive and believe on the name of Christ." (John i. 12.) They who serve the Lord Christ, are entitled to the reward of the inheritance, (Col. iii. 24;) and in keeping of his commandments, there is great reward. (Ps. xix. 11.) This reward is of *grace*, not of *debt* to any of the children of Adam: "not of works, lest any man should boast." (Rom. xi. 6; Eph. ii. 9.) And when the last elected sinner, pertaining to the whole company of the redeemed, shall have been called, justified and sanctified, then "with gladness and rejoicing shall they be brought: they shall enter into the King's palace." (Ps. xlv. 15.)

> 15. For without are dogs and sorcerers, and whoremongers, and murderers, and idolaters, and whosoever loveth and maketh a lie.

V. 15.—"Without are dogs."—These characters have been excluded by the righteous and unalterable sentence of the judge of quick and dead, having their part in the "lake of fire:" for there is no intimation here or elsewhere, of any *purgatory* or intermediate place, with the delusive hope of which, those who "love and make lies," flatter themselves and their blind votaries. Oh, that such "sinners in Zion," and out of Zion, "might be afraid!"—that timely "fearfulness might surprise these hypocrites!" that they might ponder those awful questions!—"Who among us shall dwell with the devouring fire? who among us shall dwell with everlasting burnings?" (Isa. xxxiii. 14.)

> 16. I Jesus have sent mine angel to testify unto you these things in the churches. I am the root and the offspring of David, and the bright and morning star.

V. 16.—This is the "angel" whose ministry the Lord Christ was pleased to employ in making known to the church through his servant John, most of the discoveries of this book, (ch. i. 1, 11.) Many other angels have indeed been employed by the Mediator as the ministers of his providence; but this one seems to have been the principal all along. None of these heavenly messengers, however, was found competent to reveal the purposes of God, (ch. v. 3.) To this work the eternal Son of God alone was found adequate by nature and office,—the "Lamb that had been slain." Christ has a personal property in the angels, as he is their Creator and Lord; and as they are his creatures and willing servants,—"*mine* angel."—This is perfectly reasonable; for he is the "Root of David" in his divine nature; and the "Offspring of David," in his human nature, (Rom. i. 3.)—God-Man, Mediator. And here let it be remarked, that in speaking or writing of our Redeemer there appears to be no scriptural warrant for the popular phrases,—"the *union* of the two natures,"—"Christ as man;" or, "as God." These expressions militate against the *unity* of his *divine nature* and *personality;* and are calculated,—we do not say *intended*, to mislead or confuse the mind of his disciples. "In *him personally*", not in the Father or the Holy Ghost, "dwelleth all the fulness of the Godhead bodily." (Col. ii. 9.)—By John the descent of Christ's human nature is traced through David here, because of the Covenant of Royalty; by Paul, he is represented as being of the "seed of Abraham," by reason of the more extended relation involved in the Covenant of Grace. (Heb. ii. 16.)—He is also "the bright, even the morning star." This may be in reference to the less luminous "stars in his right hand," (ch. i. 16, 20,) and by way of contrast with them: but he takes this name chiefly to intimate that he is the Author of all supernatural illumination, whether in the kingdom of grace or of glory:—"The Lamb is the light thereof," (ch. xxi. 23.)

> 17. And the Spirit and the bride say, Come. And let him that heareth, say, Come. And let him that is athirst, come. And whosoever will, let him take the water of life freely.

V. 17.—Here is the unrestricted universal call of the gospel, to "come" to Christ for eternal life.—"We do testify that the Father sent the Son to be the Saviour of the world," (1 John iv. 14.)—The invitation is manifold and pressing. "The Spirit" by the word and conscience says, "Come." "The Bride," the church militant and triumphant, says, "Come." Every one "that heareth" the invitation, is warranted to say to others, "Come." Let every one that "thirsts" for true and lasting felicity,

"Come." If any one be in doubt, whether his desire be spiritual or not, it is added for his encouragement, as well as sufficient warrant,—"Let whosoever will, take of the water of life freely." Any sinner of Adam's race may "wash and be clean," in that "fountain open for sin and for uncleanness;" may with confidence and pleasure, "draw water from the wells of salvation." (Zech. xiii. 1: Isa. xii. 3.) Who can resist these calls, invitations and persuasions, and be guiltless? or who can devise easier terms of reconciliation to an offended God, than are here addressed to the chief of sinners?

18. For I testify unto every man that heareth the words of the prophecy of this book, If any man shall add unto these things, God shall add unto him the plagues that are written in this book:
19. And if any man shall take away from the words of the book of this prophecy, God shall take away his part out of the book of life, and out of holy city, and from the things which are written in this book.

Vs. 18, 19.—"For I testify."—He who is "the faithful and true Witness" closes this book of prophecy, with a solemn and awful sanction. These tremendous threatenings by the "Lord God of the holy prophets," may well cause all who read or hear to tremble: for who can abide his indignation?—While the "prophecy of this book" is primarily intended, all other parts of the Bible are included in this solemn conclusion: for doubtless our Lord intended the Apocalypse to be a close to the whole canon. The threatening is twofold, corresponding to the criminality. Learned, bold and irreverent biblical critics; enthusiasts and pretenders to new revelations, are in danger of these judgments. "The plagues that are written in this book," are such as will utterly destroy the presumptuous sinner who "adds to these things." And he that impiously "takes away from the words of the book of this prophecy," exposes himself to the like awful punishment. "God shall take away his part out of the book of life, and out of the holy city, and from the things which are written in this book."—Tremendous doom! All that which he seemed to have shall be taken away. (Luke viii. 18.) Great will be the sudden and unexpected loss!—These awful denunciations, however, have special reference, like the rest of the threatened judgments in this book, to the great, continued and defiant impieties of the apostate church of Rome. She has "added" her *traditions* to the Scriptures, as part and principal part, of the

"Rule of Faith!" She has "taken away" the Scriptures from the body of her people; or shut them up in an "unknown tongue," so that "every man may" not "hear in his own tongue wherein he was born, the wonderful works of God." (Acts ii. 8, 11.) This is one of the articles in Rome's indictment here; and whatever modern infidelity or spurious charity may suggest, this theft of God's word, and robbery of his people, is not to be expiated with burnt offering or sacrifice. And he who scans all time, foresaw this attempt of the dragon and his allies to deprive the church and the world of the "lively oracles;" therefore, as he promised a blessing on the reader of this book, as it were on the title-page, here in the close he appends a malediction, that all who read or hear, may be deterred from such sacrilege.

> 20. *He which testifieth these things saith, Surely I come quickly: Amen. Even so, come, Lord Jesus.*

V. 20.—"He which testifieth these things" is the Lord Jesus. Again he reminds all to whom these presents come, of his certain and speedy appearance. These frequent assurances are not "vain repetitions." They are intended to strengthen the faith and counteract the despondency of the saints, and to alarm the consciences of his enemies. (2 Pet. iii. 3, 4, 8, 10; Jude 14, 15.) To this "promise of his coming," John responds in the name of the whole church,—"Amen. Even so, come, Lord Jesus," to fulfil these predictions, in their promises and threatenings; "to be glorified in his saints, and admired in all them that believe." "So shall they ever be with the Lord." (1 Thess. iv. 17.)

> 21. *The grace of our Lord Jesus Christ be with you all. Amen.*

V. 21.—These are also the words of John. He had just been addressing the "Lord Jesus," and his next words are addressed to the "seven churches," (ch. i. 4, 11,) or to all who read or hear the words of this book: but especially the church general. This is a concise form of the "apostolic benediction," (2 Thess. iii. 18,) which is sometimes amplified, by naming the Father and the Son; or, at other times, the three divine persons. (2 Cor. xiii. 14.) However, "the grace of the Lord Jesus Christ" is originally from God the Father, procured for us by Jesus Christ, and communicated to us by the Holy Spirit. And unto the Father, the Son, and the Holy Ghost, let equal, undivided, and everlasting glory be ascribed, by all the subjects of his regenerating and sanctifying grace, "throughout all ages, world without end." Amen.

APPENDIX.

THE NEW JERUSALEM.

Interpreters are much divided in opinion as to the import of this symbol. Some think it represents the church on earth during the period of the millennium; while others, no less learned and pious, consider it as an emblematical representation of the heavenly state. Of those who acquiesce in the former view, some consider the arguments "quite conclusive." It may be conceded that much may be advanced, and with great plausibility, in support of this position.

Perhaps the most specious arguments to this purpose are such as the following:—"That the New Jerusalem is distinguished from the Old, because of the superior light and grace of the present dispensation of the Covenant. Moreover, the glowing descriptions of the church militant given by the prophets, especially Isaiah, are thought to be as boldly rhetorical as those of John; yet those lofty flights are confessedly descriptive of the church on earth. Besides, who can conceive how "the kings of the earth bring their glory and honour into" the heavenly state? or how are "the leaves of the tree of life for the healing of the nations," when there *are no nations to be healed?* etc.

To these arguments the following answers may be given.

The church is one under all changes of dispensation, and by what names soever she is called: but it does not appear that we are warranted by Scripture usage to view the New Jerusalem as a designation of the church in her militant state. She is indeed sometimes called in the New Testament by Old Testament names: as when Paul calls her by the name Zion, (Heb. xii. 22.) But he does not say, *new* Zion. Again, when our Lord promises, (as in Rev. iii. 12,) to reward "him that overcometh," it must be supposed from the connexion, that, as in all similar cases of spiritual conflict, this reward is to be conferred in a future state,—heaven. But part of the reward he describes in these words:—"I will write upon him the name of the city of my God, which is New Jerusalem." Surely it may be supposed without presumption, that in this place New Jerusalem means heaven. Nor is the assumption true,—that the descriptive language of the Old Testament prophets is always to be understood of the church on earth. For instance, can the following language (Is. xxxiii. 24,) be predicated of the saints while in the body:—"The inhabitant shall not say, I am sick?" "The glory and honour of the nations" are the "saints of God, the excellent;" who while here, are "the light of the world, the salt of the earth;" and doubtless nations as well as families and individuals "have learned by experience that the Lord hath blessed them for their sakes:" (Gen. xxx. 27; xxxix. 5;)—and that he has also "reproved kings" and destroyed nations for their sakes, (Ps. cv. 14; Is. xliii. 3, 4.) And when all the saints who are to rule the nations, (Rev. xx. 4, 6,) for a thousand years, shall have been brought home to glory, then emphatically will the glory and honour of the nations be brought into the New Jerusalem.

As to the "leaves of the tree for the healing of the nations," it may be remarked, that their sanative virtue will have been experienced by national societies on earth: and there is not, there never was, nor will there ever be, any other healing medicine for them, (Ezek. xlvii. 12) In addition to what has been said, it is worthy of notice that the tree of life, in allusion to the delights of the garden of Eden, which was an emblem of heaven, is mentioned in the Apocalypse, near the beginning and near the end of the book, (chs. ii. 7; xxii. 2.) Now, we are told expressly that this tree is "in the midst of Paradise." But we learn both from our Lord and the apostle Paul that Paradise signifies heaven:—"To-day shalt thou be with me in Paradise," said Christ to the penitent thief. "I was caught up into Paradise;" that is, "the third heaven," said Paul. Did Christ and Paul mean the visible, or the invisible church militant by the name Paradise? But the tree of life flourishes there, and all the redeemed eat of its fruit. They are where the tree is, the tree is in Paradise, and Paradise is heaven itself: therefore we are warranted to conclude with certainty that New Jerusalem is a symbol of the church triumphant; and, consequently, that those parts of chapters twenty-one and twenty-two, which are of symbolic structure, are descriptive of the heavenly state.

THE ANTICHRIST.

This word does not occur in the Apocalypse, nor in any other book of the New Testament except the first and second epistles, by the apostle John. There it is found in the singular and plural form. (1 John ii. 18, 22; iv. 3; ii. 7.) The apostles in their ministry had spoken frequently and familiarly to the disciples of this personage, as an enemy of God and man. "Ye *have heard* that Antichrist shall come." "Remember ye not," asks Paul, "that, when I was yet with you, I *told you* these things?" (2 Thess. ii. 5.) Paul blames his countrymen, the Hebrews, that they had need that one should teach them again which be the first principles of the oracles of God, (Heb. v. 12.) And it is just so now, in the case of most professing Christians, learned and illiterate; they yet need to be taught again what is meant by Antichrist.

All who are acquainted with the sentiments of the reformers of the sixteenth and seventeenth centuries are aware that their conceptions of this enemy were vague and confused. Persecuted as heretics and apostates from the only true church, the church of Rome, the reformers very naturally concluded that the Pope, or the church of which he is the visible head, was the Antichrist. And this opinion is very generally held at the present day.

Mr. Faber, however, dissents from this popular notion, and with much confidence and plausibility broaches a new theory of his own. His style is always forcible, and so perspicuous that he cannot be misunderstood. In his "Dissertation on the Prophecies," he lays down the following canon or rule for expositors:—"Before a commentator can reasonably expect his own system to be adopted by others, he must show likewise that the expositions of his predecessors are erroneous in those points wherein he differs from them." To enforce this rule he adds,—"It will be found to be the only way, in which there is even a probability of attaining to the truth." I can neither admit the justness of his rule, nor the conclusiveness of his reason; for by its adoption, "of making many books there would be no end; and the world itself could not contain the books that should be written." To deduce the truth from any portion of God's word, it is by no means necessary that the expositor shall undertake the Herculean task of refuting all the heresies and vagaries which "men of corrupt minds" have pretended or attempted to wring out of it. But as Mr. Faber is not to be reckoned in this category, I shall pay him so much deserved respect as to apply to himself *his own rule* in some following particulars:—

By a formal syllogism Mr. Faber proposes to overthrow the generally received interpretation of the term *Antichrist*, that it means, the *Papacy*, or, the *Church of Rome*. Thus he reasons:—"He is Antichrist that denieth the Father and the Son: but *the Church of Rome* never denied either the Father or the Son: therefore *the church of Rome* cannot be the *Antichrist* intended by St. John." Now, in this argument, which seems to be so clear and conclusive, there is a latent sophism, an assumption contrary to the Scriptures. The false assumption is, that the word *denieth is univocal*; that is, that it has in the Bible, and on this doctrinal point in particular, only *one sense*; whereas this is not the case. The Church of Rome does indeed "profess to know" the Father and the Son, but "in works denies" both, (1 Tim. v. 8; Tit. i. 16.) Therefore Mr. Faber's conclusion is not sustained by his premises, and the Church of Rome might be the Antichrist for any thing that his syllogism says to the contrary.

Mr. Faber imagined that "Republican France,—infidel and atheistical France,"—was the Antichrist; and he labored with much ingenuity to sustain his position by applying to revolutionary France the latter part of the eleventh chapter of Daniel, together with the prophecies of Paul, Peter and Jude. I presume that most divines and intelligent Christians are long since convinced, by the developments of Providence, that he was mistaken. The commotions of the French Revolution and the military achievements of the first Napoleon, however important to peninsular Europe, were on much too limited a scale to correspond with the magnitude and duration of the great Antichrist's achievements. They were, however, owing to their proximity to Britain and their threatening aspect, of sufficient importance to excite the alarm and rouse the political antipathies of the Vicar of Stockton upon Tees! Mr. Faber's Antichrist is an "infidel king, wilful king, an atheistical king, a professed atheist," of short duration, and his influence of limited geographical extent. He is not in most of these features the Antichrist of prophecy, whose baleful influence is co-extensive with Christendom, and whose duration is to be 1260 years. Mr. Faber's erudition is to be respected, his imagination admired, but his political feelings to be lamented. Indeed, his very ecclesiastical title of office,—"Vicar," is itself partly indicative and symbolical of the prophetic Antichrist.

I do not believe that infidel France, whether republican or monarchical, nor the Papacy, nor the Church of Rome, is the Antichrist of the apostle John; yet I do believe that all these are essential elements in his composition. The following are the principal component parts of that complex moral person, as defined by the Holy Spirit, by which any disciple of Christ without much learning may identify John's Antichrist. His elemental parts are three, *and only three*, and all presented in the thirteenth chapter of Revelation. The "beast of the sea," (vs. 1, 2,) the "beast of the earth," (v. 11,) and the "image of, or to the first beast," (v. 14,) that is, the Roman empire, the Roman church and the Pope: all these in combination, *professing Christianity*; these, with their adjuncts as subordinate agencies constitute the Apocalyptic Antichrist. Besides this personage, well defined by the inspired prophets, Daniel, Paul, John and others, there is no other Antichrist. An "infidel king, a professed atheist," as distinct from this one and symbolized in prophetic revelation, I find not. I conclude that such a personage is wholly chimerical, framed as a creature of a lively imagination.

THE IMAGE OF THE BEAST.

Mr. Faber is unsuccessful in his interpretation of the "image of the beast." His reasoning is ingenious, specious and intelligible as usual. He labours to prove that the worshipping of images by the Papists is the meaning of the symbol. Material images, however, whether of papal origin or otherwise, are harmless vanities: "for they cannot do evil, neither also *is it* in them to do good," (Jer. x. 5.) The case is quite otherwise with this image. It has "life, speaks, and has power to *kill*," (Rev. xiii. 15.) These properties of John's "image" are so opposite to those of the Papal images, that they effectually confute Mr. Faber's fanciful, not to say whimsical theory. It has been already shown that the "image" symbolizes the Papacy, the *fac-simile* of the Roman emperor.

THE BEAST'S "deadly wound."

The Erastian heresy, the usual concomitant of prelacy, will readily account for Mr. Faber's explanation of the "deadly wound," which the first beast received in his sixth head. Constantine, he thinks, inflicted that wound by abolishing paganism. He writes as though the beast had been *actually killed*, and had lain literally dead for a period of nearly three centuries! (viz., from 313 till 606.) Yet the apostle assures us that the "deadly wound was healed." The *beast did not die.* Daniel gives no hint of the death of his fourth beast, which is the same as John's beast of the sea, until his final destruction at the close of the 1260 years. It was in fact under the reigns of Constantine and his successors, that ambitious pastors were nurtured into antichristian prelates, and passed by a natural transition into Popery. The empire never ceased to be a beast during the whole period of its continuance. The sixth *head* was wounded, but the beast still survived. The sixth or imperial form of government was changed, but that change brought no advantage to the Christian church either in her doctrine or order. As a distinct horn of this beast the British nation with her hierarchy is easily traceable to mystic Babylon in point of maternity. Since, as well as before the time of Henry the Eighth, spiritual fornication has ever been the crime of the "British Establishment." This historical fact requires no proof.

Mr. Faber seems to me to give too little prominence in his exposition to Daniel and John's beast of the sea, as an enemy to Christ. Indeed, he appears to overlook the leading idea involved in the name Antichrist, as a *substitutionary*, false, and therefore inimical or hostile christ. Instead of keeping before his mind the glorious person of the Mediator as the special object of Antichrist's enmity, as prophecy requires, he places before him the church or the gospel instead of Christ. Hence he writes thus:—"We find in the predictions of St. John,—(why not *St* Daniel?) two *great enemies* of the *gospel,* Popery and Mohammedism." Then he adds,—"a third power is introduced," (Preface, p. 7.) This "third power" he calls "a wilful infidel king," and, as already noticed, interprets it of "atheistical France." Now, it will be evident to the intelligent reader that among his "three powers" considered by him as "enemies to the gospel," he has entirely lost sight of the *seven headed ten horned beast,* and *his hostility to Christ*! He has, in fact, manifestly substituted his imaginary "wilful king",—infidel France, for the Roman empire, the beast of Daniel and John, the agent that slays the witnesses, (Rev. xi. 7.) To almost every expositor, and in his lucid moments, even to Mr. Faber himself, it is apparent, that the Roman empire is the primary element in the complex personage that wars against the Lamb. Even kings are but *horns of the beast,* and Popery but a *horn.* (Dan. vii. 20; Rev. xvii. 12, 13.)

It is therefore a great mistake on the part of this learned author, to feign an Antichrist distinct from the three confederated enemies of Christ and his witnesses,—enemies so clearly pointed out in prophecy by appropriate and intelligible symbols:—the beast with ten, and the beast with two horns, and the image of the first. These three, all professing the Christian religion, and practically denying it, without the shadow of a doubt, constitute the Antichrist of John, (1 John ii. 19-21.) This is the identical enemy described by Daniel, and according to the inspired predictions of both prophets, doomed to eternal destruction, (Dan. vii. 11; Rev. xix. 20.) Hence it is obvious that Mr. Faber's "wilful king" is wholly a creature of his own fancy, constituting no feature of the prophetic Antichrist.

THE LITTLE BOOK.

This symbol is in the tenth chapter evidently distinguished from the one in the fifth chapter. It is considered by several interpreters as containing all that follows to the end of the book. According to this view, it would be larger than the sealed book, (ch. v. 1.) Such a view is altogether untenable, involving, as it does, almost a palpable contradiction. The little book is indeed comprehended in the sealed book, as a part of the whole; or it may be viewed as an appendix or codicil, or perhaps still more correctly as a *parenthesis*, interrupting the series of the trumpets, that the object of the seventh or last woe-trumpet may be thus described and rendered intelligible when sounded.

Mr. Faber is correct in saying, "the eleventh, twelfth, thirteenth and fourteenth chapters, in point of chronology run parallel to each other;" but he is mistaken when he says the "little book comprehends these four chapters." It comprehends only so much as intervenes between the close of the ninth chapter and the fifteenth verse of the eleventh chapter; or, in other words, between the sounding of the sixth and seventh trumpet. To be more correct and explicit,—the tenth chapter introduces the little book, and the eleventh chapter, from the first to the fourteenth verse inclusive, exhibits an abstract of its contents,—a condensed narrative or mere outline of the contest during the 1260 years.

NOTES ON THE APOCALYPSE

THE DEATH OF THE WITNESSES.

Many divines have considered the death of the two witnesses, as consisting in a moral slaying, equivalent to apostacy. Mr. Faber views their life and death as altogether political. He censures Mr. Galloway for "want of strict adherence to *unity of symbolical* interpretation," but he inadvertently falls into the same error. Assuming, as he does, that the two witnesses are the Old and New Testament *Churches*, where is the "unity of symbolical interpretation" when he tells us that the witnesses were politically slain in the "disastrous battle of Mulburgh in the year 1547, by the total route of the protestants under the lead of the Elector of Saxony and the Landgrave of Hesse?" The *political* death of two churches in the battle of Mulburgh!—Such language exemplifies neither the accuracy of historic narrative, nor the "unity of symbolical interpretation:" nor does it accord with another rule of the writer, one of his three cardinal rules, namely,—That "no interpretation of a prophecy is valid, except the prophecy agree *in every particular* with the event to which it is supposed to relate." Mistaking the character of the witnesses, as one of the primary symbols in the Apocalypse, he is unable to ascertain in history either their identity or work, their life or their death. Having imagined their political death in 1547, he supposes their resurrection to political life in 1550,—"by the accession of Edward the Sixth to the throne of England!" and "the defeat of the Duke of Mecklenburgh in the October of that year!!" Of course, these witnesses, according to Mr. Faber's interpretation, resumed their function of prophesying so soon as they were restored to political life: but we look in vain for the prophesying of the mystic witnesses after their ascension to the symbolic heaven, (Rev. xi. 12.) As we have shown to the readers of these Notes, their lives and their testimony, or prophesying, terminate together, (ch. xi. 7; xii. 11.)

THE MARK OF THE BEAST.

"With regard to the mark of the beast," Mr. Faber "thinks, with Sir Isaac Newton, that it is *the cross*," (p. 176.) This *thought* has indeed been almost universal in the minds of protestants. So deep-seated is this conviction in the popular belief, that one is deemed chargeable with temerity, if not something worse, who would call its grounds in question. Popular opinion, or belief in matters of this spiritual and mystical nature, is, however, of very little weight in the estimation of such as are accustomed to "try the spirits." Although the mark was to be received at the instance and by the authority of the two horned beast of the earth, it was not enjoined as a mark of devotion to *himself*. It was manifestly commanded by him as a *tessera* of loyalty to the ten-horned beast of the sea, the obvious symbol of corrupt and tyrannical civil power. Instead therefore of the cross as a sign of devotion to Popery,—of membership in the church of Rome, as identifying with the beast's mark, this mark is evidently and demonstrably the tessera of loyalty to the Roman empire,—immoral civil power; and this, too, in any of the dependencies of that iron empire, (Dan. ii. 40; vii. 7.)

From the errors and vagaries of this learned and acute expositor, some of which have been pointed out, it is apparent that no amount of intellectual culture, no natural powers of discrimination, no logical or metaphysical acumen, will compensate for the want of early and accurate training in the knowledge of supernatural revelation. On the prophetical and priestly offices of our Redeemer, some of the English prelates have written with a force, perspicuity and zeal against the heresies of the Romish apostacy, not excelled by the writings of those who have dissented from the semi-papal hierarchy of the Anglican Church. But on the *royal* office of Immanuel, their prelatic training and associations seem to have blinded their minds. "No bishop, no king," is a maxim which seems to lie at the foundation of all their political disquisitions and speculations, and which gives a tincture to all their expositions of prophecy. Nevertheless, even in this field of labor, the diligent student may consult with much advantage the learned works of such writers as the two Newtons, Kett, Galloway, Whitaker, Zouch, with their predecessors, Lowman, Mede and others.

After all, the best works to be obtained as helps to understand the prophetic parts of Scripture, will be found in the labors of those who, from age to age, have obeyed the gracious call of Christ,—who have "come out from mystic Babylon," from the Romish communion,—from the mother and her harlot daughters, and who have associated more or less intimately with the *witnesses*. Among these may be consulted with profit the works of Durham, Mason and M'Leod. But while searching after the mind of God revealed in this part of his word, let us never exercise implicit faith in the teachings of any fallible expositor. Let us always regard the injunction of our apostle:—"Beloved, believe not every spirit, but try the spirits whether they are of God." Of course, the only infallible standard by which we can try the spirits is the whole word of God,—"comparing spiritual things with spiritual."

THE FIRST RESURRECTION.

Bishop Newton, among those divines distinguished in ecclesiastical history as Millenarians, may be regarded as one of the most learned, judicious and cautious. The amount of the deductions which this class of writers draw from the scripture phrase "first resurrection," and its context, confirmed as they suppose by many other parts of Scripture, appears to be the following:—All the righteous shall be raised from their graves to meet our Saviour coming from heaven at the beginning of the Millennium: he and these saints, clothed in real human bodies, are to dwell and reign together upon a renovated earth during that happy period. Indeed, writers on this interesting subject differ so much in details, that no well-defined theory or system can be discovered among them. The *literal resurrection* of the bodies of the saints, and the *corporeal presence* of Christ among them, seem to be the cardinal points of agreement with this class of expositors; and from this literal interpretation of the resurrection of the righteous and bodily appearance of the Saviour, they either took or received the name *Millenarians*. Other Christians, however, who differ from them in the interpretation of symbols, are no less believers in a millennium than they,—a thousand years of righteousness and peace *on the earth.*

Bishop Newton understands "this 'first resurrection' of a particular resurrection preceding the general one at least a thousand years." "It is to this first resurrection," says he, "that St. Paul alludes, (1 Thess. iv. 16,) when he affirms that the 'dead in Christ shall rise first,' and (1 Cor. xv. 23;) that every man shall be made alive in his own order, Christ the first fruits, afterwards they that are Christ's at his coming." It is surprising that a person of the Bishop's learning should so readily mistake the *sound* for the *sense* of the words which he quotes. While the apostle is, for the "comfort" of the saints, treating of *their* resurrection, he is evidently speaking of the general resurrection at the *end of time*. In the morning of the resurrection Christ's members will be raised after the manner and in virtue of his resurrection,—"the first fruits" securing the following harvest, in obvious allusion to the ceremonial law. In the other case, when Paul says, "the dead in Christ shall rise first," does he mean,—before "the rest of the dead?" No, but before those of their *redeemed brethren* who shall then be "alive and remain;" for these "shall not prevent (*anticipate*) them which are asleep," (*in the grave*.) That is, the bodies of the saints who have died shall be raised in glory, *before* those then alive shall undergo a change equivalent to that of the resurrection. Such is manifestly the meaning of the apostle's plain language which has no reference whatever to the millennium, not even the remotest allusion. Nothing but a groundless preconception of the nature of the millennium will account for the sound of words taking the place of their sense in the reader's mind, and no degree of mere scholarship can obviate this propensity of the human mind in "the things of the Spirit of God."

Not only does the learned prelate misapprehend and misapply the texts above quoted to support his theory, but he makes a gratuitous concession, which is at once fatal to his scheme and inconsistent with himself. He says,—"Indeed, the *death* and *resurrection* of the witnesses before mentioned, (Rev. xi. 7, 11,) appears from the concurrent circumstances of the vision to be *figurative*." The Bishop evidently viewed the witnesses of the eleventh chapter as a company altogether different from those of whom John speaks in the twentieth chapter, (vs. 4, 5.) This is another of his surprising mistakes; for that the *identical party* as a moral person appears in both parts of the symbolic and allegorical representation will readily appear to any unbiassed mind by an induction of the following particulars.

These witnesses are to continue "prophesying 1260 days" (*years*,) (Rev. xi. 3.) Then they are killed, (v. 7.) But we learn that *in death* they are *victorious*, (ch. xii. 11.) They triumph "with the Lamb on Mount Zion," (ch. xiv. 1.) In a similar attitude of triumph they again appear "standing on the sea of glass," (ch. xv. 2.) They are with their victorious King, (ch. xvii. 14.) They are exhorted to retaliate upon mystic Babylon, (xviii. 6.)

They are also engaged in the last campaign with the Captain of their salvation, (ch. xix. 14, 19, 20.) And at length they are advanced to thrones of civil power to "rule the nations," (ch. xx. 4,) in fulfilment of Daniel's prophecy and their Saviour's promise, (Dan. vii. 27; Rev. ii. 26, 27.) The death and resurrection of the witnesses is compendiously stated in the former part of the eleventh chapter, (vs. 7-14;) but these events, epitomised again in the "little book," are amplified in the subsequent chapters, where we are made acquainted more fully with their enemies, their conflicts, death, resurrection, ascension and exaltation; and in all these respects is exhibited their conformity to the example of their Captain and Leader. If, therefore, according to the Bishop's conception, "the death and resurrection" of the witnesses in the eleventh chapter be *figurative*, and if the witnesses of the twentieth be the same as those of the eleventh chapter, which identity I have proved, it follows incontrovertibly, that the "first resurrection" is to be understood in a figurative sense. This interpretation may be abundantly confirmed in the following manner:—The witnesses prophesy 1260 years. But since no individual persons live so long, a succession *must* be supposed. They are, in fact, mystic characters, having their real counterpart in actual history on this earth. The scarlet colored beast and woman, (ch. xvii. 3,) are of equal duration with the witnesses, and of similar mystic character, and have their real counterpart in history. The witnesses are slain by the beast at the instigation of the woman; but their death is only temporary, (ch. xi. 7, 11;) their enemies "have no more that they can do:" while, on the other hand, the death of the beast is "perdition,"—eternal death, (ch. xvii. 8,) and in this death the woman,—"the false prophet" participates, (ch. xix. 20.) All this symbolical language respects Christ's enemies as corporate or organized bodies.

Here it is proper to notice an objection of Bishop Newton. He asks,—"With what propriety can it be said, that some of the dead who were beheaded "lived and reigned with Christ a thousand years; but the rest of the dead lived not again until the thousand years were finished;" unless *the dying* and *living again* be the same in both places?" Very true, the dying and living are doubtless "the same in both places." The Bishop's mistake consists in taking these expressions in a literal sense, "a proper death and resurrection." He evidently assumes that "the rest of the dead," here mentioned, are to be literally raised at the last day. This is undoubtedly true, for there shall be a resurrection "... of the unjust." (Acts xxiv. 15,) but it is not the truth contained in the words in question. From the assumption of the *literal* raising of "the rest of the dead," he infers the *literal* raising of those that were beheaded. The converse of this is obviously the correct way of reasoning. We have found that the witnesses are spoken of, (xi. 14,) as *figuratively* raised by the Bishop's own acknowledgment, therefore it is most natural and logical to infer that "the rest of the dead" were to be raised in the same manner, namely, *figuratively*. As at the beginning of the millennium,—the martyrs, not some of them only, as the Bishop hints, will be raised in the persons of their legitimate successors in faith and practice; and their faith and practice will constitute the happy state of the world for a thousand years, so, when that period shall have expired, Satan, being "loosed out of his prison," (ch. xx. 8,) will deceive the nations as before, and during the "little season" of liberty, will succeed in raising from the dead as it were, a multitude of the same character as those who killed the witnesses,—"Gog and Magog." This maybe called the *second* resurrection, and there will never be a *third of that kind*, for the Lord will destroy them for ever, (ch. xx. 9.) The character of the witnesses and their unparalleled conflicts with Antichrist sufficiently identify them in the Apocalypse throughout the 1260 years, as also during the thousand years of their reign; and the character of their enemies identifies them in the time of conflict for 1260 years; but during the succeeding period of righteousness and peace for a thousand years, they will not be permitted to lift up the head. And so soon as they are organized under the conduct of Satan, and like Pharaoh, most confident of victory, (Exod. xv. 9,) then "sudden destruction cometh upon them, and they shall not escape."

THE IDENTITY OF THE TWO WITNESSES.

The late Rev. Alexander M'Leod, D. D., who had the works of learned predecessors before him, has successfully corrected many of their misinterpretations in his valuable publication, entitled "Lectures upon the Principal Prophecies of the Revelation." At the time when he wrote that work, he possessed several advantages in aid of his own expositions. He had access to the most valuable works which had been issued before that date, (1814.). He was then in the vigor of youthful manhood; and he was also comparatively free from the trammels which in attempts to expound the Apocalypse, have cramped the energies of many a well-disciplined mind, *political partialities*. At the time of these profound studies, he occupied a position "in the wilderness," from which as a stand point, like John in Patmos, he could most advantageously survey the passing scenes of providence with the ardor of youthful emotion, and with unsullied affection for the divine Master. With all these advantages, however, the dispassionate and impartial reviewer may discover, in the rapid current of his thoughts, that the active powers of the expositor some times took precedence of the intellectual. Two special causes may be assigned for this, hereditary love of liberty, and the actual condition of society at the time. Born in Scotland, the cradle of civil and religious liberty from the days of John Knox, Dr. M'Leod's traditions and mental associations were necessarily imbued with the atmosphere of such surroundings. To such causes may be attributed occasional declamation, extravagant verbosity and unconscious inconsistencies, not well comporting with the solidity and self possession so desirable on the part of an expositor. Yet even in such outbursts of impassioned eloquence we may sometimes discover noble conceptions commanding our admiration, if not altogether such as to secure our approbation. It ought to be considered, moreover, that the "Lectures" came from their author in a turbulent, if not in a revolutionary condition of society. Peninsular Europe was convulsed by the successful military career of that brilliant general, Napoleon. England and the United States were also at war. The independence and even the existence of the young Republic were apparently in peril. The lecturer very naturally sympathized with the land of his adoption, in which resided his domestic treasures and many of the "excellent ones of the earth," to whom he was bound by conjugal, paternal and covenant ties. In a condition of actual warfare, he could not but feel most keenly the constriction of these manifold and endearing bonds, especially when thought to be jeopardized.

With these preliminaries, and expressing my obligation to the Doctor's labors, to whose system of interpretation as well as to most of his details, I cheerfully give my approbation in preference to all other expositors whose works it has been in my power to consult; it is proposed briefly to review some of his expositions and sentiments, from which I crave liberty to dissent. "It is not the interest of any man to be in error."

Notes On The Apocalypse

In his interpretation of the seals and trumpets of the Apocalypse, Dr. M'Leod has unquestionably corrected many misapprehensions of his learned predecessors, especially Bishop Newton and Mr. Faber: and it is perhaps to be regretted that he did not favor the public with his view of the vials also, a work which he seems to have had in contemplation when the "Lectures" were published. The three last named interpreters did certainly improve upon the expositions of all who went before them in this field of investigation; and in most cases of disagreement the Doctor excelled in accuracy the other two, as will readily appear on careful examination.

In attempting to ascertain the import of the mystic "witnesses," as of the Antichrist, expositors widely differ. Bishop Newton says positively,—"The witnesses cannot be ... any two churches." Mr. Faber is equally peremptory, that they "must be two churches," and he attempts to sustain his position by many citations of Scripture, and by much plausible argumentation. The Bishop is substantially correct in saying, "They are a succession of men, and a succession of churches." Mr. Faber is also correct in the main when he says,—"The two witnesses signify the spiritual members of the catholic church:" but his notion of *two churches*, the "Old and New Testament churches," betrays his imperfect conception of the *essential unity* of the church of God. Both he and the Bishop overlook too often the important fact that civil magistracy is a divine ordinance, which, as corrupted, constitutes the first beast of the Apocalypse, and the most prominent feature of the great Antichrist.

Doctor M'Leod's definition or description of the witnesses is as follows:—"They are a small company of true Christians, defending the interests of true religion against all opposition, and frequently sealing with their blood the testimony which they hold," (p. 314.) This description is more definite than either of the two preceding, and is therefore worthy of preference; yet the reader will still wish for something more precise and tangible. Since the prophets of the Old and New Testaments reveal the hostility of the Devil to Christ and his people, and since both Daniel and John represent this hostility by appropriate and intelligible symbols, as carried out by corrupting the two great ordinances of *church* and *state*, would it not follow that the witnesses are those Christians who, for 1260 years, apply the word of God to these two ordinances, contending for a *scriptural magistracy* and a *gospel ministry*,—the "Two Sons of Oil;" and testifying against their *Counterfeits*? Such appears to be the import of those mystical characters of whom we read, Zech. iv. 14; Rev. xi. 4.

In tracing the witnesses through their eventful history for 1260 years as portrayed in the Apocalypse, and in fixing with precision their *continuous identity*, I am constrained reluctantly to dissent from the Doctor and agree with Faber. Adopting the language of "Frazer's Key," Dr. M'Leod says, "These witnesses differ as much from their cotemporaries, the one hundred and forty-four thousand sealed ones, (Rev. vii. 4,) as Elijah differed from the seven thousand in Israel in his time." The attempt is made to prove this assertion by the following plausible argument:—"God is never for a moment without a people upon earth." This is true,—"And the visible church is an indestructible society." Is this assertion true? It is partly true, and partly untrue:—"true of her *existence* and moral identity, but not of her *visibility* as an organized body." For example, where was the visible church while Elijah "dwelt by the brook Cherith?" (1 Kings xvii. 3, xix. 10;) or while the "woman was in the wilderness?" (Rev. xii. 6.) Is it consistent with propriety to contemplate the woman as *literally visible*, when she is symbolically "in the wilderness?" This seems to be impossible. I am therefore prepared to give my decided preference to the sentiment of Mr. Faber contained in the following words of his "Dissertation:" "The one hundred and forty-four thousand here mentioned, (Rev. xiv. 1,) are the immediate successors of the one hundred and forty four thousand sealed servants of God; (ch. vii. 4.) They are the same in short, as *the two witnesses*.... They constitute the *persecuted church in the wilderness*."—I cannot but think the evidence of identity here irresistible; and in the pithy language of the Doctor on another point, I say,—"A man must shut his eyes not to see" the correctness of Mr. Faber's interpretation of this identity. The Doctor's censure of English expositors in one of his notes will too often justly apply to other divines in expounding prophecy:—"They have greatly diminished the value of their publications, by permitting themselves to indulge so much of the spirit of political partiality." Doctor M'Leod and Mr. Faber I consider among the best expositors of the prophecies on which they severally wrote; and therefore their valuable works have been principally contemplated in these animadversions. On material points they have shed much light where those who preceded them left the reader in darkness, or involved him in perplexing labyrinths. Faber preceded M'Leod, and the latter availed himself of all the aid furnished by the former; yet till the "mystery of God shall be finished," his people will be receiving accessions of light from the "sure word of prophecy."

SOUNDING OF THE SEVENTH TRUMPET.

At the time when those learned divines wrote, the political agitations in Europe and America, as already noticed, gave a peculiar tincture to their opinions and expositions of the Apocalyptic symbols. This state of feeling on the part of these distinguished men, and on opposite sides of the Atlantic, is very strikingly illustrated in their conflicting interpretations of the "third woe,"—the seventh trumpet. Amidst the conflict of arms and the booming of cannon, in both hemispheres, those writers thought the first blast of the seventh trumpet and third woe could be distinctly heard. They differed widely, however, in their interpretations of its import and effects. To Mr. Faber, Napoleon, who was the most conspicuous figure in the passing drama, appeared as a terrific Vandal at the head of his legions, threatening to uproot and lay waste the fair fabric of European civilization. To the Doctor, on the other hand, Napoleon seemed the possible minister of Providence, destined to prepare the way of the Lord, and to introduce a better, a scriptural civilization. As time has sufficiently demonstrated the fallacy of their respective expositions of the seventh trumpet, it is needless to quote or review their speculations.

The principal defect pervading the "Lectures," and one which most readers will be disposed to view in an opposite light, appears to be, a charity *too broad*, a catholicity *too expansive*, to be easily reconciled with a consistent position among the mystic witnesses. Their author, however, deriving much information from the learned labours of English prelates on prophecy, could not "find in his heart" to exclude them from a place in the *honourable roll of the witnesses*. I am unable to recognize any of those who are in organic fellowship with the "eldest daughter of Popery," as entitled to rank among those who are symbolized as "clothed in sackcloth." The two positions and fellowships appear to be obviously incompatible and palpably irreconcilable. It is true that there have been and still are in the English establishment divines who are strictly evangelical; but the reigning Mediator views and treats individuals, as he views and treats the moral person with which individuals freely choose to associate; and we ought to "have the mind of Christ." (1 Cor. ii. 16.)

Assuming that the third woe trumpet was sounding in his ears, the Doctor, transported with the imaginary but delightful prospect, that the kingdoms of this world were speedily to become the kingdoms of our Lord and of his Christ, speaks of France as follows:—"She had given assistance to the sons of freedom on the plains and along the shores of Columbia, until the republican eagle snatched the oppressed provinces from the paw of the royal lion of England."—We may admire the metaphors of the *orator*, while we deplore the political feeling of the *divine*. It is true, as the orator in calmer moments reflects,—"The political conduct of professing Christians is generally lamentable;" and alas! this "lamentable conduct" is usually tolerated and too often exemplified by their spiritual guides. It has been generally so since the days of Jeroboam who "made priests of the lowest of the people," and thereby rendered the ministry the stipendiaries of the state. And as it was then, even so it is now, whether in the kingdoms, empires or republics of the earth. "Let us," with the Doctor, "lament the political conduct of Christians in the present age of the world."

Allusion has been already made to seeming inconsistencies in the Doctor's sentiments. There is truth in the adage,—"*tempora mutantur et nos mutamur cum illis*,"—"times change, and we change with them." And indeed changes are allowable in matters of a circumstantial nature which do not affect moral principle. Moral principle, however, is in its nature immutable. In the early period of the Doctor's public life he had nobly proved "Negro Slavery Unjustifiable." But this accursed system was from the first interwoven with the very framework of that "Republican America," which in his "Lectures" he takes occasion thus to eulogize! "We never formed a street of the mystical Babylon.... Let this be the asylum of the oppressed.... She (Republican America) has not, either by sea or land, encouraged oppression (?) or despoiled of his goods him that was at peace with us?"—I confess my inability to credit these statements, or to reconcile them with "the great moral principles" which the author justly tells his readers it was the object of the Author of the Apocalypse to illustrate before the world.

I have thus noticed some of the most important particulars in which I dissent from the interpretations of the Doctor and others, that the reader may be guided by all accessible way-marks in searching after the mind of God in this mysterious but highly instructive part of his precious word. I can again cordially recommend to his attention the Lectures of Doctor M'Leod, as the best exposition of those parts of the Apocalypse of which he treats, that has come under my notice. In the Notes will be found minor points of dissent from the Doctor's views, and from multiplied aberrations of many others. I have studied great plainness of speech, abstaining from the introduction of many verbal criticisms on the original text, and from the use of terms and phrases not familiar to the unlearned reader. Let no sincere Christian be deterred by seeming difficulties from reading the Apocalypse, or be dissuaded from searching it, by the discrepancies of interpreters; for this is equally true of "the other Scriptures." (2 Pet. iii, 16.)

THE TITLE OF THIS BOOK.

In our authorized version of the Bible, this last book is correctly translated "Revelation." It is otherwise designated "The Apocalypse," by simply Anglicising the Greek title,—*Apokalupsis*. A distinguished modern divine, Doctor Seiss, has furnished the public with a novel interpretation of the title. But it is remarkable that he does not propose an *interpretation* at all; he merely gives what he conceives to be a *correct translation*. It is this:—"The Book of the *Unvailing* of Jesus Christ!" In this singular translation two things are transparent,—affectation of scholarship, and the (*proton pseudos*) the cardinal error of Millenarianism. Learned men, however, are not devoid of fancy. Of this fact those who are historically designated Millenarians have given many illustrations from the primitive ages down to our own time. The Doctor's rendering of the name of this book discloses the predominant idea conceived in his imagination and cherished there, that Christ is to appear upon earth in glorified humanity at the beginning of the millennium, and that the Apocalypse is intended chiefly to apprize the church and the world of this momentous event.

"The unvailing of Jesus Christ," indeed! Why, the Lord Jesus Christ was revealed,—"unvailed" to the faith of our first parents in the promise of the "woman's seed" as every intelligent Christian knows, (Gen. iii. 15.) We are assured that "to him give all the prophets witness," (Acts x. 43.) Abraham rejoiced to see Christ's day, (John viii. 56.) His advent in the flesh was so well known that Old Testament believers spoke of him familiarly as of "Him that was to come," (Matt. xi. 3.) Surely he was "unvailed" to his disciples all the time that he went in and out among them before his death. And after his resurrection he appeared unto them the third time,—"was seen of Cephas, then of the twelve: after that he was seen of above five hundred brethren at once," (1 Cor. xv. 5, 6.) After his ascension Stephen "saw Jesus standing on the right hand of God," (Acts vii. 56) How preposterous then, since the whole Bible "unvails" the Saviour, to insinuate that the *specific object* of the Apocalypse is to *unvail Jesus Christ*!

That Doctor Seiss and those who endorse his *mistranslation*, or, as it ought to be called, his *false exposition* of the title to this book, do totally misapprehend and misinterpret the mind of the Holy Spirit, is further evident from the obvious import of the plain words in the first verse;—this "Revelation of Jesus Christ, God gave unto him."—Christ. Did God the Father "unvail" Christ to Christ himself? How gross the absurdity! We do not transgress the law of charity in pronouncing as impious, such manifest "wresting of the Scriptures." Moreover, the declared object of this book is to "show unto God's servants *things*,—(not to show Christ,) which must shortly come to pass:" namely, events of providence which were then future,—the evolution of the purposes of God. It is indeed true that in the sublime scenery presented in vision to John, the Lord Jesus often appears as a very conspicuous object; but he is only one among a multiplicity of other objects, and generally as the principal agent in executing the divine decrees. In this attitude he appears immediately on the opening of the seals of that book, which all sober expositors consider as the symbol of God's purposes, especially of those "unvailed" in this prophetic book. When in the sixth chapter, the "four animals" say in succession, "Come and see," is Jesus Christ the only object to be seen?—the exclusive object unvailed? or even always the *primary* object? By no means.

Thus it is evident that at the very beginning of his career as an expositor of this sacred book, Doctor Seiss gives loose reins to his fancy; and then it is not difficult to foresee through what mazes of error the credulous reader will be conducted, who in his simplicity, follows such a reckless guide. The hallucinations of Millenarians of old and of late have greatly discouraged the disciples of Christ, and seriously hindered them in obeying his command,—"Search the Scriptures," especially this precious book. Their unscriptural error, which some might call an *antiscriptural heresy*, of the pre-millennial corporeal appearance of our Saviour, with its carnal concomitants, has been a temptation to not a few to look upon this part of the Bible as wholly unintelligible, *contrary to its very name,*—REVELATION, The hereditary and inveterate misconception by Millenarians of the nature of the thousand years' reign of the saints, bears a striking analogy to that of the Jews concerning the kingdom of their Messiah, and suggests a remark by that prince of divines among English Dissenters, Doctor Owen, in his "Exposition of the Epistle to the Hebrews." He says truly,—"There are precious, useful, significant truths in the Scripture, so disposed of, so laid up, as that if we accomplish not a diligent search, we shall never set eye on them. The common course of reading the Scriptures, nor the common help of expositors, who for the most part, go in the same track, and scarce venture one step beyond those that are gone before them, will not suffice, if we intend a discovery of these hid treasures." And again he says, "How hard it is to dispossess the minds of men of inveterate persuasions in religion!"

www.ingramcontent.com/pod-product-compliance
Lightning Source LLC
Chambersburg PA
CBHW031946080426
42735CB00007B/287